THE CIVIL WAR SKETCHBOOK

OF

Charles Ellery Stedman

SURGEON · UNITED STATES NAVY

Biography and Commentary by

Jim Dan Hill

Foreword by Walter Muir Whitehill

PRESIDIO PRESS
SAN RAFAEL · CALIFORNIA
1976

The Civil War Sketchbook of
Charles Ellery Stedman, *Surgeon, United States Navy*
*

Copyright © 1976   • Presidio Press
1114 Irwin Street, San Rafael, California 94901
*

Qp 6'78

Library of Congress Catalog Card Number 76-4164
ISBN 0-89141-001-5
*

Book Design by Wolfgang Lederer
Printed in the United States of America
by Mowbray Company, Providence, Rhode Island

CONTENTS

Plates and Illustrations

The *Plates* listed below have been taken from the album prepared by
Charles Ellery Stedman in 1884 for the State of Massachusetts Commandery,
Military Order of the Loyal Legion of the United States. To preserve to the
greatest degree possible the intent and flavor of the artist, the captions used by
Dr. Stedman have been retained in their original form without change
in spelling, punctuation, or grammar. The *Illustrations* listed have been selected
from sketches in possession of the Stedman family and the Boston Athenaeum.

Plates from the Loyal Legion Album

Illustrations

Foreword

by Walter Muir Whitehill
Director and Librarian Emeritus, Boston Athenaeum

THE GHOST of Charles Ellery Stedman, a Boston physician who died in 1909 when I was four years old, has materialized in my presence several times in the last thirty years through the agency of good friends of mine who never knew each other. The first was Alexander Crosby Brown of Hilton Village, Virginia, a stalwart collaborator in *The American Neptune, A Quarterly Journal of Maritime History*, whom I saw constantly when we were both on active duty at the Navy Department during World War II. After being graduated from Yale in 1928, he and a couple of friends spent two years circumnavigating the globe in the schooner yacht *Chance*; his account of this adventure was published under the title *Horizon's Rim* by Dodd, Mead & Company in 1935. Although he was originally drawn to the James River by the Mariners' Museum at Newport News, he has for the past thirty years been a journalist and writer on maritime history. Soon after I moved from the Navy Department to the Boston Athenaeum in 1946, Alec Brown began investigating the authorship of an amusing album of lithographs that he had inherited, entitled *Mr. Hardy Lee, His Yacht, being XXIV Sketches on Stone, by Chinks*. This thin volume, published in Boston in 1857 by A. Williams & Co., had no text beyond the captions that accompanied lively sketches of what William Hogarth would have entitled "The Yachtsman's Progress." The plot concerns a young man who, having come into a fortune, wonders how he can most quickly spend it. His solution is admirable: "By Jove, I can keep a *Yacht*!"

As Alec Brown pursued efforts to identify "Chinks," he discovered that *Mr. Hardy Lee* was unknown in most research libraries; indeed he located only four copies other than his own: one in the library of the New York Racquet and Tennis Club, another in the collection of Mr. Harry T. Peters, Jr., and two in the hands of dealers. One of the latter I promptly bought for the Boston Athenaeum to add to its collection of Boston lithography. As reviews in Boston newspapers intimated that "Chinks" was young, a recent Harvard graduate, the son of a Boston physician, Harvard class reports were searched, and the author's identity established as Charles Ellery Stedman, A.B. 1852, M.D. 1855. Doctor Stedman's daughter, Mrs. Gorham Dana of Brookline, and his niece, Miss Anne B. Stedman of Boston, confirmed the identification.

As Alec Brown's researches created a new interest in *Mr. Hardy Lee*, both among institutions and in the book trade, a few more copies came out from hiding;

the Peabody Museum of Salem and The Mariners' Museum appropriately acquired copies for their libraries. Alec was determined to give Doctor Stedman a wider audience. Trade publishers not sharing his enthusiasm, I proposed that the Club of Odd Volumes in Boston, of which I was then Clerk, republish *Mr. Hardy Lee* in facsimile in a limited edition for its members. So in September 1950, one hundred and fifty copies, reproduced in offset by the Meriden Gravure Company, appeared. As the number was determined by the advance subscription of members, the book never went on public sale. But the club had followed Thomas Jefferson's admonition in regard to historical documents "to save what remains, not by vaults and locks, which fence them from the public eye and use in consigning them to the waste of time, but by such a multiplication of copies as shall place them beyond the reach of accident."

I thought, erroneously, in 1950 that I had seen the last of Doctor Stedman; he has continued to appear at intervals from surprising and unrelated directions. In 1956 the late Mrs. Edward Cunningham, a valued friend of the Boston Athenaeum whose shelves and cupboards seemed as bottomless as the widow's cruse of oil, gave the library an autograph book which Doctor Calvin Gates Page of the Harvard Class of 1852 had circulated among his classmates. This little leather-bound book contained chiefly nostalgic sentiments in prose until it reached Charles Ellery Stedman who, after explaining "It's pretty hard, dear Cal, for a fellow who could only get a 36 in his best theme

to have to follow the class poet in these pages," began to draw pen-and-ink sketches of members of the Class of 1852 engaged in wasting time in the manner familiar to undergraduates before and since. I reproduced in my Athenaeum annual report for 1956 the sketches of a studious gathering (with bottles and pipes) in 14 Hollis Hall and another under a tree in the Yard (with only pipes). In addition Stedman drew sketches of his classmates lolling on cushioned window seats, smoking huge German pipes, and venturing onto Fresh Pond in rowboats. These indicated that, even as an undergraduate, Charles Ellery Stedman could not resist sketching and gently satirizing his friends and neighbors.

Nineteen years later, in January 1975, Miss Anne Stedman telephoned to ask my thoughts about a Texas historian who wished access to various papers of her uncle Charles in connection with a book on the Civil War. On learning his name, I assured Miss Stedman that Major General Jim Dan Hill was an able scholar and delightful person whom I saw at least every eighteen months at the meetings of the Secretary of the Navy's Advisory Committee on Naval History, of which we have both been members for many years. I pointed out that his military career in two branches of the service had been similar to a mirror image of that of Samuel Eliot Morison, who was a private of infantry in the First World War but in the Second rose from lieutenant commander to rear admiral in the United States Naval Reserve. Jim Dan Hill reversed the order, having been a signalman in a destroyer during World War I. Liking the sea, he acquired a third mate's license after leaving the Navy and served for a time in the merchant marine, but he came ashore, took a Ph.D. at the University of Minnesota, and turned to college teaching of history and economics. In 1931 he became president of the state teachers college at Superior, Wisconsin (now Wisconsin State University—Superior), of which he became president emeritus after more than forty years service. Having long had an extra-curricular interest in national defense, President Hill served as a colonel, Field Artillery, during World War II; he commanded the 190th Field Artillery Group, a Pennsylvania National Guard unit, attached to V Corps, European Theater, from the Normandy beaches to VE day at Pilsen, Czechoslovakia. During the Korean War, he served as a major general on the Reserve Forces Policy Board.

Although Jim Dan Hill wound up as an artilleryman, he always maintained a scholarly interest in the sea. His first book was *Sea Dogs of the Sixties*; in 1937 the University of Chicago Press published his *The Texas Navy*, a work so valuable that it was reprinted in paperback twenty-five years later, with a highly complimentary foreword by the Director of Naval History. The title brings a smile to the faces of those who only know the twentieth century "Kentucky colonel" version of that naval force. A few years ago, when visiting Austin, I myself received a commission as an admiral in the Texas Navy. In thanking Governor John B. Connally for this honor, I pointed out that,

had I not first known him when he was President Kennedy's Secretary of the [United States] Navy, I would not have so greatly appreciated being promoted through five grades in a single day. But during the 1830s and 1840s there *was* a Texas Navy that operated at sea and contributed materially to the victory that Houston won at San Jacinto.

In the foreword to the original edition, Colonel Theodore Roosevelt rightly observed that the author "has not merely given the bare bones of the naval narrative. He has also skillfully drawn the whole sequence of events in the fumbling but powerful movement of Anglo-Texans which led to Texas statehood." He further remarked: "True historian that he is, Jim Dan Hill has not attempted to paint these early characters as fabulous heroes. He has shown the good with the bad, the competent with the incompetent." As proof that this Texan has resisted the temptations of mythology in dealing with his native state, one has only to read these sentences on the action at San Jacinto. "Houston hoped that the Mexicans would attack him. But Houston's captains urged an offensive, to which the General reluctantly agreed. When the motley Texan troops were paraded, shortly after noon of the 21st, a number of rabble rousing speeches were made, at the end of which the Texans stealthily advanced through the woods and noisily hurled themselves upon the Mexican encampment. Fortunately for the attackers the Mexican officers were taking their afternoon *siesta*. Enlisted men were working about routine camp duties. Though a bayou cut off a

Mexican retreat, no sentries were posted. The rout was complete. Less than twenty surviving Mexicans reached the Brazos and Gaona's main column, now commanded by General Filasola. All other Mexican survivors, including Santa Anna, were captured. The Texans lost but two killed and a number severely wounded. Sam Houston was among the latter."

I have always marveled how, between Army service and a college presidency, Jim Dan Hill managed to get so much written. In 1950 he inaugurated a weekly column, syndicated among Wisconsin newspapers, entitled "Let's Look at the Record," in which he expressed his views on current topics with a pungency and forthrightness similar to that of his fellow-Texan, the late J. Frank Dobie. In 1964 he published *The Minute Man in Peace and War, A History of the National Guard*. This 585-page work is characteristically dedicated to the officers and men he commanded in World War II, "who not only maintained the highest military traditions of their States and their Nation but they also often made their Colonel appear better than he really was, which he deeply appreciated." After retiring from his long college presidency, Jim Dan Hill returned to Abilene, Texas, where he keeps steadily at his typewriter.

Soon after talking with Miss Stedman, I heard from General Hill and learned that Colonel George S. Pappas of Presidio Press was contemplating the publication of another album of drawings by Doctor Stedman, based on his experiences as a naval surgeon during the Civil War. As with *Mr. Hardy Lee*, the doctor retreated behind a pseudonym and invented fictitious names for his ships and people. This considerably larger album, entitled *Doctor Squillgee's Four Years in the U.S. Navy*, was created in 1865 after Stedman's return home, on the basis of sketches that he had made during the war. In 1884, however, he made a fair copy of the series for the Military Order of the Loyal Legion of the United States, to which he added his signature and a pair of photographs of himself, then and now. For over eighty years this album remained in Boston with other records of the Loyal Legion, long housed in a tower room of the First Corps of Cadets Armory at Arlington Street and Columbus Avenue.

As participants in the Civil War died, interest diminished in the great collection of books, photographs, prints, portraits, and memorabilia of the conflict lovingly assembled by the Loyal Legion; it became a forgotten and unfrequented resource, tucked away in a tower of a building that no longer served a current military purpose. After the armory was sold, Colonel Pappas mercifully arranged to transfer the Loyal Legion collection to the U.S. Army Military History Reserach Collection at Carlisle Barracks, Pennsylvania, of which he was then director. There he came upon *Doctor Squillgee's Four Years in the U.S. Navy* and was as delighted with the drawings as Alec Brown and I had been with *Mr. Hardy Lee* a quarter of a century before. Having turned publisher upon his retirement from the Army, Colonel Pappas wished to assure "such a multiplication of copies as shall place them beyond the reach of accident." He persuaded General Hill to make a study of Doctor Stedman and his drawings, and set them in reference to the naval activities of the Civil War. With the hearty cooperation of the artist's family, which produced a richness of letters and information, the book that follows came into being. Having had a hand in reviving the memory of Charles Ellery Stedman a quarter of a century ago, it delights me to be allowed to introduce this far more extensive publication, which represents a collaboration between two valued friends, one in Texas and the other in California.

A BRILLIANT IDEA
"By Jove, I can keep a YACHT"
Sketch from Hardy Lee . . .

Preface

CHARLES ELLERY STEDMAN, M.D., Harvard Medical School, 1855, wantonly and needlessly rejected any possibility for distinction or fame as a Civil War artist. It was indeed a highly competitive field. An often noted phenomenon of the Civil War and its immediately following decades was the vast pictorial proliferation in the expanding news media. Much of it was a result of the increasing popularity of lithography and the better wood engravings that came with improved inks and more refined techniques. It was an increasingly competitive field.

Doctor Stedman, however, was without a rival. The scores of "field artists"; the ambitious, would-be Thomas Nasts and Winslow Homers who sought distinction among the later nineteenth century artists, could not have been rivals of Doctor Stedman. They had been so completely absorbed by the great drama of the more easily understood armies that the men and the lives they led on the ships at sea were all but ignored. Accordingly, Stedman was a narrative artist without competition. Nevertheless, he brought to the self-assigned task a sharp eye for significant, human interest details and a skill as a draftsman far beyond that of many shore-bound contemporaries.

The printed pages of this volume attempt an emphasis upon the time, place, circumstances, background of events, the persons involved, ships concerned, their guns and capabilities, plus some of the laws and customs of the Navy. One or more of all of the foregoing considerations provided the inspiration for each of the fifty-four plates reproduced. A sometimes digressive commentary is offered on each. Stedman's art cannot be fully appreciated without such treatment. Standing alone, even if numbered, dated, and arranged in correct sequence, the pictures and captions would tell no coherent story to modern viewers, not even to the more ardent Civil War devotees.

The Stedman caricatures are heavily laden with the substance of history. They merit recognition and treatment as such. Stedman has, perhaps unwittingly, provided us with some long overdue human interest illustrations for the greatest period of change in the world's naval history—the transition from sail to steam and from wood to metals. Of scale drawings, mechanical designs, marine architectural specifications, and printed memoirs of participants in this technical revolution, there is a large and bulky literature. Other than Stedman, however, no artist has given us a sustained, graphic portrayal of the impact of that revolution upon the daily lives of the Civil War sailors who served through the transition. If he allowed himself a light satirical touch, no one can accuse him of romanticism, though he did have a thin streak of such in his system. It was a part of his era.

Through constant use of the *Official Records of the Union and Confederate Navies,* Series I and II, supplemented by other contemporary sources and a representative number of his letters to his beloved wife, Edith, we have been able to bring more than fifty of his caricatures into a correct sequence and to fit them into a narrative of his naval service and experience. At times we have been able to reveal his emotions and reactions to men and events.

As usual in historical writing, the author is deeply indebted to many and wishes to give public expression of his thanks to them. Under a succession of dedicated, retired flag officers; Rear Admirals John B. Heffernan, Ernest M. Eller, and now Vice Admiral Edwin B. Hooper there have been brought together and retained a group of alert and imaginative historical staff specialists who can hardly be equaled by any other similar departmental agency in the national government. It was Vice Admiral Hooper who first told the author of the existence of the Stedman drawings. As the Director of Naval History and Curator for the Navy Department, he and his staff have given valuable assistance and advice. Staff members are: Dr. William James Morgan, Head of Historical Research Branch; Miss Mary F. Loughlin, Historical Research Branch; Mr. W. Bart Greenwood, Librarian; Mr.

Frederick S. Meigs, Assistant Librarian; Commander Richard T. Speer, USN, Head of Ships' Histories Branch; Captain Roger Pineau, USNR, Director Navy Memorial Museum; Mrs. Agnes F. Hoover and Mr. Charles R. Haberlein, both of the Photographic Section, Curator Branch.

It was Colonel George S. Pappas, U.S. Army (Ret.) and President of Presidio Press who insisted I should become involved in the publication of the album and such other pertinent sketches as I might find incident to research on the subject. His enthusiasm was contagious. Between an author and his publisher a certain amount of collaboration is absolutely necessary. In this Colonel Pappas has been tireless and most helpful.

No area is more hospitable to historians than Boston and nearby Cambridge. Their enviable libraries can always provide something of vital interest to all, regardless of the fields the visiting historians may represent. Walter Muir Whitehill personifies this scholarly hospitality. Harvard's Widener Library, the Francis A. Countway Library of Medicine, and the Boston Athenaeum have made substantial contributions from their holdings, not only informative material, but also some of the lesser black and white sketches in the first two chapters. Mrs. Janet F. Regier, Curator of Harvard Medical Archives and Mr. Richard J. Wolfe, Librarian, the Countway Library, were most generous with their time and assistance. It was Mr. Wolfe who sent the author to Miss Anne Bradstreet Stedman and who quite favorably mentioned Mr. Eric Rudd. I had no meeting with Mr. Rudd, but two telephone conversations were indeed quite helpful.

A special note of thanks must be directed to the members of the Stedman family: Miss Anne Bradstreet Stedman, Eleanora Stansbury Peacock, Edith Wilson Saville, Thomas Hale, and John W. Stedman, Jr. Their complete and wholehearted cooperation in providing letters, sketches, and recollections of Charles Ellery Stedman made my task much easier and far more pleasant.

Jim Dan Hill
Abilene, Texas

August 1975

PUBLISHER'S NOTE

THE DRAWINGS OF Charles Ellery Stedman represent a wide variety of artistic techniques. Some, such as U.S.S. "Huron" . . . on page 3, were drawn in pencil. An unusual technique was used in preparing the caricatures, such as Tidings of War shown on page 21. Stedman first covered his paper with a thick layer of blue-grey paint. When this had dried, he drew the caricature in black paint; when this had dried in turn, he chipped away bits of the grey paint to provide white highlights. Other drawings, such as The Monitors . . . in action on page 149, were drawn in black ink with heavy overtones added in charcoal. The resultant effect was intended to provide the feeling of semidarkness and murky cloudiness caused by gun smoke. Other drawings, such as the nautical scene of Onward and Vandalia on page 83, were sketched using a combination of his caricature technique amplified with black ink shadings. The sketches from the Stedman family albums and the Boston Athenaeum collection were drawn either in pencil or in ink. Several of the Hardy Lee . . . illustrations were copied from the lithograph album.

Every effort has been made to reproduce Stedman's drawings as identical to the originals as possible. The fifty-two plates used in the Civil War Sketchbook are the exact size of the originals; the background blue-grey color matches the tint of Stedman's paint. Differences in tone have been retained untouched; hence the variations in texture of various printed plates. Some of the sketches have faded or been stained during the passage of nearly 100 years since they were drawn. Although the fading has been compensated for to some degree by careful attention in copying the originals and in making the plates for printing, the stains have been left virtually untouched, for to do otherwise might materially alter Stedman's work. Lastly, the captions have been reproduced exactly as prepared by Stedman; spelling, grammar, and punctuation are unchanged. This volume uses photocopies of the original hand-letter captions in the Loyal Legion album. We at Presidio Press hope that you, the reader, will enjoy the drawings of Charles Ellery Stedman as much as we have thoroughly enjoyed preparing this book for you.

The Civil War Sketchbook of Charles Ellery Stedman, *Surgeon, United States Navy*

These drawings were made in 1865, some from sketches taken during the War, but mostly from memory. They have been copied from the original series in lead-pencil, for the Military Order of the Loyal Legion of the United States, this year.

1884

C. Ellery Stedman

CHAPTER ONE The Education of Charles Ellery Stedman

The "lost" Civil War Sketchbook of Charles Ellery Stedman, Surgeon, United States Navy, lay relatively unknown and unused for almost a century after he made the series of drawings in 1884. Drawn from sketches prepared during and immediately following the Civil War, the Sketchbook included fifty-four lively caricatures of life afloat, an intimate and factual glimpse of duty on board ships at the time the United States Navy was moving rapidly from sail to steam and from wood to iron. But who was this Charles Ellery Stedman? Where did he serve during the War? How did a surgeon develop such an artistic capability coupled with such keen and humorous appreciation for the everyday events on board a Navy combat vessel?

Doctor Stedman first broke into print as early as May 1857 when his black and white sketches were published as a lithographic pictorial narrative entitled *Mr. Hardy Lee, His Yacht, Being XXIV Sketches on Stone by Chinks.* The thin album was published by A. Williams & Co. of Boston. The light, satirical darts of the sketches were carefully blunted by proper Bostonian gentility and restraint, since hurtful innuendoes toward identified persons were not considered good form although clubs, institutions, fads, and social trends were always fair game. Expensive yacht-ing was the new, "in-thing" since 1851. That was the year the schooner *America* brought national joy and pride to sportsmen of the United States by winning the first international yacht race in history—and that in British waters with no less than Queen Victoria as a disappointed onlooker! The victory sparked an already burgeoning saltwater enthusiasm into a booming extravagance that continues to the present day. Accordingly, Mr. "Hardy Lee," a convenient pun on a frequent yachting phrase, and his expensive schooner, the *Windseye*—also a borrowed term—appear to be mere allegorical names for an enviable trend among the wealthy, a foible of the rich. The light and thin volume was not reprinted; its author-artist, soon forgotten. As the years rolled by, however, it became a book considered both unusual and rare.

There are definite parallels between this first published work by Stedman and his Civil War Sketchbook. Exactly what purpose Stedman had in mind when he adopted a pseudonym for these drawings is not known for he included no preface with the album. We can safely assume that his shipboard drawings were not to be viewed by his shipmates. Otherwise, why did he attribute them to a mythical "Doctor Squillgee" serving aboard the nonexistent man-of-war

"*Fornots*" commanded by a Captain "Rumbelow" whose name appears on no American naval list or directory? Obviously, thin subterfuge though it would have been, Stedman was prepared to disclaim any effort toward realistic innuendoes should his sheets fall into unfriendly hands while he was still aboard or assigned to the ship. In some drawings that he sketched while on shore duty or while a convalescent at home, he gave his ship its actual name.

In light of the foregoing, it is reasonable to assume that Doctor Stedman's artistic efforts were primarily for his own amusement and intended to make more pleasant the many lonely hours of dreary idleness that come to a doctor when surrounded by so many disgustingly healthy people. He had full knowledge of the scrimshaw carving and ink work done on bleached whale bone or the ivory teeth of sperm whales and sharks. Scrimshaw made the long and tedious whaling voyages more acceptable to another breed of sailor. Perhaps Stedman's whimsical but often realistic art did the same for him. It might have supplemented his letters in bringing cheer to his family and friends in Boston.

We now know that his mythical warship, "*Fornots*," was actually USS *Huron*, a new, Boston-built, wooden, steam corvette, complete with two tall masts and a wide spread of sails. Like all twenty-three "90-day gunboats" of her class launched in 1861, she was given only four cannon, all much heavier than the old style, seagoing ordnance. When combat loaded, *Huron* displaced 691 tons and carried a crew of about ninety officers and men. She was 158 feet long and twenty-eight feet at the widest point amidships. Stedman's drawing of *Huron* on page 3, stripped for action and operating under steam only in the Stono River near Charleston, South Carolina, is an excellent likeness of his ship. For offshore duty on the blockade, the long main and fore topmasts were hoisted and stepped; all standing and running rigging was replaced; and sails were bent aloft and alow. The exceptionally large mainsail and foresail were rigged fore-and-aft, schooner style. The topmasts carried yards and square sails, and there were the usual jibs, staysails, and the studdingsails for the yards. Under steam alone, *Huron* could make nine knots. A stiff breeze with all sails drawing could easily add four knots to her speed, hopefully five. Stedman's pun-like name for *Huron*, "*Fornots*," could have been his recognition of the many times those *four knots* were not forthcoming. In earlier sketches drawn before he prepared the Loyal Legion album, Stedman referred to *Huron* as the "*Squidnocket*." Possibly considering that name too flattering, he chose "*Fornots*" for use in the album.

Huron's Captain "Rumbelow" of "*Fornots*," proved to be a crusty seagoing officer of the Old School. He probably had more saltwater in his system than he had blood in his veins after twenty-three years service as midshipman, passed midshipman, master, and lieutenant in the United States Navy. Moreover, he was the son and namesake of the renowned Commodore John Downes, a distinguished small ship com-

The U. S. S. "Huron" in Stono River, S. C.

mander through much of the War of 1812. The senior John Downes had also served as Commodore David Porter's Executive Officer aboard *Essex* during her famous Pacific cruise which ended with her overpowering defeat by two British men-of-war in Valparaiso Harbor, Chile. The Commodore was a hard taskmaster and stern disciplinarian. In 1831, for example, while commanding the new heavy frigate *Potomac*, he had had twenty-five of his crew of 500 men "flogged with the cats" for "skulking," a naval term which covered foot-dragging at drills and laying on hands without pulling their weight. This, however, was a familiar incident in the Old Navy. The Commodore's theories of discipline and order were undoubtedly passed on to his son—in one way or another. He, in turn, was a stern disciplinarian although his methods differed from those used by his father. This might explain why the sensitive Doctor Stedman never warmed up to his pseudo-Captain "Rumbelow."

The real life "Rumbelow," Lieutenant John Downes, Jr., had no such mental reservations concerning his Assistant Surgeon. After each had seen the other through heavy artillery duels with Confederate shore batteries, Downes was promoted to commander and posted to command a new monitor-type ironclad, USS *Nahant*. He promptly recommended that Stedman be transferred from the List of Volunteer Officers, integrated into the Regular Navy, and that he be transferred to *Nahant*. Nevertheless, Stedman retained his thinly veiled mental reservations about Downes. In his pictorial autobiography,

Nahant became the fictitious *"Semantocook."* Not until she had distinguished herself in battles with the Charleston forts and the capture of the Confederate ironclad *Atlanta* did Stedman concede that her real name was *Nahant*. Captain "Rumbelow," however, does not appear in any of Stedman's drawings other than those concerning the steam light corvette *"Fornots."*

It is also interesting to note that Stedman's portrayal of 'Captain Downes' wrath against the seaman who had "expectorated generously on the quarter-deck" was the last time the Doctor attempted to personalize anyone other than himself. Stedman's drawing on page 9 shows his obvious sympathy for the sailor who stands in a classic Greek stance, frozen in his tracks with bowed head while the Captain indulges in explosive vituperation. In truth, the sailor merited no sympathy. With the entire Atlantic Ocean to spit in and with the lee rail seldom more than fourteen feet away, any sailor who expectorated generously upon the open deck of a ship that size deserved all of the verbal abuse within the resources of any well seasoned officer. Few junior officers could do the job properly although, conceivably, a chief bos'n (boatswain) could have risen to more colorful blasphemy had the deed been done in his presence. Among the other faces present, there is surprise and silent amusement but no evidence of any sympathy. Perhaps that is all the more reason why Stedman felt sympathetic toward the abused individual. While a student in college, he described himself as "weeping profusely at every untoward occurrence" in the Boston Latin School.

Perhaps we can better understand and interpret the pictures from the pen of Doctor "Squillgee," illustrating life on board the USS *"Fornots"* and the monitor *"Semantocook,"* by becoming better acquainted with Doctor Charles Ellery Stedman of Dorchester, Massachusetts.

STEDMAN, CLASS OF '52, HARVARD

The artist's father was Charles Harrison Stedman, M.D.; his mother, Lucy Rust, daughter of William Ingalls, M.D. They lived in Chelsea, then a Suffolk County village three or four miles north-northeast and across the Mystic River from Boston. Their son, Charles Ellery, was born in the Chelsea Naval Hospital on 23 March 1831.

The pink and squalling infant was received into the most prominent heritage of medical practitioners and specialists in nineteenth century Massachusetts. From 1829 to 1841, the father was "Physician in Charge" of the famous naval hospital in which the boy was born. In 1834, the senior Doctor Stedman revised and edited an American edition of J. G. Spergheim's *Anatomy of the Brain with a General View of the Nervous System*, "with an appendix of eighteen plates." The preface is modestly signed "C.H.S." After moving to Boston for general practice and consultation, Doctor Stedman soon accepted the responsibilities of Superintendent, Boston Lunatic Hospital. As a consultant, his testimony was often sought in medico-

*Professor Rich and students
at the Boston Latin School*

legal cases.

On the baby's maternal side, Grandfather William Ingalls had graduated from Harvard Medical School in 1801. He was Professor of Anatomy at Brown University from 1811 to 1823 when he returned to

Boston to resume private practice and to teach. Ingalls wrote *Malignant Fevers* in 1847.

In the Boston of that era, there could be no escape from the same profession for Charles Ellery Stedman. The same was true for his younger brother, Henry Rust Stedman, who was a highly respected specialist on brain and nervous disorders until his death in 1925. This heritage also brought to both sons the interlocking marriages and kinships within the lace-like fabric of family trees which continued to distinguish the Proper Bostonians.

Little Charles Ellery showed the usual, built-in antipathy for learning that was enjoyed by all boys of that era—if not of all eras. His *bete noire* was a Chelsea governess who, poor soul, had Charles Ellery and two other boys in her "school." One little toughie—not Charles Ellery—would stomp on her feet with his new cowhide boots when he disapproved of her

A studious gathering in 14 Hollis Hall

pedagogical procedures. In 1841, the family moved to Boston where the boy was entered in Mr. Thayer's School. After two years with Thayer, he was enrolled in the Boston Latin School whose headmaster had the exacting reputation of making ignorance uncomfortable. Accordingly, young Stedman passed into Harvard without difficulty in 1848.

Boston in the 1840s was a far cry from the Boston of today. Charles Dickens, who visited the Intellectual Hub in 1842, found it to be a charming city of clean streets, white houses, and bright green shutters. The dock where the Boston Tea Party had taken place was still on the waterfront. Dickens met the intelligentsia and better educated politicians on more or less even terms. Most of the former were Harvard faculty members, successful clergymen, and a few currently successful authors such as Richard Henry Dana whose brilliantly realistic *Two Years Before the Mast* was in full popularity. The difference between the Harvard of Stedman's day and the modern multi-fountain center of knowledge is even more astounding. Not until forty-four years after Stedman's graduation was compulsory attendance at prayers relaxed for undergraduate students. Throughout Stedman's student days, Trinitarianism versus Unitarianism versus Transcendentalism were hot issues concerning the future of mankind.

When Stedman entered Harvard College and what we would today call the undergraduate School of Letters, Arts, and Sciences, the College had a faculty of fourteen full-time tutors, instructors, and professors. No other faculty, however, has included more great names in proportion to its size. Each of the eight full professors was expected to cover wide fields of related subjects. Henry Wadsworth Longfellow, for example, taught German, French, and Spanish; Louis Agassiz, zoology and geology. Edward Everett was President of the University during Stedman's freshman year. He was followed by Jared Sparks, the famous editor and historian, who also continued his professorial duties.

Most likely, Longfellow was the best and most impressive classroom instructor during Stedman's undergraduate years. Which of the three languages taught by Longfellow was studied by Stedman does not appear to be a matter of record; it can be assumed that it certainly was not all three. Longfellow was approaching the crest of his popularity. His *Evangeline*, published in 1847, established him as a master of narrative poetry in England. Throughout sentimental America, readers were dabbing their eyes over the well-metered wanderings of the poor Acadian maiden searching for her always farther-wandering Cajun sweetheart. There can be no doubt that Longfellow left an indelible imprint upon the admittedly sentimental and sensitive Stedman. In later years, it took no more than a Class of '52 reunion or a meeting of the Knights of the Punch Bowl for Stedman to bring forth a few verses of his own. Some have survived though published only in the Harvard *Annals* of its classes.

All freshman, sophomores, and juniors followed a prescribed and identical series of courses. A limited number of electives were permitted in the senior year. Latin, Greek, religious philosophy, history, mathematics, and modern languages dominated the first three rigidly-structured years. With so small a faculty no student could escape any professor, for their schedules were arranged in that manner. In his senior year, Stedman undoubtedly chose the science courses and lectures which would best serve him in the medical school of his future. Nevertheless, for his baccalaureate disquisition, he must have felt more at ease in Latin and Greek. His subject was "Anna Comnena," said to have been the first woman historian. She wrote extensively in Greek about her father, Alexius I, Roman Emperor in the East from 1081 to 1118 A.D., although Latin was still the official language of the court. Few baccalaureate candidates today could qualify for the degree with that assignment.

Under a tree in the Harvard Yard

Among the science professors who had a profound influence upon Stedman was Louis Agassiz, a research scientist far ahead of his time. A much younger professor, Benjamin Peirce, must have held Stedman spellbound. Like Agassiz, Peirce was groping from the knowns into the unknowns. He was Professor of Mathematics, Astronomy, Analytical Mechanics, and all else remotely associated with such subjects, including chemistry. Peirce was more approachable than Agassiz for he was warm, friendly, and brilliant in his conversations with students. Some, however, considered him pedantic in the classroom. In Peirce's opinion, mathematics and the sciences were the "unchanging truths of God." Within that premise, he lost few, if any, arguments to the theologians who dominated the philosophical cleavages on the campus.

It must be kept in mind that Harvard, although over two centuries old at that time, had far more coming during the next eighty years than had evolved from its slowly moving past. The University Library numbered less than 80,000 volumes. Harvard College each year enrolled about 375 undergraduate students in all four classes; the university schools added an additional five or six hundred. At the same time, the population of Massachusetts was about one million; that of Boston, slightly over a hundred thousand.

The faculty of the Law School consisted of three practicing attorneys who ran an apprentice clerk's reading course of eighteen months' duration. They received nothing from the University, not even library facilities. The three lawyers pocketed the student fees for their trouble and for the use of their own law library. On their "faculty certification," the University conferred the LL.B. degree upon the finishing "students" at the end of their eighteen months of study. A similar situation existed in the other university schools with only the faculty of Harvard College drawing fixed and guaranteed salaries. Full professors lived rather handsomely on $1,500 a year. An instructor or tutor, such as young Charles W. Eliot who was employed in 1854, might well be satisfied with $750 or $900 as an understudy to a great mind. Eliot was destined to be the greatest of Harvard's many famous presidents for, during his four decades as president, he lifted Harvard to its present status in education.

There were eighty-seven members in the graduating Class of 1852, somewhat more than the average number for that era. In keeping with the sound of the last digit, they were known as the "Toodles." Young Stedman was neither Valedictorian nor Salutatorian, those coveted honors going to the Choate brothers, William and Joseph H., respectively. The latter, as a New York lawyer and diplomat, became one of the most famous of the class. Today, however, the most widely remembered member of the Class of 1852 is Horatio Alger. With instinctive and uncanny accuracy, his classmates at once nicknamed him "Holy Horatio." Alger wrote more than a hundred juvenile novels predicated upon the simple plot and theme of youthful success and early wealth through diligence, integrity, piety, and considerable luck. All had titles

Ship on fire? Bless you, no. But the American Tar has expectorated generously on the quarter deck, and Captain Rumbelow is expressing his disapproval.

such as *Tom the Bootblack, or How Honesty Wins*. Although no complete list of his book titles exists, Horatio Alger's name is still synonymous with such platitudes. Nevertheless, the legend that one of his titles was *Paul the Piano Mover, or Four Square, Upright and Grand*, has never been validated!

THE MEDICAL STUDENT

At the Massachusetts General Hospital across the Charles River, Stedman encountered another Boston poet of more than passing repute: Oliver Wendell Holmes, Dean of the Harvard School of Medicine. With more than average New England modesty, Doctor Holmes had more or less suppressed his emergent proclivities toward poetry, "....a dangerous affliction for a doctor of medicine!"—a statement based upon his own retrospective testimony. Unfortunately for him, during the summer of 1824, the year before he entered Harvard, Holmes had written an unsigned poem for a local newspaper under the title of "Old Ironsides." It was an impassioned protest against breaking-up and selling as junk the famous old 44-gun frigate, *Constitution*, known among veteran sailors of the War of 1812 as "Old Ironsides." Other periodicals picked up the poem and the protest spread across the nation. The ship was saved as she would be again and again in future years.

That Holmes was the best educated doctor of medicine in New England at that time, there can be little doubt. His erudite contributions to professional journals won medical prizes. Dartmouth Medical School invited him to a professorship of anatomy which required only three months of teaching during each summer. Although he still had to cure people to make a living, he did not enjoy sick people; and his miserable, unhappy patients did not appreciate a wise-cracking doctor who tried to cure them with jokes, impromptu rhymes, and jingles along with his pills and powders.

In all probability young Stedman, with the ink not yet dry on his college diploma, had more than a passing acquaintance with Doctor Holmes prior to his entry into the Medical School. Both his father and his maternal grandfather, William Ingalls, had been practicing medicine in Boston for many years. Consequently, Charles Ellery must have been fully aware of all of the requirements and some of the personalities involved in the acquisition of the M.D. degree. Most likely he viewed the three years ahead with some impatience, if not with trepidation. Latin and Greek declensions could be difficult, but how about dissecting tissues of a cadaver?

Actually, the Medical School had much the same relationship with Harvard as the abbreviated Law School. Harvard provided neither funds nor other support. It merely conferred the degree upon those certified by the self-created and accepted "Medical Faculty." This faculty consisted of nine or ten practicing physicians and surgeons, including the Dean whom they elected. Most, if not all, had access to the corridors, wards, and facilities of Massachusetts General Hospital as did some practitioners who were not on the faculty. Not every doctor cares to be bothered with a teaching responsibility be it ever so short and brief in its scheduling. Tight commitments elsewhere can damage a good practice.

The faculty members were willing to make that sacrifice. The result was a fairly well thought-out trade school proposition whose rules' requirements sounded much better than were the actual procedures. Quite often, the requirements were negotiable. In effect, an entering student apprenticed himself to a practicing physician in Boston or elsewhere for a period of three years. The fees paid to the School entitled the student to attend sixteen weeks of lectures from November to February. The following winter, the student returned to the lecture hall for a second academic treatment of sixteen weeks. Entering students that year received the same instruction as second year students. This leads to the conclusion that the course content of both the first and second years was substantially the same. The faculty apparently believed that repetition was the first and only law of learning.

The emphasis of academic requirements was upon the need for thirty-two weeks of instruction. Should a student be in a hurry to graduate, he could attend Dartmouth initially for sixteen weeks of instruction there, and then attend the winter session in Boston for completion of the thirty-two week requirement. If a doctor could be found to certify that the student had been under his tutelage for thirty-six months, that student could be admitted to practice within a year

Medical student deep in
the study of anatomy

should he feel himself ready to write an acceptable treatise upon a medical subject and pass the oral final examinations just prior to the June University Convocations.

The medical paper was read to the faculty in a convocation of other candidates and students. Normal enrollment was 250 to 300 students. The diploma fee was thirty dollars; like all other fees, nonnegotiable and paid in advance. Stedman's Harvard College classmates thought it a good joke that he was permitted to read his medical dissertation since he had been required to memorize and deliver in Latin his baccalaureate disquisition on Anna Comnena.

The final oral examinations were somewhat farcical. The man who designed them was endowed with an abiding faith in the democratic process for each and every situation. He also must have had a rare sense of gamesmanship and humor. One instinctively suspects Doctor Oliver Wendell Holmes. A series of nine conference stations were prepared in a large room. The stations were as far apart as the size and conformation of the room would permit. Each station was manned by a faculty member representing his responsibilities to the curriculum. A tenth station, for the Dean, faced the array of professors. A group of nine students was admitted. Each student took a seat opposite a professor. In exactly ten minutes, a bell clanged. The line of candidates displaced to the right by one station with the last man filling the vacancy at the first station. This shift, precisely on the clang of the bell each ten minutes, was repeated until all professors had enjoyed ten minutes with each student.

The nine candidates were then dismissed from the room. Before the decisive voting began, the Dean gave each professor a large white card with a large black spot in the middle of one side. The Dean then announced a name from his list of the nine candidates just examined. Then the question: "Are you ready to vote?" There being no dissent, the next word was "Vote." Each professor flashed his card toward the Dean. If he counted more than four black spots, the Dean announced that the candidate had failed; if there were four or less spots, the word was "Passed." At no time was there a conference of the whole or a discussion about any candidate between professors. In other words, a candidate could be mentally inept

on forty-four percent of the medical curriculum and still be qualified to administer to the woes of the sick, the lame, the halt, and the blind throughout the Commonwealth of Massachusetts.

There is little wonder that the medical doctors of that era often disagreed as to whether the successful practice of medicine was a science or an art. But who are we to criticize? That question continues to haunt some areas of the curative skills—subjective psychiatry, faith healing, and acupuncture, for example. In defense of the medical generation of Doctors Holmes and Stedman, it must be admitted that an attentive student could acquire a fair mastery of the limited and accepted body of medical and surgical literature of the day during the thirty-two weeks of concentrated study, lectures, and demonstrations— and through the observation opportunities in one of the largest and best equipped hospitals of that time.

Each working day of those thirty-two weeks, the students attended five hours of lectures and demonstrations. They were assigned readings in the best medical libraries. The same was true of the laboratories which had the best instruments, equipment and apothecary supplies. That Doctor Holmes much favored microscopic work and photography was not an idle or groundless rumor. In company with a physician, each student had access to the sick and operating rooms. Student volunteer help was appreciated. Most of the clinical experience of the student, however, was expected to be the responsibility of his preceptor, the practicing physician to whom he was apprenticed. In other words, the learning opportunities were there and specific.

Even so, it is significant that it was against the schools of Law and Medicine that the young University President, Charles W. Eliot, first moved in 1869. He listed the integration and upgrading of these two professional schools as numbers one and two among the widely recognized improvements made during his forty years of Harvard administration.

STEDMAN'S BACHELOR YEARS AND MARRIAGE

This brief review of Stedman's schooling raises many questions concerning the man. How healthy was he? How well disciplined his mind? How active and eager his pursuit of knowledge? Was he fully committed to attaining an objective?

The best testimony concerning his health is the physical examination he necessarily took to become a commissioned officer in the United States Navy. There is an often repeated theory that doctors are always easy on one another. The reverse was—and is—true when the examiner is already a commissioned officer in the armed services and the examinee is a candidate for a commission. No member of a comparatively small technical or professional corps of officers wants a weak brother in its midst.

Stedman has made it a matter of record that a three-man board of naval surgeons descended upon him for he pictorially recorded the Board in the sketch on page 29. They probed the depth of his

". . . George Head's happy misery in smoking"

medical knowledge and training far more than did the Harvard School of Medicine. He also passed the rigorous physical examination.

In passing, we might note that in the sketches of himself before the Examining Board and elsewhere, Stedman tacitly admits that he was a rather handsome chap, slightly taller than average with a thin, well-groomed figure. The photographs at the frontispiece (this page was also the frontispiece of the Loyal Legion album)—one in uniform taken about 1865 and the other in civilian clothes about 1875—sustain the veracity of his drawing pen. For health in mind and body, Stedman should be marked "superior" on almost everyone's rating sheet. He lived until 1909 and age seventy-eight.

Stedman might be rated the same on mental discipline. Much has been said and written in denunciation of the old and inflexible curricula. There has been even more said against the driving, drill-sergeant teaching techniques in the writing of English, the demanding translations of Latin and Greek, and the precision required in the use of the irregular verbs in modern languages. There are today few kind words spoken for sending a mathematics section to the blackboards for competitive speed and accuracy in the solution of the same problem, with the teacher roving about with a pointer, prepared to nudge any eye-rolling student hoping to pick up a fortuitous equation from a speedier neighbor. The fact remains that such curricula and such teaching procedures as those experienced by Stedman's generation did develop a broadly based mental discipline that should not be discounted when subsequently applied to self-motivated interests.

After three years in the Harvard School of Medicine, much of that time being spent as an apprentice with an established physician in Boston, Stedman began his own practice of medicine. It can be assumed, with little doubt, that the young doctor may have encountered difficulty in obtaining his own patients. Those of us who are older well remember the time when the family doctor retained his patients throughout their lifetimes—and added their children and even their children's children to his list of patients. Such was undoubtedly even more true in Stedman's day.

It may have been the paucity of patients which sent Stedman to Europe as a ship's doctor in 1855 or 1856. Although there is no record of his writing any letters or keeping a diary during this period, he did record his experiences in a series of drawings which he entitled "Reminiscences of a Voyage to Liverpool by One of the Experienced Surgeons That Are Attached to Each Ship." Stedman's keen humor becomes immediately apparent, even in that title, for he is pulling his own leg by designating himself an "experienced surgeon" no more than a year or so after completion of his medical education. His drawings, however, are much closer to being an historical account of ship's travel at the time than a humorous tale of his voyage. The vivid representation of sail against sea, the minute descriptions of life on the packet ship, and the humorous portrayal of everyday incidents provide an insight into marine travel of the mid-nineteenth century not found elsewhere in either pictorial or written sources.

Stedman actually drew two groups of sketches concerning his trip. One must be considered to be a preliminary set of drawings for many of the individual caricatures are obviously incomplete; the second small album contains sketches which are more polished and more detailed. It is interesting to note

Resigned.

"E.E.P. was Mother"

that Stedman often drew at least two complete sets of drawings for his major groupings. This is evidenced by the preliminary sketches for *Hardy Lee . . .* and the lithograph volume which resulted from these sketches. It is also shown by the two groups of drawings portraying his Civil War service.

These drawings also provide an insight into Stedman's character, a view which is substantiated later by his Civil War sketches. Compassion and sympathy for his fellowman appear in his drawing of the steerage which appears on page 18. The packed and crowded conditions for "passengers," the noise which must have reverberated throughout the steerage area, the lack of privacy, and near-inhuman conditions must have shocked the sensitive young "experienced surgeon." Stedman's sense of humor becomes even more

apparent in his caricature of "Cruelty of the Mate, (2d day out) 'Come, have a cigar, Doctor!' The Beast!", shown on page 19 with both versions. Any seagoing traveller who has felt the power of the sea as he leaned against the rail can sympathize with Stedman's opinion of the mate. One must wonder, however, if the young doctor's desire for anonymity through use of fictitious names for individuals and ships was evidenced in these drawings as it was in both *Hardy Lee . . .* and his Civil War sketches.

This interest in people and events had fascinated Stedman throughout his school years. While others "doodled" to give the appearance of taking notes during a boring and unproductive lecture, Charlie Stedman could not resist making a few deft lines to record a fleeting thought of a situation or to capture a sharp image that he saw—or thought he saw. This sincere interest in the everyday events taking place around him and the tendency to record these events pictorially characterized Charles Ellery Stedman throughout his lifetime. His sketches which have survived the years start with those drawn during his student days at Harvard and continue through the antebellum period and the Civil War to some which he drew only shortly before his death in 1909. As an entity, they provide a truly intimate and detailed glimpse of life in another era, an era of comparative simplicity and tranquility.

Be that as it may, the quantity and increasing quality of his spontaneous sketches quietly brought him an unrivaled and undisputed status—even before his graduation from Harvard College—among his peers and to an extent seldom enjoyed by any member of a baccalaureate graduating class. It was a status increasingly respected by both earlier graduates and subsequent alumni. His many sketches, some hasty and some polished, tell more about his contemporary antebellum collegians—their attire, habits, customs, and the limited and almost-quaint knowledge being purveyed to them—than do most books on American higher education. These same sketches tell even more about Stedman and the warmth of his growing friendships.

While at Harvard, Charles Ellery had been elected to various clubs and societies: the Natural History Society, the Institute of 1775, the Odd Fellows, and the Knights of the Punch Bowl (K.P.B.) whom he appears to have served at times as both poet and orator. He was also for a time Vice President of the Hasty Pudding Club. Throughout his bachelor days both as a medical student and as a young practitioner, Stedman developed closer ties with these friends, especially with the hilarious graduates from the K.P.B. The dinners of those punch bowl cavaliers were a monthly must. But marriages began to thin their sturdy ranks. Each defector was given an extremely rough time before and after the ceremony.

Wedding bells were often followed by a "resignation." Because he had a sardonic aptitude for restrained satire and nifty witticisms, undoubtedly as a result of the influence of Doctor Oliver Wendell Holmes, Stedman usually led the attack.

Then, of course, came the inevitable day when Cupid registered a direct hit upon Stedman himself. Both former members and the continuing punch bowl cavaliers had a field day heaping some of Stedman's erstwhile abuse of others back upon his own shoulders. But his love for Edith Ellen, daughter of Isaac Parker of Parker's Hill, withstood all the jibes. They were married on 1 November 1859, and made their home in Dorchester.

Since Charles Ellery Stedman, the artist, seldom bothered to either date or number his pictures in series, error in positioning any single drawing is possible. Although the wedding sketch on page 15 was the last drawing in Stedman's Loyal Legion album, it is entirely possible that it may have been the first sketch drawn for the original series prepared in or before 1865. It may easily have been his own silent, self-serving retort to the jests and jibes at that memorable dinner of the Knights of the Punch Bowl.

CHAPTER TWO Doctor Stedman and Winslow Homer

THE INFLUENCE of such great teachers as Henry W. Longfellow, Louis Agassiz, Edward Everett, and Oliver Wendell Holmes upon young Charles Ellery Stedman cannot be overestimated. It would be easy to brush off further review of his formative years by insisting that he was just another product of the often cited "Flowering of New England." Such would be unfair to both Stedman the artist and his times. Although his interest in human nature and its foibles, his fondness for puns, and his

The steerage in a packet ship

restrained satire bear the unmistakable stamp of Doctor Holmes, there are major factors involved in addition to the preceptorial influences of Harvard College and the Medical School. What developed and fostered young Stedman's urge toward pictorialization of what he saw?

The initial impetus could not have come from the crude cartoons that appeared in the newsheets and magazines of his childhood years. Crude to the point of being almost repulsive, these cartoons were normally gross woodblock prints in the worst of inks, frequently further burdened by libelous political themes and words. From the mouths of public personages, necessarily identified by a label, lines led to balloons filled with unfounded accusations, idealogical retorts, and election year slanders. Much of this form of political graffiti continued from the bitter years of the Jacksonian era to and through the disastrous election of 1860. A century earlier, William Hogarth, the great caricaturist of London themes, streets, and people, would have considered any one of the American news cartoons far worse than the juvenile designs to be found on the sidewalks and corner walls of London's Lime House district. Stedman could not have found a childhood inspiration in the cartoons he saw. His source must have been something else.

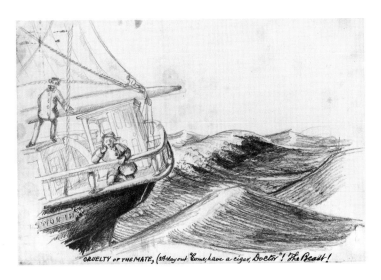

CRUELTY OF THE MATE, (2d day out) "Come, have a cigar, Doctor"! The Beast!

The Preliminary Sketch

Cruelty of the Mate, (2d day out)

"Come have a cigar, Doctor!" The Beast!

The Finished Sketch

THE IMPACT OF LITHOGRAPHY

About 1795, Aloys Senefelder, son of a Bohemian actor, accidentally discovered that a clean, smooth slab of carbonaceous limestone from a quarry near the village of Solenhofen, Bavaria, possessed an equal affinity for water and oil although the two liquids were hostile toward one another. Lines could be drawn upon the stone with a greasy black or colored crayon. If the remaining white area of the stone was merely moistened with water and a greasy roller run over the stone's prepared surface, the greasy lines already drawn upon the stone would be activated in such a way as to absorb some of the grease from the roller while the white, unmarked moist areas resisted the grease. A sheet of paper, placed on the stone under proper pressure, would reproduce the desired pattern, design, or image. Senefelder's discovery and invention acquired immediate popularity.

The simplicity of using the ground and polished slabs of limestone brought participation in art as well as art for art's sake to the masses. The first impact was upon those individuals with the most spare time. Possession of one small brick of that most wonderful limestone was sufficient to identify any man as a putative artist. Caricature, basic art since the days of the caveman, became the first principal art form for this expanding generation of homespun artists. By 1845, lithography was a far-flung hobby and fad throughout Europe; and making one's own designs, maps, and sketches on the wonder-stone was the "in-thing" among the lively smart sets, the puzzled intelligentsia, and the proud wealthy.

Commercial printers were even more prompt to sense the potential of this original and primitive forerunner of the modern offset printing processes. They eventually found themselves installing a series of large limestone slabs for creating shades of color traced or stamped upon the stones. The lucrative market of the masses was the goal which the commercial lithographers sought throughout Stedman's lifetime. While publishers always welcomed new sketches, caricatures, and original scenes, they were more than willing to use similar themes and drawings of the great masters. Copyright laws, if such even existed, were only lightly enforced, even when violations were discovered and prosecuted. International copyright was a utopian dream cherished only by a few popular authors such as Charles Dickens and William M. Thackeray. Commercial lithographers stole copy and ideas whenever and wherever they found them; great masters were pirated without a blush.

Historians are not in complete agreement concerning the exact time and place that lithography first surfaced in the United States. Boston possibly can make the best claim; for a date, 1828 is close enough for all practical purposes. By that time, London's Cruikshanks, father and sons, were making a financial success from their caricatures. Reproductions in print—sometimes made from steel etchings, sometimes from lithograph stones—multiplied their impact beyond the limits of statistical imagination. Copies of the Cruikshank drawings appeared throughout the United States with increasing proliferation during Stedman's Latin School and Harvard College years. America was literally flooded with Cruikshank reproductions for they embellished the narrative lines of serialized English novels in London periodicals such as *Bentley's Miscellany* and *Ainsworth's Magazine*. Americans did not even have to subscribe to the London periodicals to benefit from the novels and their illustrations. Both were pirated and serialized in American magazines and newspapers as fast and as regularly as the twice-a-month Cunard Line mail service could deliver the sequels to the earlier chapters. Meticulous tracing of Cruikshank's illustrations on limestone or on a block of fine grain boxwood required no more labor than handsetting the type for an equal amount of textual page space. This semi-monthly wave of literature and art had a profound influence upon Stedman and his contemporaries during their formative years. It would be a pleasure to find documents and other evidence which would indicate the exact manner by which Stedman developed into a gifted and productive amateur artist. Without accurate source information, however, one can only hypothesize.

As a child, Stedman may have been influenced by the constant inflow of lithographed caricatures into the homes of the proper Bostonians; he may have responded to these stimuli by producing a precise imitation of Cruikshank's lawyer Grimwigg in *Oliver Twist*. A bit of praise from the elder Doctor Stedman might have led Charles to draw an original and con-

Tidings of War.

vincing caricature of a neighbor which, in turn, would bring even greater praise from the father. The next logical step would be the purchase of a lithograph stone or the reproduction of some of Charles' drawings by a nearby lithographer's shop. Many an incurable amateur artist has been created in this way. But all of this is pure hypothesis for there are no definite indications of when or how Charles Ellery Stedman first developed his interest in and talent for portrayal of the life of his times.

YOUNG STEDMAN DABBLES IN ART

Despite this lack of information concerning the start and development of Stedman's interest in art, there is a more definite indication of a probable artistic influence exerted during his student years and immediately following his graduation from the School

Porter: "Half past 5? No, Sir. New York train goes at 5, time altered yesterday."

of Medicine. A family of distant relatives lived in nearby and much more rural Cambridge, on its outskirts but still near Harvard College. Charles Savage Homer was a well-to-do importer; his adored and appreciated wife, Henrietta Marina Benson, was an amateur painter of more than passing skill whose canvasses today would probably be classified as "Primitives" or "Early American." Most people agreed that the second of the three Homer sons, Winslow, was fully endowed with Mrs. Homer's fondness and aptitude for art. Sixteen years old at the time, distant cousin Charles Ellery Stedman was graduating from nearby Harvard College. Winslow Homer was not destined for college for he was a mediocre student at best. His family, however, was willing to extend financial backing to Winslow's growing artistic ambitions. His fame as an artist-journalist came initially from his black and white sketches, his wood gravures, and his lithographs. These earlier drawings and his subsequent successes with pigments and oils were to earn him worldwide fame as one of the few truly great American artists during the highly competitive second half of the nineteenth century.

Winslow Homer's formal art training began in the lithography shop of John H. Bufford, who had advertised for a teenage boy of unquestioned sketching ability; none other should apply. Despite his son's talent, Mr. Homer had to use a bit of personal influence to·get the appointment for Winslow, now nineteen years old and with a yen for little else than drawing. Drawing upon his personal relationships with

Bufford—both were members of the same volunteer fire company—Homer was able to persuade Bufford to accept Winslow as an apprentice. Bufford, however, demanded $300 as the apprenticeship fee, and required the young man to be bound to him until he reached the age of twenty-one. Similar arrangements were not unusual for young men desiring vocational training. There is little doubt that Winslow Homer learned quickly and well.

It can be assumed that Charles Ellery Stedman also learned from Bufford—directly by hanging around his lithography shop during nonacademic seasons or indirectly from Winslow Homer. By 1857, we find the two young worthies in an odd publishing partnership; Homer was freshly free of his bonds as an apprentice and welcomed lithographic chores. Young Doctor Stedman, after his trip to Europe as a ship's doctor, was still pinch-hitting for older family practitioners in Dorchester. With time on his hands, the doctor had amused himself by drawing some light, satirical caricatures which he would not mind seeing in print—but only under an assumed name. Oliver Wendell Holmes' expansive mixing of levity and laughter with his practice of medicine was not to be repeated by young Doctor Stedman. Holmes' pleasant pun that "the smallest fevers are thankfully received" was funny only to people who had no fevers. Fond as Stedman was of humor and puns, he could not afford the admitted mistake of his medical school mentor in permitting his name to be used as an author, poet, humorist, and essayist. Stedman preferred to remain anonymous.

Mr. M——— is annoyed
by the scrutiny of the tavern loafers

THE TALENTED BUT UNKNOWN "CHINKS"

Accordingly, a thin, hardback, album-shaped volume, *Mr. Hardy Lee, His Yacht, Being XXIV Sketches on Stone by Chinks*, was published in Boston on 27 May 1857. It has been reviewed briefly—or, rather, characterized—in the opening pages of this book. Boston's local reviewers gave it prompt attention in the *Advertiser*, the *Transcript*, and the *Journal*. Homegrown art of such high quality was heartily welcomed in the Hub City. It was not necessary for the reviewers to say that American art was in its infancy; most Bostonians already believed that Bufford's lithography shop was the first in the United States. The craftsmanship of the unknown Mr. "Chinks" was praised; the volume was generally accepted as a pleasant and humorous commentary upon current social trends. However, the *Journal*'s reviewer, possibly a vulgar, off-duty news reporter with no knowledge of sailing but with a keen ear for titillating gossip, missed the pun on the nautical phrase "hard-alee." He was certain that *Hardy Lee* was a lampoon against a well-known man-about-town, Henry Lee who was often called Harry Lee. That supposition may have been correct, but current research reveals that Henry Lee, a member of the Harvard Class of 1836, had married in 1845; there is no indication that he was the target.

Further research also fails to disclose any unmarried, rich, or young yachtsman of the right name and of sufficient prominence to rate the honor of such a mild and almost flattering lampoon. It is far more likely that the name *Hardy Lee* was simply a good nautical pun and that the association with a real Henry Lee was only the ill-founded guess of a newspaper gossip reporter.

All three reviewers, however, speculated upon the identity of the talented "Chinks." The *Advertiser* critic was quite close to the truth for he was certain that "The sketches are by a young gentleman of this city who could be recognized, if the anonymous veil were lifted, as the author of many a striking little sketch which has afforded amusement and pleasure at Harvard and in social Boston circles." Some Knights of the Punch Bowl obviously had been talking out of

school. Years later, Stedman's daughter, Mrs. Gorham Dana, confirmed the identification hinted at by this mass of contemporary evidence.

For a time, the single edition of *Hardy Lee . . .* graced the parlor tables in many Boston homes. Then, with many casualties along the way, the edition almost exhausted itself in attics, rubbish heaps, secondhand bookstores, and eventually on the shelves of rare book collectors. By the late 1940s, Alexander Crosby Brown, as mentioned in the introduction, was able to locate only four copies in addition to his own. During this same passage of years, Winslow Homer became famous at home and in Europe. Every secondhand book dealer knew that Homer had started as an obscure lithographer and illustrator in Boston prior to the Civil War and that he had continued to turn out hundreds of unsigned lithographs and drawings as a field artist with the Union armies for *Harper's News Weekly*. With sound logic and in good faith, some dealers undoubtedly sold unsigned lithograph works as "early Winslow Homers"—possibly even some of the rare copies of *Hardy Lee. . . .*

When Brown brought the album to the attention of Doctor Walter Muir Whitehill, Director of the Boston Atheneaum, the two conspired to bring Stedman into his proper place in American art history. Their discussions resulted in the preparation of a limited special edition for an advance subscription list under the imprint of the Club of Odd Volumes. Mr. Brown provided an excellent introduction while Doc-

Surgeon Leeshaw, U. S. N. advises the Navy as the best way for a man to serve the country.

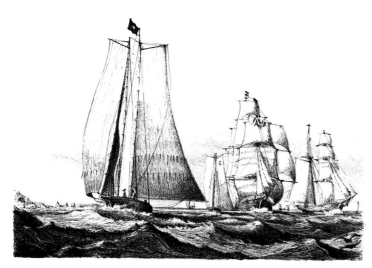

WING AND WING Sketch from *Hardy Lee . . .*

tor Whitehill handled production details. Thus, after almost a hundred years, Charles Ellery Stedman, M.D., was finally recognized as an artist.

But, other than for the possible sale of the rare original volume by an occasional dealer as a work of Winslow Homer, is there any actual and factual evidence which would tie the cousins together in the production of *Hardy Lee . . .*? Eric Rudd, a student of American art history with a primary interest in Winslow Homer, recently began a search for recondite material concerning Homer's early years in Boston. Although there are today no direct descendants of Charles Ellery Stedman, Rudd's research led him to Miss Anne B. Stedman, daughter of Ellery's brother, Henry R. Stedman. Miss Stedman sent Rudd to her cousin, Thomas Hale, who had in his possession the original sketches from which the lithograph illustrations for *Hardy Lee . . .* were produced. Rudd studied these sketches and the original lithograph volume carefully and in much detail. His findings were revealed in a beautifully illustrated article, "Winslow Homer and Mr. Hardy Lee, His Yacht," which was published in *Antiques Magazine* in November 1974. Rudd insists that Homer must have been the lithographer who transferred Stedman's twenty-four sketches to the stones.

Rudd's assertion could be true; if so, it subtracts from the reputation of neither man. To the same degree that a good poet deserves a good printer, a good artist requires good craftsmen for the multiplication and publication of his pictures. Because of their long friendship, and other associations, Stedman may have considered Homer the best—and probably the cheapest—lithographer in Boston. Homer's first and unsigned illustrations were yet to appear in *Ballou's Pictorial Drawing-Room Companion* for he had completed his apprenticeship only three months earlier, in February 1857. The publication of *Hardy Lee . . .* in May represented a wonderful and ambitious project for both Stedman and Homer. Its splendid renditions are remarkably mature. Although the *Journal*'s reviewer assured his readers that "The designer himself has lithographed his pictures and so has retained all the humor of his original conception," Rudd nevertheless suspects that Winslow Homer actually performed that routine task, basing his arguments upon clues he uncovered in his study of the lithographed prints and the original drawings. The presence of frills and lines forming numerous *W*'s and *H*'s and a cryptic pew number which can be interpreted to indicate Homer's date of birth are the major substance of Rudd's argument that it was indeed Winslow Homer who lithographed the drawings of Charles Ellery Stedman for *Hardy Lee.* . . .There is no strong reason to challenge his interpretations, but they are highly presumptive.

Taken too seriously, however, Rudd's assertions might be mistakenly used to claim the entire series and volume as the work of Homer. There is massive and conclusive evidence to the contrary which completely contradicts any such extreme thought. The original sketches, drawn at least a year before the appearance of the lithograph volume, are definitely the work of Stedman. There is the contemporary statement that the creator of the sketches also transferred them to the stones. Although there are admittedly many improvements and finishing touches in the lithograph prints which are not present in the original sketches, most artists add final touches and make changes to a drawing before releasing it for publication. Stedman himself did that in copying his Civil War sketches for the Loyal Legion album; he did the same in preparing a more detailed and polished version of his drawings about his trip as an "experienced surgeon" and ship's doctor. Such additions and changes are trifles that only add to the overall perfection of a drawing.

BOARDING MADE EASY.
"I never shall get down this awful ladder in the world!"
Sketch from *Hardy Lee* . . .

Collaboration between Stedman and Homer at this time may well have existed to some extent. It is possible to develop an interpretation which does, to some degree, make the apparent contradictions more compatible. In 1857, Stedman was a young doctor trying to build a sustaining practice from among patients who had rejected older doctors or from other patients whom older doctors had rejected for non-payment of bills. Doctor Stedman needed medical creditability far more than he needed—or wanted—artistic recognition and distinction. Indeed, he considered such distinction a liability; he wanted and needed anonymity. Winslow Homer's desires and needs were the exact opposite. Having completed his apprenticeship, he had immediately opened a lithography shop in competition with his master, the long-established Bufford. Homer's requirements were those of a tradesman with artistic skills to supplement his technical ability: publicity and recognition. Two months after publication of *Hardy Lee* . . . his unsigned drawings began to appear in Boston periodicals. Thus it may well be that the respective desires and needs of both Stedman and Homer were used to confuse the contemporary and local public regarding the identity of the talented but unknown Boston artist, "Chinks." They could hardly have flattered themselves that their deception, if such it was, might confuse others for nearly a hundred years.

NEGLECT OF THE NAVY IN CIVIL WAR ART

Neither Homer nor Stedman could have even remotely dreamed what their immediate futures would bring. In four short years, Homer would find himself in sharp competition with swarms of war correspondents and their associated "field artists"; Stedman would again be a ship's doctor, but this time in a warship instead of a packet.

In its pictorial representation, the American Civil War attracted more artists and produced more artwork than any other war in our history prior to World War II. While tremendous improvements in weaponry since the days of Wellington and Napoleon expanded the fronts and changed the face of battle, giant strides improving pictorial techniques took place almost at the same time. The competition of lithography had forced the clumsy woodblock craftsmen, little changed in their methods since the days of Benjamin Franklin, to take a harsh and critical look at their own inks, cutting tools, and techniques. Seasoned boxwood, heavily coated with white paint, made faster production possible; inscribing finer lines with lighter tools resulted in major improvement in every phase of delineation. The deterioration of woodblocks caused by heavy press runs would soon be solved by transferring the image to metal plates. At the same time, lithography continued to move forward from its humble beginnings.

Even more startling was the development of the muddy and always ugly daguerreotype into a comparatively clear and realistic photograph. Some individuals even predicted that all art in its historic forms would ultimately perish, replaced by photographs. Matthew Brady and his fellow cameramen in the field apparently tried to hasten that day. However, about all that was definitely proven was the limitation of the cameras, lenses, and wet plate negatives. There was also the additional problem of translating a glass plate negative into a printable image. It would be many years before the actual photographic print could be directly reproduced for publication purposes. During the Civil War, photographs were often used by staff artists to provide basic images to be used for woodblock engravings.

The increased use of illustrations by newspapers and periodicals brought increased demands for illustrative coverage on all fronts. Field artists accompanied correspondents. Many news magazines and major newspapers maintained editorial art studios to

The Board of Examiners: Surgeons Weatherly, Bilger & Tompkin, U.S.N.

"Melancholy termination of this season's boating."
The original sketch

translate field sketches and photographs into gravure plates. Never were American newssheets more scoop-hungry; they had to be for the thirst of the people, North and South alike, for news from their embattled armies was at times unquenchable. When telegraph lines were cut and dispatches were so brief as to merely stimulate the imagination, "news" was created within the publisher's own resources. When no drawings were available, editors and craftsmen frequently improvised pictorial coverage "from the front." The political and social nature of the conflict and, most of all, the composition of both the Blue and the Gray armies were responsible for this chronic and extraordinary thirst for news.

At no time during the entire four years did the Union ever have a Regular Army of more than 25,000 officers and men. Although the South did have a Regular Army on paper, it was never able to bring that Army into being. Both central governments fought the war with regiments, brigades, and even some divisions which were *requisitioned* from their states on a more-or-less pro rata basis. President Lincoln's initial "call" to the loyal states, for example, was not for the 75,000 officers and men so often cited by careless historians. He asked for armed and marching regiments, totalling that number, to be brought into Federal service. Volunteers were so numerous that many of these state regiments reported at full wartime strength instead of their smaller peacetime numbers. The first call actually brought 91,000 men and officers from the Volunteer Militia, the equivalent of today's National Guard, instead of the 75,000 asked by Lincoln. During the war, a city such as Chicago often raised a brigade of three regiments of 1,000 men each. By contrast, a small rural county might be called upon to provide ten companies of one hundred men each, organized into a county regiment. These county companies and city regiments, both North and South, campaigned and fought alongside each other for the duration of the war or for whatever length of service the unit had volunteered.

The intense interest of home-front families in what their sons and fathers were doing and where they were levied an obligation on national, regional, and local newspapers to provide that information. It was this massive public interest which led the press lords of the era to recruit hundreds of correspondents, field artists, and engravers. Although correspondents and artists accompanied all of the armies on their various campaigns, none were assigned to the ships of the Navy. There was no naval militia; volunteers such as Ellery Stedman entered the Navy as individuals because of prior nautical interest or because they possessed special skills and experience needed by the Navy. No single crew came from the grass roots citizenry of a single community as was true for so many companies, batteries, regiments, and brigades of the armies. Public thirst for information, human interest stories, and scenes of life afloat did not exist in the same degree as the demand for information about the armies. Consequently, publishers and editors tended to ignore the Navy except in those instances where ships and armies were engaged in joint operations such as McClellan's Peninsular Campaign or the attacks on Roanoke Island, Hilton Head, Mobile, and New Orleans.

The lack of artists with the fleets resulted in artwork which was notoriously bad and often improvised by craftsmen who were not on the scene. Pictorial representations of Farragut's ships battling the forts below New Orleans, for example, were highly imaginary. Both *Harper's Weekly* and *Frank Leslie's Illustrated* showed Union ships deployed as if the Confederate barrier across the Mississippi had been completely removed. Depiction of various ships was highly inaccurate. Early drawings of the clash between the ironclads *Monitor* and *Virginia (Merrimac)* were also improvised from the imagination of staff craftsmen and artists. The representations of *Monitor* were not too bad. Someone had reported that she looked like a cheesebox on a raft which, in truth, she did. The staff artists in residence far from the Hampton Roads scene of action were able to picture *Monitor* with reasonable fidelity; this was not true of their concept of her adversary.

It is a remarkable and unusual coincidence that the two cousins, Winslow Homer and Charles Ellery Stedman, artistic collaborators before the War, would both record pictorially some of the events of that conflict. It is even more remarkable that Homer, the artist seeking a reputation, achieved his goal because of his sketches prepared as a field artist with the armies. Stedman, the reluctant artist, recorded his experiences afloat but without publicity or public exposure.

"Melancholy termination of this season's boating."
The lithograph from *Hardy Lee . . .*

Homer's war drawings are well known; Stedman's almost completely unknown.

STEDMAN, THE RELUCTANT ARTIST

When Stedman drew this collection of sketches representing his naval service, it is doubtful that he realized his lack of competition from the professional field artists. Why he initially veiled the name of his ship with a pseudonym and why he styled himself as "Doctor Squillgee" (a squilgee is a mop or device for cleaning the deck) is a matter for conjecture. It could not have been necessary to shield himself from an unsympathetic medical public for that public no longer existed. We can only attribute his restraints to his innate modesty which had been bolstered by the constantly repeated admonitions of his much admired teacher and exemplar, Oliver Wendell Holmes.

As Dean of the Harvard School of Medicine, Holmes had often warned his students and young graduates that:

> *Medicine is the most difficult of the sciences and the most laborious of the arts. It will take all your powers of body and mind if you are faithful to it. Do not dabble in the muddy sewer of politics, nor linger by the enchanted streams of literature, nor dig in far-off fields for the hidden waters of alien sciences. The great practitioners are generally those who concentrate all of their powers in their business.*

She's got all she wants, now.
Old Graves says: "A reg'lar muzzler."

In effect, what the wise and experienced Dean was telling young Stedman and his other students was "Do what I am now telling you to do; under no circumstances do what I am now doing." Holmes, at that time nearing the peak of his fame as a poet and author of whimsical essays, undoubtedly knew that there is often a tendency for the student to imitate the much admired professor and preceptor; hence his admonition.

Although it is quite likely that Stedman may have wondered why he should not follow Holmes' example by developing a reputation both as an artist and a physician, it is clearly apparent that he decided to accept Holmes' advice. His desire for anonymity was carried almost to an extreme even before he entered the Navy, as exemplified by *Hardy Lee.* . . . That same desire resulted in the "loss" of his Civil War drawings for over a century.

CHAPTER THREE Doctor Stedman Joins the Navy

As ELLERY STEDMAN and Edith Parker were exchanging their wedding vows on 1 November 1859, the headlines and editorial pages of the nation were heavily laced with news and views of an abortive slave revolt at Harpers Ferry, Virginia. Its leader, John Brown, was a notorious fanatic and a deliberate murderer of record. At the same time, it was being truthfully whispered in Boston that one of its most prominent philanthropists was a principal money raiser for financing the debacle. Brown's son and nine of his fifteen black followers had perished during the revolt; Brown had been wounded and was being held for trial in Virginia. He was promptly and legally hanged under the criminal code of Virginia on 2 December 1859. It would have been far better for the nation had Brown also perished with his followers.

With equal promptness, passions in both the North and South were brought to white heat by irresponsible news media and the rampant rhetoric of ambitious politicians and propagandists. In this artificially created crisis, the nation suddenly found itself bereft of leadership. About the only thing that extremists on both sides agreed upon was the complete failure of the Federal Constitution and the necessity for dissolution of the Union. William Lloyd Garrison,

revolutionary leader of the Abolitionists, was more vicious on this theme than anyone in the South.

If any of this social and political turbulence bothered the divinely happy Ellery and Edith, there appears to be no record of it. Only one sketch from Stedman's pen has been found that carried a political message. This was actually more personal than political but it did present a dim view of Nathaniel P. Banks, state and national politician and Civil War general. Stedman apparently took quite seriously his Medical Dean's admonition against a doctor "dabbling in the muddy sewer of politics."

It is not likely that even the chaotic election year of 1860 materially jolted the Stedmans' equanimity nor did it seriously disturb the much admired Doctor Oliver Wendell Holmes. As late as two weeks before the inauguration of President Lincoln, Holmes expressed optimism in a letter to his friend, John Lothrop Motley, in Europe. He was equally disgusted with the "Abolitionists, as bent on the total separation from the South as Carolina is upon secession from the North." He considered the victorious Republican party an uncertain factor: perhaps willing to listen to further compromises, but fully accepting the leadership of the new President should he call for a showdown on any form of secession or nullification of

Federal taxes and laws.

The views Doctor Holmes expressed to Motley were typical of contemporary attitudes of Boston's medical practioners, well-to-do businessmen, and in Harvard College social circles other than those of the Divinity School and its graduates. In all probability, Holmes and Stedman voted for neither Mr. Lincoln, the Republican, nor Mr. Douglas, the Illinois Democrat. If they voted at all in November 1860, it was most likely in support of the Constitutional Party which had John Bell of Kentucky heading the ticket and Harvard's former professor and president, Edward Everett, for Vice President.

When Lincoln subordinated all other issues, including slavery, to the preservation of the Union, he alienated William Lloyd Garrison and his Abolitionists until 1863 when they decided that Lincoln was a winner. By contrast, the New England moderates, such as the Constitutional Unionists, had no choice other than to support Lincoln. This they did enthusiastically from the day Fort Sumter was fired upon by the South Carolina regiments.

EVENTS OVERTAKE STEDMAN

Thus we find newly married, young Doctor Stedman picturing himself for the first time as a concerned citizen. In his caricature on page 21, he tells us far more than his own contemporary concern for national news. The portraiture is that of a medical practitioner before the horse and buggy became a luxury in a doctor's life. Although the one-horse shay was already in vogue for a Boston city practice since most of the important streets and thoroughfares were cobblestoned, the heavy sands and sticky clay of the rural paths and roads in small and scattered Dorchester made a saddlebag practice mandatory.

One can easily see the professional dignity inherent in the tall hat of the era, the riding crop under his left arm, and the relaxed ease of his seat in the English saddle. The long tight trousers, strapped tightly down under the instep of the shoe, kept the trouser legs from creeping up to form punishing woolen wrinkles. These trousers were the antecedents of the jodhpurs in vogue today. If the bangtail horse appears to be more concerned than his tidings-eager rider, he has just cause to be considering the long-shank spurs with tiny rowels attached to his master's heels. For a general-purpose horse of the time, such spurs could be worse than a war. No inkling is given of what the news may have been that day, but it could not have been good.

Stedman's second self-portraiture on page 25 shows him on foot but wearing essentially the same, or similar, riding attire. The riding crop and spurs have been left in the horse barn in favor of a walking stick. In his caption for the sketch, Stedman makes his first use of a fictitious name for an actual individual; "Surgeon Leeshaw, U.S.N." was probably Surgeon William M. King, U.S.N. There can be no doubt as to what Surgeon Leeshaw is advising him to do. The service needs him. Ships are being taken out of "ordinary" and fitted for high-seas service. New warships

Commission - with orders to the U.S. Steam Sloop "Fornots," 12.

are being built. Acting volunteer commissions as lieutenants are being offered to qualified merchant ship officers. Yes, surgeons are wanted. Doctor Stedman should hasten over to the Navy Yard and talk to the Captain Commanding. From the end result, we know exactly what was said. Nevertheless, Ellery Stedman might have done much better in terms of rank and pay had he conferred with the well-groomed volunteer militiaman, strolling with his wife and proud son, who at the moment wanted the latest paper from a busy newsboy.

Far more regiments than ships were needed and were being activiated. With his credentials and experience, Stedman could hardly have been offered any less appointment than that of a regimental surgeon, with two assistant surgeons and a medical detachment of his own. Such an appointment would have come his way without the bothersome oral examination by a board of crusty old seagoing doctors who had little to do on long voyages other than constantly read the latest books and journals on surgery and medicine.

But Ellery Stedman had been born in the Chelsea Naval Hospital. The clean, salted airs of the wide Atlantic had been filling his lungs since childhood. Sailing on the bay had been great fun. He had sailed to Europe as a ship's doctor. Family associations with the sea and its sailors had been too long. If the Navy needed him, he could not turn his back, not even if the Army had offered an assignment as surgeon general to an army corps. Following the usual delays in

paper work going to and from the Navy Department Personnel Office in Washington, D.C., Stedman was given the physical and professional oral examinations by Surgeons "Weatherly, Bilger, and Tomkins," as portrayed on page 29. These names are also fictitious; Bilger might have been Surgeon William S. Bishop, U.S.N., who was then on duty at the Boston Navy Yard. Finally, Doctor Charles E. Stedman, from Massachusetts, was duly commissioned as a Volunteer Acting Assistant Surgeon, U.S.N., to rank from 16 September 1861.

The fall of Fort Sumter was no longer news. The great and sovereign states of Arkansas, Tennessee, North Carolina, and Virginia were horrified when they were required to provide regiments for the invasion of their seven sovereign sister states who had already seceded. They belatedly joined the Confederacy. Within Missouri, Kentucky, and some counties of Maryland, little revolts and counter-revolts were in progress. The agony of defeat at Bull Run late in July had plunged the North into despair. Ellery Stedman had hardly picked a period of optimism for his entry into a combat profession.

Stedman continued to wait. Older ships were still to be put in commission; new ships were still to be launched. He was informed that his name was on the "Awaiting Orders List." In that status, the pay scale allowed him about seventy dollars a month. But "unemployed" Naval List surgeons were permitted to maintain a private practice ashore. In the piping good times of peace, naval surgeons often avoided sea duty, seeking just enough to protect their status on the seniority list. After twenty years, if the usual calendar rate prevailed, one could reach the rank of surgeon with "Awaiting Orders" pay of over two thousand dollars a year. Sea duty pay for such an officer was twenty-eight hundred dollars. Given good health and enough years, becoming a fleet surgeon at sea with a salary of thirty-three hundred was a dream to be cherished.

In other words, Stedman was starting at the bottom, but he would be able to care for his Dorchester patients until the reporting date of his orders. Thus he was able to remain happily at home until shortly after New Year's Day, 1862. A few days later we find him with sword properly belted but doffing his cap instead of saluting as he reports for duty to Captain "Rumbelow." Stedman pictures this in the drawing on page 39.

By 8 January the entire crew of the new fourth rate, USS *Huron,* was on board at the Boston Navy Yard. The vessel was about to be commissioned. In time of peace, the commissioning might well have been an auspicious occasion with an improvised platform, the Navy Yard Band crashing out martial tunes, and forensics and compliments from the Yard Commander. But warfare provides little time for unctuous ceremonies. Opening music was probably restricted to the shrill notes of the pipes of the boatswain's mates calling "All Hands" and passing the word, "Ho, spar-deck." The Executive Officer would have introduced Captain Downes in one sentence. He, in turn,

would have said little or nothing and then nodded toward a Marine Corps bugler who would have blown "To the Color." Downes would have jerked a halyard that broke the stops on the ship's commission pennant at the main truck. He would then have lifted his voice with a loud "I hereby declare the United States Ship *Huron* in commission." The Executive Officer would have followed with "Go to your work, men. Dismissed."

HURON PUTS TO SEA

Huron did not immediately cast off her mooring lines and majestically steam down the bay. Bunkers had to be filled with coal and magazines stocked with ammunition. Barrels of fresh water to an aggregate of 3,000 gallons had to be stowed below. The men of the crew were but little more than a list of names for they had arrived aboard that day from the old, semi-dismantled, 86-gun ship-of-the-line *Ohio* which had long served as the station receiving ship. Each man had a warrant rank or rating, from cook to sailmaker, with presumed skills for every essential assignment. Sorting them out and putting them on the job would come when the basic chores were finished. Captain John Downes and his officers had about thirty days in which to do all of the initial tasks and to organize the crew into functional teams for every major and minor duty. *Huron* soon cast off her mooring lines and put to sea for shakedown and training in coastal waters.

Meanwhile, the war that never should have happened was dragging through its first winter. There was some local and significant fighting in Missouri and Kentucky, but very little east of the mountains. General George B. McClellan, with an army rapidly growing to 138,000 men, was intent upon defending Washington against Confederate attacks that never came.

In Maryland, Massachusetts Volunteer Major General Ben Butler, an erstwhile Democrat who a year previously had tried to get the party's presidential nomination for Jefferson Davis instead of Stephen Douglas, was a restless man. He teamed up with the Navy to seal the Pamlico and Albemarle Sounds of North Carolina by seizing and holding Hatteras Inlet. This would simplify the blockade problem and would keep Confederate privateers from sneaking out into the sea lanes to capture Yankee merchantmen. It would also give Flag Officer Silas Stringham a smooth haven for coaling and servicing his men-of-war. Butler with 860 of his soldiers went along for the ride and to act as marines. Stringham could muster a few companies from within his fleet. It was a brilliant stroke. During the first week of September 1861, they captured two forts, three vessels, thirty coast artillery pieces, 750 prisoners, 1,000 small arms, and much ammunition.

On 21 October, General McClellan permitted a Union brigade to venture across the Potomac at Ball's Bluff. It narrowly escaped capture, and its casualties were proportionally heavy. Three of the regiments of infantry were from Massachusetts. Oliver Wendell Holmes, Jr., a lieutenant in the 20th Massachusetts, was hit by two bullets; one really hurt. He lived to fight many more days and battles. In later years, although he called himself an old soldier, he was more famed as an Associate Justice of the United States Supreme Court. The war had come to Boston; local headlines were tall.

A short time later, on 7 November, Flag Officer S.F. DuPont struck at Hilton Island with sixteen warships and chartered transports for a sea lift of 14,000 soldiers commanded by General T.W. Sherman (no kin to "War is hell" Sherman). The heights of the island dominated Port Royal Sound on the South Carolina coast thirty air miles northeast of Savannah, Georgia. The fortified heights were captured, but the garrison escaped to the mainland. The South Atlantic Squadron had come to stay. As a naval base, Port Royal with its potential for supporting further invasions toward Savannah or Charleston was to be a bleeding wound in the side of the Confederacy for the remainder of the war.

Throughout most of January and the first week of February, rumors swirled about the future of *Huron*. The Rebels were striking back in the Hatteras area. *Huron* would certainly be rushed there with additional troops and other ships. General Ambrose Burnside and Flag Officer Louis Goldsborough were known to be planning a counteroffensive there. The same was being said about Port Royal and Hilton Head. Other rumormongers insisted that the next real big show was shaping up for the Gulf. Ships were being chartered to move General Ben Butler and an

Reports to Captain Rumbelow, commanding U.S.S. "Fornots."

unknown number of men to that region, possibly to Pensacola. But where from there? *Huron* could hardly miss that buildup.

Meanwhile, on *Huron,* training was progressing by day and night exercises. There was little time for songs or high jinks during the dogwatches. Furthermore, it was too cold on the spar-deck. This training in home waters was distasteful to Stedman—so near home and yet so far. On 5 February, *Huron* was back at the shipyard dock topping off stores, coal, and water. Captain Downes came back aboard with sealed orders which he opened when *Huron* was well out at sea. At their evening meal, Lieutenant George E. Belknap, the Executive Officer, told the wardroom mess that they were going to Port Royal.

In the light of his greater experience, he probably explained that all the other rumors were as erroneous as most shipyard rumors usually are. He may have indicated that Port Royal and the South Atlantic Squadron were nothing less than the best of luck: Flag Officer DuPont's zone of responsibility extended from the northeast boundary of South Carolina, excluding only Cape Fear, to Cape Florida at the extreme tip of Key Biscayne. No squadron had a better hunting preserve for capturing blockade runners. There would certainly be prize money bonuses for all. Whether Belknap actually believed this is beside the point although logic was on his side. It is a basic duty of a good second-in-command to make things look good whether they are or not. The Executive Officer's attitude was almost immediately reflected by the junior officers who passed the word to their division chiefs and gun crews.

Belknap was a good Executive Officer. He would ultimately retire in 1894 as a rear admiral, the highest rank then available in the Navy. His is a distinguished name in the period of the Navy's transition from sail to steam, from wood to iron, and from iron to steel. Like Alfred Thayer Mahan, the naval strategist and historian, Belknap was one of the giants in an era when great strides were taken in the development of the modern Navy.

Stedman left a good wardroom scene in his Loyal Legion album; this is reproduced on page 41. The officers depicted can be identified if they were with *Huron* at the time of its arrival at Port Royal on 13 February. A name or two may be in error since Stedman did not date the sketch. The faces from left to right are: Acting Master W.H. Baldwin; Paymaster Thomas T. Caswell; Lieutenant George E. Belknap; standing is the wardroom steward; Acting Master J. W. Gill; and Acting Master Joseph Blake. The officer with his back to us, at the foot of the table seated on a folding chair, is none other than the artist himself, Volunteer Acting Assistant Surgeon Charles Ellery Stedman. Captain Downes, of course, ate alone in his own comparatively spacious quarters. The ship was not at sea during that rather relaxed meal for one of the three masters would have been absent on duty as officer of the deck. Had that been the case, Stedman would have rated the arm chair occupied by Mister Blake. "Mister" was almost an official title for masters

The ward-room mess in a screw gunboat.

and passed midshipmen, and the latter title soon to be replaced with the new rank of ensign.

Though he was low man on the totem pole as the ship's only surgeon, Stedman was not without some enviable perquisites and rights. One of the doors back of the chairs in the wardroom opened into his own little cabin, complete with bed, desk, and a porthole as shown in Stedman's drawing on page 47. He also rated a surgeon's steward who bossed a well equipped little sick bay stocked with drugs, instruments, and beds suspended from the overhead. Sick bay was manned by a detachment of hospital corpsmen.

Above and beyond these tangibles, the Surgeon —his title, like "Captain," was automatic—shared with the Paymaster and the Executive Officer the privilege of a conference with the Captain, each at his own initiative. All others talked to the Captain only when and where he demanded a response to a vital situation, such as when a seaman in his presence "expectorates generously on the quarterdeck" as noted in Chapter One. Nevertheless, the Captain was always responsible for everything that occurred on his ship. If the weather was fair but the Captain nervously paced the quarterdeck with glances to windward, everyone knew that the barometer was falling. Entering or leaving ports, in other narrow waters, during storms, fogs, and battles, the Captain assumed direct command.

The ship's engineers had not yet achieved full recognition as commissioned officers and held warrant ranks as did the Gunner, the Boatswain, the Carpenter, and the Sailmaker. Their pay scale at times did exceed that of the junior deck officers, the three masters already mentioned. *Huron's* Chief Engineer was actually rated as a First Assistant Engineer while his three engine room watch officers were rated as Third Assistants. The warrant officers had a mess and steward of their own but not a separate cook. Their hot food, tea, or coffee came from the ship's galley. If the crew was being fed "salthorse," so were the warrant officers. However, when the ship was in port, they were able to embellish their mess with cakes, fruits, and "warrant officers' champagne," another name for grog mixed with ginger ale. The entire crew officially received grog only when the Captain gave the order, "Splice the Main Brace," as Stedman illustrated in his sketch on page 119. On special occasions such as Washington's Birthday or following a victory over an armed and resisting foe, a squadron commander might hoist a flag signal for the same order.

The wartime shortage of Regular Navy officers is further revealed by the *Huron's* list. Only the Captain and his Executive Officer had served prior to the firing on Fort Sumter. Her three junior deck officers, although appearing old for their rank, were Volunteer Officers and had probably commanded a merchant ship or a whaler. The Paymaster was a Regular, but he had been commissioned since the beginning of hostilities. Another peculiarity of *Huron's* officer list is the absence of a midshipman or passed midshipmen. Apparently the only midshipmen in the Navy were those in the Naval Academy. The entire Class of

1860, which included future Admirals Alfred T. Mahan and Winfield S. Schley of the Spanish American War era, were at sea as lieutenants. Schley was second in command of *Winona,* a sister ship of *Huron.* The ship also had no Marine Corps lieutenant although there was a small detachment of Marines aboard. The detachment probably included fourteen privates, a bugler, a drummer, a fifer, and three corporals, all commanded by a gunnery sergeant. Conventionally, the sergeant would have been allocated a seat at the steerage mess.

Beneath the warrant ranks, the stratification of the crew of a warship at sea continued downward through sundry ratings. There were the chief petty officers, gun captains for each gun, captains of the maintop and foretop, and a captain of the head. In terms of pay, there were stewards, cooks, painters, yeomen, storekeepers, and other specialists, all stratified among themselves. However, they were rated above the able seamen, numerically the largest rating group aboard. Beneath this rate were the partially trained ordinary seamen and landsmen. This last and lowest mudsill of seagoing society was seldom called anything other than "greenhorns."

A boy from twelve to eighteen years of age could be signed on legally but only with the Captain's specific permission since the boy became his legal ward if under eighteen. Most captains rejected all young applicants unless there was an officer kinsman aboard to whom most of the responsibility could be delegated. A boy was usually called a "powder monkey" for this was his normal assignment as a gun-crew member. His pay would be half that of an ordinary seaman which was sixteen dollars a month. Greenhorns drew fourteen dollars a month under the pay tables of 1864.

It can be readily seen that a warship away from her home port is populated by a thoroughly stratified masculine society, a stratification demanded by both the power and majesty of the sea and the stern requirements of naval warfare. The shape and interior arrangement of any seagoing ship are dictated by the all-powerful sea; its management necessitates a crew properly stratified, thoroughly disciplined, and skilled to perform their respective duties efficiently and promptly. This was the stratified society in which Volunteer Acting Assistant Surgeon Charles Ellery Stedman found himself as *Huron* steamed south toward Port Royal.

CHAPTER FOUR USS *Huron* Goes to War

MASSACHUSETTS BAY and neighboring New England waters and coves offered ample opportunities for shakedown, local cruising, and training of officers and men. Coordinated teamwork was essential for a ship scheduled for a war zone. In a way, it was worse for all personnel than being on the high seas for homes and friends were so near and yet so far. Nevertheless, New England winters were superb for training for the weather was a worthy foe.

Steam was used in the narrow waters although the sails were set when well offshore. Exercises in ship handling and team techniques in all conceivable crises plus the rapid rhythm in service of the big guns occupied eight or more hours every day. Added to other routine ship duties and learning to live with one another, training more than filled the short daylight hours. *Huron* was having the breath of life activated within her own man-made organs. At sea, especially in combat, a ship must have robust health or perish.

At fifteen minutes prior to six bells in the morning watch, 5:45 AM, the little marine bugler sounded his brassy notes. The Master-at-Arms, or one of his corporals, assisted by the boatswain's mate from the on-deck watch would begin running the length and breadth of the berth-deck. They occasionally bent low

to avoid a head collision with a lower than average, heavily sagging hammock. They would be shouting: "Rise and roll out! Get up and lash-up!" This last command required the use of the head line to lash the hammock and bedding into a tight, waterproof, round bundle. These orders were often accentuated by painlessly hitting the bottom of a slow hammock with a resounding loud slap of a flat board. Men who have been off duty only two hours from the midwatch (midnight to 4:00 AM) were billeted separately and permitted to "sleep in" until 7:30 AM. To say that anyone ever slept through this furor would be an undue strain upon the imagination.

Sailors from the watch-on-duty would receive the rush of arriving hammocks at the spar-deck's bulwarks where they would be properly and uniformly stowed in the "nettings." The misnomer was applied to the heavy, rope nets that were normally carried along the bulwarks and sometimes over the hammocks. Stowing hammocks within the bulwarks provided additional protection from small arms fire and flying wood splinters created by cannonballs crashing through the bulwarks. Nettings could be instantly triced up as a barrier to any hostile or unwanted boarding party; they could also be dropped over the side at swimming call to be used by men entering or climbing out of the water. Used as cargo nets with lifts rigged from convenient yardarms, nettings were often employed to hoist recalcitrant or drunken sailors aboard after the shore patrol had poured them into the night's last liberty boat.

With the decks cleared of personal effects and with seabags and ditty boxes in their assigned places, the ship received its daily cleaning, both alow and aloft. The berth-deck was saltwater swabbed, swept, scrubbed, and squeegeed. Any soiled or stained areas or spots would be attacked with a holystone at the end of a stick; or, if in a nook or a corner, by a sailor on hands and knees using a "prayerbook" or small holy-stone. The spar-deck would be completely holy-stoned by teams moving with the speed and precision of a drill exercise under the sharp eyes of the bos'n and his mates. They would point to additional "prayerbooking" needed here and there. The wide and curving metal tracks for the four gun carriages would be burnished and polished as would all other topside brightwork. Aloft, standing rigging was checked, rewound when needed. Halyards and brace blocks were also checked and the nightly acquired "Irish pennants" carefully tucked in. Before the ship's buckets were returned to their racks, sailors filled them from saltwater spigots for use for washing face and hands and perhaps for shaving. Shaving was con-sidered fastidious at best and self-punishment under all circumstances. The Navy's special "saltwater soap" was a fair cleaner but never foamed or "sudsed."

Doctor Stedman promptly grew a beard much to the amusement of "The Toodles" (the Harvard Class of '52) back in Boston. What Edith thought of this is not known for only a part of his letters home have survived the years. In any event, most sailors' wives reserve such opinions until "her man" returns home. There is certainly no known reason for Mrs. Stedman to have departed from this general rule.

With hands and faces washed and with beards and mustaches properly stroked and caressed, *Huron's* crew was ready for breakfast which, for most, came at 8:00 AM, the beginning of the forenoon watch. At that time, the clock and the quartermaster who struck the bells were in agreement. Thereafter, the bell was struck each half hour up to eight bells which ended the four hour watch with the sound being a signal for the watch below to relieve the watch on duty. A full twenty-four hour cycle was: midwatch from midnight to 4:00 AM; morning watch to 8:00 AM; forenoon watch to noon; afternoon watch to 4:00 PM; first dogwatch to four bells or 6:00 PM; second dogwatch to eight bells or 8:00 PM; and night watch to mid-night.

Although warrant and chief petty officers were served by stewards, the ship's cooks issued food for each mess of lesser ratings and seamen to rotating orderlies, a seagoing form of kitchen police. Messes were generally grouped according to the watch to which its members were assigned or by gun crews, topmen, the "black gang" of coal heavers and firemen, and marines. *Huron's* seventeen marines, including the corporals, might have become Messes 7 and 8.

Each mess could rotate the orderly job among the privates or hire a messmate to do it permanently, most likely the latter. The orderly was trusted with the key to the food locker for his mess. This contained the rations issued to the mess and any collective purchases made in port to supplement the issue rations. If cheese was issued once a week, the members of the mess decided whether they would eat the issue on the day it was received or to spread it out over certain days of the week. The members of each mess also decided when supplementary provisions would be used. Sundry utensils were also kept in the food locker, but the individual "tools" (knife, fork, spoon, and mug) would be stored in the locker only if there was space and after negotiations with the mess orderly.

The mess orderly delivered ration items to the cook and his assistant. The orderly also brought the hot food in a brightly scrubbed kid and the coffee pot to the white sailcloth he had spread on the deck at an assigned place. In foul weather, this was on the berth-deck; in fair weather, on the topside. The messmates sat on the sailcloth and served themselves from the kid—or ate directly from it! Some messes of marines and sailors were more meticulous and required tin plates for all members; others heavily supplemented their issue rations and acquired a reputation for good living and verbal jollification. Most messes, however, quietly took what the government offered and lived meagerly on "dogs' bodies." Transfer from one mess to another could be arranged, but

this took a bit of politicking in the forecastle to get the best results. An "invitation" to join another mess could often be arranged in advance. If this was not done, there was the risk of rejection by a majority of black spots on the blank ballots dropped in the hat when the mess members voted upon acceptance of the transfer candidate.

TRAINING FOR COMBAT

Captain Downes had the option of dividing his crew into three watches with each serving four hours of deck duty or in the tops with eight hours of relief from such calls. In the listless, offshore months of the blockade, he might well have cut to quarter-watches as did some skippers, but cutting that thin in hostile waters was always a doubtful decision. However, Downes, a heavy-handed follower of old traditions, instructed his much younger Executive Officer, Lieutenant Belknap, that he would stick to the two-watch organization of four hours on and four hours off with a switch in the daily cycle by changes between the first and second dogwatches. By doing this, neither watch would have to take the midnight to 4:00 AM duty two nights in succession. For the Captain, this had the added advantage of maximum utilization of his limited number of experienced and seasoned sailors in the on-the-job training of his excessive number of "greenhorns" or landsmen.

Daylight hours were dedicated to the combat training of all hands in drills, exercises, speed, and techniques of ship handling in every conceivable

He wishes he had joined the Army.

combat situation. Throughout the shakedown cruise, everyone was on call during daylight hours for *Huron* had to have the appearance of being combat ready by the time the anchor was dropped in Port Royal Sound off Hilton Head. Downes would necessarily report substantially as much when he reported to Flag Officer DuPont aboard the 50-gun steam frigate, *Wabash*.

From breakfast to the first dogwatch, all officers and men were constantly piped, bugled, and drummed from one routine and repetitious drill or practice exercise to another. However, they did not follow the same training sequence on any two successive days. This meant that through each scheduled activity there could be no prediction as to what might be coming next. There were collision drills, abandon ship drills, explosions aft and explosions forward drills, and fire drills, although the only fires aboard were under the steam boilers and amidships in the galley stove. The other disaster drills were also conducted *in absentia*.

Even more mythical were the hostile ships that attacked from the starboard and then from the port, often closing rail to rail for a grapnel embrace and possible victory by boarding. At times, it was presumed that *Huron* was closing in on a cannonball-battered foe with *Huron* throwing the grapnels for a certain victory on the absent, hostile decks. These heavy demands upon the imagination came when the marine drummer rolled the "Beat to Quarters" which actually meant "all hands to battle stations." When beaten at night, everyone turned out under the eerie glow of battle lanterns. Hammocks were lashed and stowed; decks were cleared for action; and the guns were cast loose although not provided with ammunition. Rosters were called within each division. All being present and the ship in battle order, the bugler would sound "recall," and the off-duty watch would retrieve its hammocks and go below to sleep until the next eight bells.

THE MEDICAL DIVISION AT BATTLE STATIONS

The boredom and seeming futility inherent in constant practice drills usually fall heaviest upon those who have the most time to think about them because they have the least to do while the drills were underway. First among these usually would be the Chaplain for there hardly could be any mortally wounded men to be comforted or burials to be performed. Since *Huron* had no Chaplain, these non-arduous duties were assigned to the Surgeon during drills.

The beat to general quarters or battle stations held little or no challenge for Stedman for his seasoned and experienced steward promptly and properly took charge. Hospital linen was spread over the wardroom mess table. Glasses and flatware disappeared from the buffet to be replaced by another white spread which was quickly adorned with various oddly shaped instruments and shining pieces of surgical cutlery flanked by sutures, absorbents, and bandages. The operating room was prepared for patients although, in the absence of hostilities, no one was being crippled or hurt.

While the wardroom was being transformed, previously designated stretcher-bearers with stretchers under each arm hastened to the foot of the companionway, ostentatiously opened one stretcher, and stacked the others to one side. Another hospital corpsman was posted at the spar-deck head of the companionway to pass the word if and when disaster struck, knowing full well that there would be no call for help unless a dropped cannonball injured a foot. At the same time, the remainder of the Surgeon's division was suspending additional seagoing beds from the berth-deck overhead.

When all of this had been accomplished, it was Stedman's duty to go topside, salute the Executive Officer, and report: "Medical Division is prepared to receive casualties, Sir." He then returned to his own duty post in the wardroom where he could slide into a comfortable wardroom chair to meditatively wait for some landsman to drop a cannonball. In the sick bay, the enlisted men resumed the fan-tan game which had been interrupted by the drum's irregular rumble. At times Stedman might have used this period for instruction in patient care routines; but, without patients, this soon became empty and repetitous rhetoric.

How to get regimental and ship surgeons and their personnel into and geared with field manuevers and naval combat training has long baffled some of the best military and naval minds. A totally absent armed foe has never wounded or killed anyone; and

the law does not permit mayhem on one's own troops or sailors merely to get the medics into the spirit of the game. Some unheralded and unsung but imaginative regimental or naval commander came up with a solution that continues to be used with some variations. It consists of merely harassing the medics with a deluge of pseudocasualties—and, at the same time, provides a bit of rest for worthy and perspiring sailors or soldiers who merit a respite from the heavier training routines.

A score or more tags are marked to indicate wounds from bullets, shell fragments, and splinters from ship's timbers shattered by enemy projectiles, a source of most casualties in wooden ship artillery duels. The location and nature of the wound is also written on the tag, sometimes with more frivolity than combat probabilities. One tag, marked "Killed-Dead," might be pinned on the alert hospital corpsman stationed at the scene to send word that the ship was being punished by enemy fire and that men were being wounded. Ordered to stretch out on the hatch as if he were a *corpus delicti,* he could hardly send the word to the waiting surgeon!

Young Surgeon Stedman and his medical team, alone on a new ship and without a senior surgeon to brief them on all of the arcane arts of combat training, certainly received the full treatment. Although none of his letters mention any details, his own caricatures provide conclusive evidence. As a satirical sketch, "Give 'em another eight-inch, lads, before they haul their flag down!" on page 51 is one of his best. He must have drawn it as a silent retort to the subsequent jibes and jests. Below in the sick bay or the operating room, Stedman could only interpret the usual clatter on the spar-deck as the normal daily routine of shadowboxing with phantom foes. The flat bang of a salute round from one of the howitzers could have caused him to raise his eyebrows. Quicker than an echo, the full-throated roar of the 11-inch Dahlgren Columbiad told him something was happening. Then came the bang of the other howitzer followed by the sharp bark of the smaller rifled gun on the forecastle. Not having heard them fired before, he could not have known that they were all using blanks. Nevertheless, they merited the Doctor's personal attention in his drawings.

His caricature tells us that up the companionway and on the spar-deck, Stedman found himself in a dress rehearsal for an 1812-style boarding action to capture a hostile ship by laying alongside, holding with grapnels, and fighting hand-to-hand on the enemy deck. Not even Stephen Decatur actually enjoyed hand-to-hand combat on a strange deck. There was always hope that the enemy would surrender by hauling down his colors before the actual rail-to-rail closure was completed. One can almost hear the exhortations of the young officer commanding the gun; he is eager for himself and the gun crew to have the fun of pumping out another blank before the obsolete dress rehearsal ends. The gun smoke in the rigging is real gun smoke, probably the first time most of the crew smelled it. This is a happy appearing crew considering that number three, the side tackle man, is "bleeding" to death on the deck and another shipmate has already turned up his toes on the booby hatch. This is probably the medic who should have been bringing up the stretcher-bearers.

The satirical peak of Stedman's picture is reached along the row of hammocks topping the non-embattled bulwark. The 1812 tradition held that the Captain should lead the boarders, and most of them actually did. Captain Downes, son of an 1812 valiant, has dutifully honored the dress rehearsal by buckling on his side arms and drawing his sword to lead "the forlorn hope" as the first five men aboard a hostile deck were usually called. Stedman does not identify Downes as "Captain Rumbelow," but he leaves no doubt for the sword-waving, corpulent figure astride the hammocks could be no other. The young junior officer at the upper left intends to share the forlorn hope honors. He will be followed by the party of sailors between the gun and the Captain if and when they get alongside that mythical foe. The marine guard with bayonets fixed will support the spearhead of the Captain's attack. The boy bugler from the marine unit is blowing "boarders away"; the marines are ready for action. Their commander, at a lower level and back to the rail, is directing their movement. If the Captain does not promptly sweep his sword downward and yells, "Halt! As you were. End of exercise," some marine just might march right over the rail and into the Atlantic! We would like to think that the enthusiastic gun commander had the pleasure

"Give 'em another eight inch, lads, before they haul their flag down!"

of shooting the bag that the powder monkey is rushing to the howitzer's muzzle. If the crew can ram it home before the exercise ends, the only really safe way to remove it would be to shoot it out. That is why the shout for one more round "before they haul down their flag" is directed to the boy instead of the entire gun crew.

Viewed with full understanding of its time and place, this caricature offers the sharpest and most unrestrained, satirical comment on shipboard exercises. Usually, Stedman's sketches have a lighter touch. It is not likely that either the Captain or Lieutenant Belknap ever said an official word of criticism to Stedman about the belated medical attention of the "suffering wounded" for they knew it to be unnecessary. Should he be too obtuse to "get the message," they could throw him in the lap of the Fleet Surgeon upon arrival at Port Royal, and ask for a more experienced seagoing doctor. That they did not do so negates the adverse opinion.

Actually, there was little for Stedman to do other than order his men to clear the decks of the "dead and dying." The "dead men" were marked duty and put to work. The inert "wounded" were rolled onto stretchers. The bearers had the superficial practice of getting them down the narrow companionway into the sick bay or the wardroom. There Stedman and his men "splinted and bandaged" according to the tagged wounds; wrote the treatment into a training medical log; solemnly painted all others in sundry places with iodine and marked them duty. Of course, none of the

patients were retained beyond eight bells, the beginning of the first dogwatch for that was mealtime for the lower ratings. Stedman's sketch on page 55, "The Surgeon's station in the 'Fornots' is in the wardroom," continues the satirization of the all-out dress rehearsal throughout a general quarters exercise. None of the men pictured had been hurt; they were merely the still-living casualties from topside. The "dead" were already back at work.

Line officers of the armed forces have always been quite tolerant toward "spot commissioned" staff specialists such as doctors, engineers, and chaplains, especially on their first tour of duty. Most of them are so eager to learn the unwritten environmental rules, to do the right thing in the right manner and at the right time, and to comply with written and published requirements that a harsh rebuke would be more harmful than helpful. To a limited degree, that same tolerance continues through subsequent tours of duty. It is a tolerance, however, that line officers seldom allow themselves and almost never extend to other line officers.

In the light of Stedman's complete service record, we can safely assume that he was a fast and pleasant learner and that he did not have to be hit on the head with a reprimand. To scornfully tell him that he had not properly crewed-in his men with the general quarters exercise would have been a waste of Belknap's breath and would have caused undue injury to a professional man's pride. At dinner, however, the Executive Officer might have offered a mild witticism about the steward's diligence in bringing the wardroom back to its more conventional and convivial use, in view of all the "casualties" so recently treated therein. Such would have been a cue to all members of the mess that there was an open season on the Doctor and that any additional pungent remarks they might see fit to offer on the same theme could be made at that time or later.

For some reason, however, the young Surgeon remembered the boarding exercise with dark resentment or his ridicule would have been more bridled. Although the sketch was his retort to a situation, it might have been drawn for his own spiritual benefit, something he was getting out of his system and sending home without admitting to his messmates that some of their darts had found a target.

Stedman's shyness concerning his own sketches—at times almost to the point of timidity—is most regrettable. In an age of self-proclaimed artists who tack their signed and dated, ill-shaped, graphical maunderings on every available corridor wall, it is refreshing to learn that there once lived a modest, reticent artist of far more than passing ability. It is all the more reason for recognizing him now and enjoying his works today.

A TASTE OF EXCITEMENT

Captain Downes, son of a famous commodore out of the War of 1812, had lived his childhood, boyhood, and manhood years on the decks of ships of that war that were as famous for their battles as his father was for the battle that had brought him promotion and fame. With good reasons, Downes believed that boarding actions would occur throughout the Civil War for boarding or the threat of boarding had been a winning factor in every major sea battle since a Roman admiral invented such tactics to win complete control of the Mediterranean Sea in 241 B.C. By contrast, Lieutenant Belknap, then thirty years of age and a few months younger than Doctor Stedman, represented what historian and Rear Admiral Mahan considered to be the New School of naval officers. Belknap had entered the newly created Naval Academy for its five year course. The first year he studied at Annapolis; the next three he served as a midshipman afloat. At the end of that cruise, he returned for his final year at Annapolis, graduating with the Class of 1853. Modernization and fleet expansions brought him a lieutenancy in 1855. When naval ranks were modernized during the summer of 1862, Belknap became a lieutenant commander; on the same list, Downes became a commander.

Old School officers such as Downes argued that steam would create more boarding actions than ever because the slower ship would always be boarded if the faster steamer had the purpose of and manpower for boarding. The New School maintained, however, that new, more accurate, and heavier guns would destroy or disable any attacker before ship-to-ship contact could be made. The Old School countered this argument by insisting that the motion of ships through normal waves made consistent artillery hits impossible at a distance of more than 200 yards. They also believed that the relatively small number of the heavy new guns and their slow rates of fire could not prevent closures. Both sides, however, did agree that boarding action exercises were valid means for training a crew.

Even the Civil War did not settle the argument. The New School happily pointed to the *Kearsage-Alabama* battle. The two equally matched wooden ships steamed in circles off Cherbourg, France, both refusing to close because they were receiving hits and did not dare risk a fore-to-aft raking broadside. *Kearsage's* two 11-inch Dahlgren Columbiads, indentical with *Huron's* largest gun, were the margin which sank *Alabama*. Equally happily, the Old School used the action between the ironclads, CSS *Virginia* and the *Monitor,* to support its argument. The ships were repeatedly "rail-to-rail," and *Virginia* should have boarded and captured *Monitor* for she had a much larger crew. The entire argument, however, was more specious than analytical; and it would appear that the New School was right. Surgeon Stedman obviously would have happily pronounced a curse upon both schools!

During the shakedown cruise, *Huron* had stopped and boarded several vessels well out to sea when their recognition signals were nonexistent or flawed. Dropping boats into the water to put a party aboard while an officer examined the stranger's papers and manifests was well within standing orders for all men-of-war. Although no blockade runner was intercepted by *Huron*, these boardings offered good training for all concerned.

Toward the end of the training period, *Huron's* men on watch in the tops sighted a smudge of smoke and then a ship which Captain Downes and all hands would have gladly boarded. The new stranger, under full steam, was an admitted blockade runner. *Huron's* hoist of signal flags demanding that the ship "make her number" was ignored. Both ships were off the North Carolina coast; the runner was probably headed for the north entrance to Wilmington, back of Cape Fear Island. The thin-hulled, big paddlewheeled stranger promptly stepped away from the puffing *Huron*. Downes could not chase her forever and should have left her to the South Atlantic Squadron's blockaders off Wilmington for he would have had to stand farther out to sea to avoid Frying Pan Shoals off Cape Fear.

The lure of prize money galore within the first day of his arrival in the zone of the North Atlantic Squadron held Captain Downes in the wake of the elusive blockade runner beyond the limits of caution. As Surgeon Stedman's drawing on page 59 reveals, both ships were headed southwesterly and tightly inside the thrust of the Gulf Stream. In "The Blockade-runner they did not catch," Stedman has given her lines which suggest that she was one of 13½-knot packet steamers designed for coastal runs from England to continental ports and overnight service from Liverpool and Glasgow to Irish ports. A number of these packet steamers had been immediately diverted

The Surgeon's station in the Fornots is the ward-room.

to blockade running because of the soaring profits inherent in that trade. *Huron* was rapidly nearing her first adventure. Surgeon Stedman promptly wrote details home to "My dear Edith" in one of his better narratives, dated 12 February 1862:

> *. . . We were sitting around in the wardroom & having a pleasant chat, & singing sailor tunes, after which we went to bed. . . . It was about ½ past when I heard from Gill [Volunteer Acting Master J. W. Gill] who had been suffering from a terrible inflamed eye—making a tremendous row about some application for his peepers. That woke me & soon after I heard a sound which made me crawl all over. Still I heard no one on deck messing about, & I thought I must be mistaken; but soon after the lookout sung out "Breakers" & soon the vessel touched bottom & ground along and "Stop her," screamed the officer of the deck.*

> *"Ahead fast," yelled the Captain who had jumped on deck in his night clothes. "Put on all steam and push her over." The vessel continued stuck in the sand. . . & the mischief of it was that it was apparently high tide when she struck. All hands, officers were now on deck facing into the mist and rain. Sail was set and the screw propeller applied, but it was soon taken off because it was impossible to tell the direction of the nearest deep*

> *water. Sails were flapping, the steam roaring, the sea beating against the unyielding ship, officers shouting and men answering.*

> *Daylight came & revealed our position & a specially nasty one did it look to be. . . .*

A defect in the paper used by Stedman precludes an accurate transcription as to the location of the grounding and the course being steered at the time. It does suggest, however, that the ship was badly off course. The Confederacy had blacked out all light houses—such as the one shown in the background of Stedman's drawing—and removed all other aids to coastal navigation because they were more helpful to blockaders than to blockade runners. Each outbound blockade runner carried a pilot who knew South Carolina better than he could recall the hallway to the kitchen in his father's house. Even more important, the pilot knew the most recent or planned future locations of frequently shifted "range lights," and could signal for partial exposure of their flashing signals by displaying his own screened identification signal light. Captain Downes should have been aware of these conditions.

Huron had grounded in darkness. At dawn, activities on the near and hostile shore were disconcerting. Downes promptly dropped a boat overside manned by a relief team of oarsmen and equipped with a sail should the light dawn and morning airs prove helpful. Downes was obviously thinking of the frigate *Philadelphia* which had grounded off Tripoli and had been captured by Barbary pirates in a night boarding action before she could be floated. Downes handed Acting Master Baldwin a letter to be delivered to the first man-of-war off Charleston Harbor, nearly forty miles southwesterly. It was a note of alarm. For one who had never before had command experience in the possible presence of an enemy, his concern is excusable:

> As I am near the shore and have probably been observed, it is possible that I may be carried by boarding during the night. If possible, after making what defense I can, I shall spike my guns and thus make her helpless to resist your attack, should you be disposed to attempt recapture. When you appear off this place and signalize by firing a gun, I will hoist colors at the peak and the cornet at the fore if all is right. Perhaps I may get off during the night. In that case, I shall proceed to off Charleston and there pick up my officer.

This was also Surgeon Stedman's first experience and he continued his description for Edith:

> What the capabilities of the natives for attacks might be, we of course could not tell. A small steamer, apparently a coast guard & a schooner, when they saw us, put for the interior, either in fear or to bring men to pitch into us at night.
>
> Work was begun in earnest to get us off at the next tide. The Launch was got out, & the boats lowered & anchors carried out in the direction of deep water, ascertained by sounding from the gigs.—I never shall forget the aspect of that beastly coast. Across the dirty brown water; the white sand below the low foliage; the shore lighthouse with the tall unfinished tower beside, paid for by Uncle Sam, the lights put out by those lunatic rebels to get U. Sam's fastest gunboat ashore!
>
> The decks, but yesterday so clean & trim & orderly was cumbered up with cables & hawsers, & lines; the Square Yard awry, & the little Huron looked like a wreck. At high tide the greatest efforts were used to get her off by heaving on the anchors before laid out & steaming at full power. While loosing the main sail, crash down from the mast a lad by the name of Lewis, striking a man on the back with sufficient force to start blood from the latter's nostrils. Lewis was taken below, bleeding from a large wound in the head & with a broken collar bone. He died the next morning. . . .
>
> Capt. Downes behaved splendidly, never losing heart, & never leaving the deck. At dark a boat was gotten ready & provisioned, Mr. Baldwin & a Master Mate were sent off with a crew armed to the teeth, to communicate with the Squadron off Charleston, about 30 miles distant. Efforts to heave off were resumed next tide.

Downes was lightening ship by dumping coal and heavy equipment overboard and by shifting other stores aft. At the same time, kedge anchors for warping off were put out astern. Among the forward gear put over the side was the starboard chain, marked with a buoy for subsequent retrieval. All hands looked suspiciously at the 16,000-pound, 11-inch Dahlgren smoothbore, but putting that overboard would be the last resort for they might need "Brother Ephraim." When all was ready, Downes tried to get *Huron* free with propeller churning astern and with another all-hands heave-ho against capstan bars and lines leading to the kedge anchors astern. The effort was aborted, however, when the propeller picked up six turns of the buoy line marking the jettisoned anchor chain. Even worse, the churning fed a number of links into the shaft and propeller before it could be stopped. *Huron* would be dead in the water when and if she could be pulled free. Downes had to wait for another high tide. To Surgeon Stedman the next tide was really low. That hostile shore looked more grim than ever:

> "Boat ho!" sang out the lookout, "where-away?" "Two boats putting off, six." "Go to quarters quietly without the drum," says the Capt. The ports were opened, the guns loaded with shrapnel, the rifle guns pointed to starboard, Brother Ephraim to port, our howitzer shoved out of an after port, the other abeam. The muskets and revolvers were loaded, & the crew arrived with them & cutlasses. I got all my traps ready, but it was a false alarm; luckily for them unless they were double in numbers.

That night the men slept under arms on deck. Efforts to free the propeller continued without success. More stores were dumped overboard to further lighten the ship. About noon on Tuesday—*Huron* had grounded Sunday night—two friendly ships appeared. After exchanging the signals arranged for by Downes through his messenger, Mister Baldwin, they closed in and were identified as the large armed merchantman, *Flambeau*, nearest ship from the blockade cordon off the Charleston approaches, and the small armed steamer, *Penguin*. *Penguin* would tow *Huron* when she had been freed from the shoal. The shape of the shoal, however, kept *Penguin* from approaching near enough for a good pull. With this help at hand, Downes did not hesitate to dump all remaining coal overboard; even the water was removed from the boilers. All was set for another mighty heave by all hands against the kedge anchors aft. Stedman described the results:

> . . .And just before daylight, they began to heave again. Thump, as the sea lifted her. Thump, thump & at last a slide! There must be something to keep us troubled, & it was soon seen the Penguin was aground. She backed off in ten minutes. You must know . . . that she could not get near enough

The Blockade-runner they did not catch.

to haul us off, & we had still to depend on our own worn & raw crew. I never shall forget the first roll . . . as we left the ground. It was the most exhilerating sensation I ever felt. We anchored as soon as were clear of the bank and gave the crew a rest of a couple of hours.

Huron received a towline from *Penguin*, and they were off to Port Royal. Stedman was sure that:

We have been in the most unpleasant scrape we can get into, and I shall have no apprehension of getting into a worse one anywhere or how. . . . To be 48 hours ashore on a hostile coast, with a prosepct of a S. Easter coming on and everything failing you as you tried your best to get off, is no joker. Everyone on the ship said it was the worst spot they were ever in. I am about done up with fatigue, want of sleep, excitement & suspense, and can write no more. Our ship, as light as she now is, rolls like a beast but, it is a delicious motion after grinding and thumping on the shoal 2 days.

In his formal report to the Navy Department through channels, Downes blamed "a considerable error in my compasses and the imperfection of the chart." He indicated that *Huron* had grounded on

Tower and flute.
Tower was Chief Engineer on the Huron.

Cape Romain Shoal where the range of high and low tidal water is about six feet. *Huron* drew twelve feet when heavy, nine when light. Fortunately for Downes, so many Federal blockaders had been grounded throughout the winter of 1861-62 that *Huron*'s trouble was accepted as almost routine by the Navy Department.

CHAPTER FIVE Hostile Inland Waters

W HEN *HURON* ARRIVED at Port Royal Sound, off Hilton Head Island, at the end of a towline from *Penguin*, she found the Sound to be a swarming beehive of shipping. Over a hundred coastal steamers were present, many commanded by their owners and with five or six-man crews composed of sons, in-laws, and neighbors. All were loaded with coal from Pennsylvania mines which they discharged directly into the bunkers of fighting ships, transient supply ships, and a few steam-powered transports. When empty, each schooner pulled out into the Gulf Stream for a leisurely voyage back to the Delaware River estuary for more coal. In addition to the mosquito-like swarm of coal schooners and service ships receiving coal or discharging cargoes on Hilton Head Island, there were improvised docks and warehouses on the near shore.

At the top of the island was a large old plantation house. The Stars and Stripes flying from the tall pole in front identified it as Major General Thomas West Sherman's Army headquarters. The frowning fortifications built by the departed Confederates had been expanded and reshaped, and the batteries now covered the upper stretches of the sound and narrow lagoon between the island and the mainland. Partially visible from the deck of the arriving *Huron* were the growing rows of hutments built to replace the tents of the 15,000 soldiers who had come to stay.

A brigade composed of the 6th Connecticut Infantry, the 4th New Hampshire Infantry, and the 97th Pennsylvania Infantry with an aggregate strength of 2,400 men and officers was already aboard transports when *Huron* arrived. The transports and six shallow draft warships had moved to Wassaw Sound and into the channel between Tybee and Wilmington Islands. This move was a demonstration, a threatened landing which might capture Fort Pulaski from the back door. The purpose of the move was to draw more Confederate men and guns to Georgia by demonstrating against Savannah and thus screen the true mission and objective of the unusual Federal activities in Port Royal Sound and Hilton Head Island. The threatening force remained in Wassaw Sound until the remainder of DuPont's armada was ready to move; the demonstration force would then move out and fall in line as the armada steamed down the coast to Florida. This was the situation when *Huron* arrived at the end of a tow line. For the first time her officers and crew were privileged to see a large and fully functioning squadron moving out on a definite mission and responding to the signals from a flag officer's command ship.

DuPont's amphibious force sailed from Port Royal the last day of February. *Huron* and two sister ships, *Ottawa* and *Seneca*, did not sail with the main force. Ellery Stedman explained this in a letter to Edith dated 1 March 1862:

> *On the 27th at four in the afternoon, the Wabash made signals for the fleet to follow her and off she started and the other vessels steamed after her excepting Huron and two or three others who were to receive fresh ammunition. Accordingly, at evening a tug came alongside and deposited a lot of eleven inch shell on board, and then supplied the Ottawa and Seneca, like Upham's cart going round Downer Court.*

The net result of this delay put *Huron* at the end of the big parade moving down the coast, much of it under cover of darkness. Being the last to leave Port Royal, however, in no way dampened the rising enthusiasm of *Huron*'s crew. In his letter to Edith, Stedman makes it quite clear that the arduous past training had shown results:

> *Everyone has been expecting the expedition to sail daily, . . . On board ship there has been great sharpening of cutlasses, testing of pistols and drilling. The men whack the big and little guns round with great facility, considering the short practice they have had. They are very cool in prospect of a fight and one hears no bragging or nonsense about it.*

A CHANGE IN PLANS

Flag Officer Samuel F. DuPont's original plan was to close his force in St. Andrews Sound between Jekyl and Cumberland Heights. He would then steam in line ahead inside of Cumberland Island and emerge with his entire force in Cumberland Sound to strike at St. Mary's and Fernandina through the side door. Thus he would isolate each in turn and capture Fort Clinch which was sited with its heavy guns trained to control the conventional approach and channels to Fernandina and St. Mary's. Another strong battery on the south end of Cumberland opposite Fort Clinch would be even more isolated and even easier to capture.

"Wise men change their minds occasionally; fools never," is an old axiom. Flag Officer DuPont and his nephew, Major General Henry A. duPont, appear to be the only members of that distinguished family who were foolish enough to seek further distinction by shooting ammunition instead of manufacturing more of it. Even so, both proved to be quite ready to change their minds when it appeared to be the better part of wisdom. Accordingly, Flag Officer DuPont, when his armada had closed in St. Andrews, decided to defy an equally old axiom against dividing one's forces beyond immediate support distance when closing in on an enemy. Actually, however, the Flag Officer had little choice in the matter. The inside channel, such as it was, did not have enough water in it for his larger and heavier ships. Still intent upon the

The Leadsman.

side-door approach and attack, DuPont created a flotilla of lighter ships to be led by "third rate" *Pawnee* whose captain, Commander Percival Drayton, also would command the flotilla of "fourth rates" assigned to him. The advent of steam and the increasing weight of naval guns had prompted a system for rating warships by displacement tonnage with machinery and guns only aboard. Vessels of 2,400 tons or more were rated first rate; those between 1,200 and 2,400 tons, second rate; between 600 and 1,200 tons, third rate; and all armed vessels of 600 tons or less, fourth rate. *Huron* was 600 tons. DuPont, with the heavier ships, would proceed via open water for ultimate entry through Fernandina's front door and past its batteries.

This change in plans called for a conference of captains on board first rate *Wabash*, fifty guns and 3,274 tons. Although there was no time to draw pictures, Stedman watched and described what he saw in a letter to Edith:

> *The Commodore [DuPont] stopped and signalled for Captains to come aboard. The fleet all closed together to read the signals; the answers flew up the mastheads. The boats with their little pennants and flags darted along, converging to one point .... The sun flashed out clear from under a cloud and on the wet oar blades, the laced uniforms of the captains, and the long, low, smooth waves.*

All of the "signalizing" had intrigued and fascinated Ellery Stedman from the day of *Huron*'s arrival in Port Royal Sound. It stimulated his admiration even more when the coastal scene increasingly appeared "to be solid with Lincoln's Pirates." The business of sorting themselves out pursuant to the new plan extended into darkness. The flags gave way to colored lights. This is how Doctor Stedman saw these lights from the deck of *Huron*:

> *Imagine a large fleet lying in smooth water with everything as quiet as if the 10,000 men in it were sound asleep. Suddenly a brilliant white light breaks from the stern of the Commodore's ship, changes to red and back to a white. A moment or two of darkness, and out flashes from each ship of the squadron a green, white, and red light; all reflected from the water with the masts cutting dark lines of shadow on the smoke. The ships have intimated that they are wide awake and paying attention. Then off goes a series of red, white and green, which is answered in the same way. Another constellation from the Flagship flashes and goes out, and over the still water come the shrill notes of the boatswain's whistle, followed by the clank of the capstans as the anchors are hove up.*

By early forenoon, Captain Drayton and his *Pawnee* had sorted out the flotilla of more or less light draft, weapon-bearing craft and began to advance through the tortuous inside channel. Following *Pawnee* in order came, *Ottawa, Seneca, Huron, Pembina,*

Isaac Smith, *Penguin*, *Potomska*, *Ellen*, three armed launches with a company of sailors from *Wabash*, transport *McClellan* with a battalion of marines on board, and transport *Boston* carrying the 97th Pennsylvania Infantry, all followed by the little armed cutter, *Henrietta*. By and large, it was a well balanced force for the side-door thrust.

As the column progressed, it became more and more apparent that the twisting and turning inside channel was completely without any defending artillery. The only enemy present was the ill-defined, unmarked channel. A leadsman was in both the starboard and port chains every moment *Huron* was in motion. Stedman portrayed the leadsman in the drawing on page 63. A good pair of leadsmen will so time their rhythms of winding up and heaving that neither will exactly duplicate the other unless each successive heave of both continues to find exactly the same depth. In an environment such as the narrows of the inside channel, the leadsman is the most attractive target for a hostile sniper concealed in the always-near-at-hand shoreline trees. The line about the leadsman's body is to prevent his falling from the chains—the unexplainable name for the links of iron bolted to the ship's side with deadeyes in the upper end to which the shrouds are connected. In this case, the shrouds are those of the foremast.

The lead at the end of his line weighs seven pounds. The coil of the line in his left hand dimly reveals marking tags. His report, when he reads the depth will be in fathoms, six feet to a fathom. Two

fathoms from the far tip of the lead, the marker is two short strips of leather; three fathoms, three strips; five fathoms, a white rag; seven fathoms, a red rag; ten fathoms, leather with a hole in it; twenty fathoms, two knots. Thereafter, the line was marked with an additional knot for each ten fathoms. For depths beyond seven fathoms, forty-two feet, however, a much heavier lead and a different technique normally would be in use. The so-called deep-sea lead is actually a scientific instrument and need not be discussed here.

As Stedman pictures the leadsman, the sailor is not actually heaving the lead. The ship is moving slowly to his left. He is in the last, fore and aft, pendulum swing before he goes into his windup. His next pendulum swing will be forward and even higher than the back swing shown in the drawing. As the line comes back, he will carry it into his final forward, overhead windup of two or more complete circles. This creates centrifugal force for the heave. At the top of the second or third circle, he will release the lead into the actual overhand heave. He will nurse the distance by flowing the light lead line from his left hand. If he is as good a leadsman as Stedman pictures him, the lead will splash fathoms forward of *Huron*'s jib-boom.

As the ship moves slowly over the distance of his heave, usually at four knots in waters such as these, he has time to gather in the line until he can "feel the lead" as his station is passing over it. He then reports his reading in loud, slow, clearly enunciated words: "By-y-y the mark three-e-e." This means eighteen feet of water, six feet of which are under the ship's keel. The navigator or the Captain supplanted the routine officer of the deck although all three are still on the bridge which, on *Huron*, was just forward of the mizzen mast. The Captain would be to starboard, the navigator to port, and the officer of the deck standing by or immediately behind the man at the wheel. Six feet of water under the keel would give all of them a comfortable feeling.

If the water is deepening, the next reading, perhaps from the port leadsman, might be "By-y-y the deep four-r-r." The five fathoms marker being about six feet above the ship's waterline, this reading would indicate that the leadsman has split the difference between the three fathom and five fathom markers for twenty-four feet of water. Since tidal flows create runnels and sand ridges and even cross channels, this would be no time to bring in leads despite the reading. "By the deep six" would be a similar split between the five and seven fathom markers. Such depth would have been good news on a ship as large as the Flagship, *Wabash*. Aboard *Huron*, the next command would be "Belay the leads and stand by." Samuel L. Clemens, the famous author, adopted Mark Twain as a pen name. To his ears, it was always good news with a pleasant sound when he was a Mississippi River steamboat pilot on vessels with a draft of three to six feet. Aboard *Huron*, "By the mark twain" would have been a most unpleasant sound.

Surgeon Stedman's drawing of "The Leadsman," is one of his few sketches that exudes admiration rather than mildly cynical reporting. It is one of the best in this collection of his Civil War drawings. The inspiration for the picture may have come during subsequent and similar operations up the Ogeechee and Stono Rivers when *Huron* was under fire and received hits, for Stedman did not date his drawings. Within such coastal rivers and sounds, the leadsmen were constantly in the chains. The man in the port chains was usually left-handed or was at least ambidextrous. Even when lying to offshore at night or in fog, the 14-pound lead was often used to test for any onshore or lateral drift. The lead was often loaded with tallow to take a sample of sand or clay from the bottom, but then it was thrown from both hands over the side.

SCENERY AND INCIDENTS ALONG THE SHORE

The flotilla's pause for the first night within the serpentine inside channel left *Huron*

> *. . . abreast of a large, splendid mansion with quarters and factories lying around it. The owner, a Mr. Stafford, had said he would not leave it, but some boats went ashore from Pawnee. . . . We sent a boat ashore after beef, a little further up, as some cattle were seen on the beach. They brought back a portion of a miserable cow.*

The next day, the movement continued toward Fernandina, but with increasing apprehension. Sted-

Eleven-inch gun drill.

man thought danger could be lurking in every foot of the heavily wooded shore:

> At every point we rounded we expected a shot from a rebel battery and there were a hundred places from which we might have been knocked to smithereens. . . . The shores were sandy, low and reedy, so that when the fleet moved along through immense marshes, the ships looked as if they were ploughing through land, for it was seldom that the crookedness of the stream allowed the water to

"Jimmy Legs"
Master at Arms with handcuffs

> be seen. About ten, the Pawnee grounded in a sharp turn of the river, when the whole fleet took occasion to do the same. By and by she got off, also the Ottawa and Huron and one or two others but the rest were jammed together in the most absurb manner. We got up to within six or seven miles of Fernandina and the Pawnee took the ground again. After lying some two hours, she signalled the Ottawa and Huron to steam up towards the town.

Stedman apparently mistook the tidal flows for the current of a river for they came into the inside channel from around both ends of Cumberland Island. Where the two opposed tidal flows met, sandy shoals were created which is where the entire flotilla was grounded. With *Pawnee* aground, *Ottawa* took the lead with *Huron* close on her stern. Once clear of the shoals and in deeper and stronger currents, they anchored. In the twilight, *Ottawa* sighted a strange small steamer and went southward in pursuit. The chase led *Ottawa* near a railroad and a standing train headed inland. There was a volley of musketry from the shore; the shrubbery along the railroad erupted with hostile soldiers running to the train. *Ottawa* returned the fire, but the train escaped. *Ottawa* captured the strange craft, a small inland-waters steamer named *Darlington*. She was, for the most part, burdened with civilian escapees and their private property. She had hoped to escape northward up the inside channel when DuPont's heavy ships appeared from the open sea.

Meanwhile, *Huron* was still anchored in the channel. Came midnight, Stedman heard the drums rumbling in anger for the first time. The tune was "Beat to Quarters," battle stations all hands, ". . . on account of a strange steamer coming. . . .We fired a signal rocket which she did not answer, and we were on the point of blazing into her when a boat came from the *Pawnee* to say the steamer was a prize of the *Ottawa,* being the one she was chasing in the evening." At daybreak *Pawnee* resumed her place at the head of the flotilla. *Huron* and the remainder of Commander Drayton's column proceeded in line ahead to the water front of Fernandina without drawing a hostile shot.

The little city was blossoming with white flags. To Surgeon Stedman, it was a beautiful day with handsome scenery:

> *The shores became bolder and the foliage more varied. Every now and then we could see fine mansions "bosomed high in tufted trees" with clipt hedges and lordly oaks with long grey mosses sweeping down to the ground, and footpaths, roads, fences, and landing places. The situation of Fernandina is beautiful, on a gentle hill with those splendid live oaks hiding all but the larger houses.*

But, getting back to the grim thoughts on warfare, Stedman decided:

> *A battery commanded the river with two guns—eighty-pounders, looked like—which might have knocked the Ottawa into a cocked hat, had the Seceshers had the nerve to work them for half an hour. In fact, the run of the Ottawa up to the town was one of the boldest things done during the war, and great was our indignation at being kept back. Had all the rest of the war been conducted like this burst, Savannah would have been ours two days after the battle of Port Royal [DuPont's capture of Hilton Head Island]. The panic of that fight has not subsided.*

DuPont's reconnaissance in force was an astounding success. The Confederate garrisons for the formidable positions on Amelia Island (Fort Clinch) and the recently emplaced guns on the southern end of Cumberland Island were completely isolated by Commander Drayton's large force of shallow draft men-of-war and the accompanying regiment of seaborne infantry. The garrison was in the process of removing the guns and ammunition when the heavy ships and transports appeared offshore. There was no opposition, and the positions were abandoned. Only a few prisoners were taken although a number of Negroes remained to tell what had happened.

While Brigadier General H. G. Wright's infantry occupied the abandoned positions and sent a force into the city of Fernandina, DuPont moved his flag to *Mohican,* a more shallow draft vessel than *Wabash,* in order to get across the bar into the harbor and nearer any action that might occur. At the same time, *Ottawa* continued to function as the advance guard of the shallow draft column. Reinforced by two armed launches of *Wabash,* she pushed onward and up the St. Mary's on the Georgia side of the river. The old city surrendered though there was a regiment of Confederate cavalry in the vicinity. *Ottawa* continued upriver fifty miles to Woodstock. At various landings and plantations, her commander, Thomas H. Stevens, posted notices that people and property would be protected as had already been done at Fernandina.

It was later learned that the withdrawal of 1,500 men had been approved four days earlier by General Robert E. Lee in Richmond. Consequently, only thirteen guns were found in the defenses of Fernandina and St. Mary's; only two were rifled. Eighteen other guns with all of their ammunition had been removed to fight elsewhere. Some, without a doubt, were sent to Charleston and Savannah. Stedman and his shipmates were to hear from them again and again.

THE WIDER FRONT

DuPont promptly planned to expand deployment of his ships and infantry southward to include Jacksonville and St. Augustine. With equal promptness, he reached northward to seize and hold Brunswick, Georgia, and to take control of all the sounds, inlets, and offshore islands from St. Simons to Mosquito Inlet—not a nice name for the modern real estate development now known as Ponce de Leon Inlet, thirteen miles south of Daytona Beach!

While DuPont's plans were being initiated, *Pawnee* and *Huron* remained anchored in the stream off Fernandina, although *Huron* was to have one more minor adventure. A number of locomotives, cars, and coaches had fallen into Federal hands. The Confederates tried to isolate this rolling stock by burning a railroad bridge connecting Amelia Island with the mainland. The Federal armed launch posted there to "protect property" found itself involved in a skirmish just a few hours after Fenandina surrendered on 4 March 1862. The launch was forced to withdraw, but *Huron* arrived in time to put out a small fire and save the bridge.

Downes then pushed *Huron*'s bow slightly aground and into a muddy creek which would permit him to defend the bridge with gunfire. All was quiet for a while. Downes, Lieutenant Belknap, and Mister Baldwin lowered boats for a bit of onshore scouting while Mister Gill backed *Huron* clear of the creek which was crossed by the endangered railroad drawbridge. Stedman's narrative in his daily, continuing letter to Edith initially dated 1 March 1862 described the action which followed:

> *After they had been gone for an hour we saw them making tracks with great expedition for the boats, for it seems that a picket came from a house a half mile from the bridge, fired at the Captain's boat and might easily have cut him off. When they got back we fired from the Parrott* [bow, 20-pounder rifle] *a shot at the house, which fell short. "Oh—what a shot!" says Downes from the main rigging*

Six bells in the dog watch.

where he was perched. "Mr. Gill, fire that eleven inch at them!"

You never saw a piece come round as that sixteen thousand pounds of iron did, as it was trained on the house. Mr. Gill leveled his glass along the gun, got his elevation, squinted along the trunnion sight. "Fire!" Roar—yell of shell—strikes the ground—ricochets and bursts almost on the house.

So splendid was the shot that everyone jumped right up on the deck, clapped his hands and gave a cheer. We tried two or three more with great success. . . . By this time we were hard and fast aground again and remain so to this day, being twenty-four hours to this time of writing, March 5th. [Stedman depicts the eleven inch gun in the drawing on page 67].

The tide had fallen from under *Huron*, but this did not interfere with the continued performance of her mission. Shortly after Stedman made the above entry in his letter, *Ellen,* a sidewheel oceangoing tugboat armed with two light smoothbores and two 30-pounder rifles, joined *Huron. Ellen* drew only seven feet and had a crew of fifty officers and men commanded by Volunteer Acting Master William Budd. A bold and audacious Irish skipper, Budd was a great favorite of all commanding officers including Flag Officer DuPont. At one time or another, he had marked devious channels and led various ships through them,

turning back to offer a tow line to each in succession when they went aground.

Downes ordered Budd to explore the creek beyond the bridge. Downes, Belknap, and Tower, with armed crews in their boats, were towed along for the ride and reconnaissance. They soon found an abandoned, stranded Confederate government schooner that had come to grief while transporting civilian passengers, officers, soldiers, and sundry public, private, and personal property during the hasty withdrawal from Fernandina. On board, Tower found surgical instruments and medical supplies charged to the post surgeon for the garrisons of the abandoned Fort Clinch and its associated batteries. Stedman closed his letter to Edith by describing the return of the boats:

The Surgeon of the post had all his traps aboard and Tower had the sense to hook the lot of medicine and surgical traps, including two ounces of quinine, which is worth $2.50 an ounce in Boston and was charged at $10 for the lot on this doctor's invoice. Pistols, chickens, and women's skirts were brought off, and a most absurd sight was presented at the unloading of the boats. . . . It is said we are going next to St. John's [River]. When <u>shall</u> *I be where I can get your letters?*

Stedman may or may not have heard the sequel to this incident. After returning to his anchorage near the temporary flagship *Mohican,* the bold Acting Master William Budd had claimed the schooner as a prize of war. Should she be successfully salvaged and sold as such, he and the crew of his little *Ellen* would get the lion's share of the prize money, small though that might be. The Confederate schooner was a small prize at best, but the enemy property aboard, such as the ammunition and army equipment in her hold, could easily make her worth much more. Unhappily for Budd, the post surgeon, a Doctor Lungren, and the State Adjutant General of Florida were among the few prisoners taken at Fernandina. Flag Officer Du-Pont was of the Old School which believed in the principle of courtesy toward captured and defeated officers. Doctor Lungren obviously used the opportunity to vent his spleen with unrestrained gusto. He protested that the medical supplies and instruments aboard the schooner were his personal property, making no mention that these were included in Confederate army inventories. About the time that Stedman was concluding the long accumulative letter quoted above, DuPont was dictating a sharp reprimand to one of his yeomen, or ship writers, for prompt delivery to Acting Master Budd: ". . . you will see that they are instantly returned to Dr. Lungren, a prisoner of war, whose private chattles should be respected. I understand that Dr. Lungren, having permission, visited your ship and was rudely treated by you. I desire explanations on this head also."

Captain Budd's corrective actions, if any, are not of record. The same goes for his explanations, if any. He may have offered some oral remarks on the sub-

ject by going aboard *Mohican* without delay and asking for a conference with the Flag Officer. On the other hand, Budd may have filed the communication in "The Deep Six," and waited for the possible reprimand for not responding to a reprimand. That is another way of silently saying: "Sir, I'm forgetting it; am hoping you are doing the same. We are both busy men and, of course, I will not be doing it again." That formula works surprisingly well when a junior commander is in a combat operation; but it is not recommended in army field or fleet wargame maneuvers.

Budd, however, continued in DuPont's highest esteem. He was ordered to take *Ellen* over the St. John's River bar alone and defended by no more than a hoped-for acceptance of a flag of truce. He was to steam past the frowning batteries believed to be in position without making any overt movement of his own. At the Jacksonville waterfront, he was to contact the city authorities and would have the widest discretion in negotiating the surrender of the city. He was to state that the fleet was there to see that the laws of the United States were observed as well as to protect all peaceful citizens' lives, liberties, and their legal possession of property. This Captain Budd did successfully.

Actually, the reprimand sent to Budd should have been sent to *Huron* and Captain Downes. Budd went up the creek and beyond the bridge at the order of Downes. Furthermore, Downes was the senior officer present when the dastardly deed was done. Some of the loot was on his ship. Downes, however, had been

Fernandina Lt House, 1862

wise enough in the ways of the service not to claim the schooner as a prize of *Huron*. It is also likely that Downes heard of the Confederate surgeon's complaints and the ensuing reprimand to Budd. This might have prompted him to go to the flagship, assume full responsibility, and present the facts as he knew them to be. He would have insisted that enemy equipment and medical supplies were contraband of war in every struggle known to history and that they were subject to confiscation and use without referral to a prize court verdict when needed by one's own forces and useful in field operations.

Downes would have cited the example of *Ottawa's* capture of the Southern steamer *Darlington* which had been confiscated without verdict from an Admiralty Court and was being used to transport Federal troops in operations against Jacksonville. Had the loot aboard *Huron* been brought up, he might have stated that his boys wanted the dresses for a theatrical skit in the second dogwatch, a time for normal "skylarking." Stedman pictured the second dogwatch in the drawing on page 71. Downes would have the dresses rounded up, have them washed, starched, ironed and returned to the lady, presumably still in Fernandina. Some such explanation from a seasoned senior lieutenant with twenty-five years of service could have been most persuasive to another older sailor with DuPont's service or more than forty-five years. In any event, Budd's reprimand remained in "The Deep Six," or wherever else Budd may have filed it.

Flag Officer DuPont was most meticulous in his

Mail from the North.

relations with the normally hostile coastal communities. He did not view his operations as being typical of warfare between nations. His often proclaimed purpose was to restore the authority and laws of the United States to a people who had been misguided and betrayed by dissident and treasonable state officials. The troops and patrol ships left behind were to protect the municipal governments and all peaceful, law-abiding citizens who were expected to return to their homes and to live in peace under the protection of the Stars and Stripes. The response of the people was astoundingly good. They obviously felt they had been badly let down by the central government of the Confederacy in Richmond and by state authorities in distant Tallahassee. The guns and equipment sent to protect them had been improperly placed; and were then hauled away in flight to be used in defense of other cities in other states.

With a few thousand men, General Wright could have made a sustained thrust westward to Tallahassee and Pensacola along the line of the Florida, Atlantic, and Gulf Central Railroad. He could have driven the secession government of Florida into exile and replaced it with a loyal regime under a military governor. Such an early loss to the Confederacy of one of its eleven states would have impressed the diplomatic leaders of England and France. Confederations of states that cannot maintain their integrity seldom win; there is no diplomatic joy in backing a potential loser.

It is a basic rule of strategy that a successful reconnaissance in force of the vast magnitude of DuPont's expedition should be exploited by heavy rein-forcements. However, throughout those first two weeks of March 1862, no one in either Washington or Richmond actually realized or cared what DuPont was doing from Savannah, Georgia, to Mosquito Inlet, Florida. While Jacksonville and St. Augustine were surrendering to the first truce flag that came across the harbor bar, the ironclad CSS *Virginia* (the former USS *Merrimac*) was calmly sinking USS *Cumberland* and USS *Congress* while their most modern projectiles were bouncing off her armor. These two sturdy old ships had been rearmed with the most modern guns in the Navy's inventory and had been positioned so that *Virginia* would have to come under their fire in order to get well into Chesapeake Bay. The arrival of the ironclad USS *Monitor* on 9 March 1862 was a timely and dramatic checkmate. At the same time, Major General George B. McClellan's Army of the Potomac was concentrating against Richmond on the Yorktown Peninsula. A week later, the amphibious expedition of Commander Stephen C. Rowan and Major General Ambrose E. Burnside captured a depot of munitions, ordnance, and other equipment at New Bern, North Carolina. Of more importance, some generals in the West named Grant, Sherman, and Pope, with artillery support provided by improvised river gunboats under Flag Officer Andrew H. Foote, were beginning to win battles although Major General Henry W. Halleck in St. Louis was getting the lion's share of the credit and praise. In the Gulf of Mexico, Flag Officer David Farragut was moving his squadron and flotilla of mortar schooners up to the head of the passes in the Mississippi Delta prepara-

In the launch.

tory to his assault on Forts Jackson and St. Philip; his objective New Orleans.

When considered against this background of contemporary and momentous events, it is not surprising that the remarkable achievements of DuPont and his South Atlantic Squadron were viewed as a routine, blockade enforcement operation. DuPont, however, considered his expedition a probe for a soft sector in the defenses of the Confederate States of America. He had certainly found a soft spot and convincingly demonstrated its weakness.

As for *Huron*, Surgeon Stedman was almost right when he wrote Edith that their next destination would be Jacksonville. *Huron* almost immediately returned to Fernandina from her bridge duty and received aboard a captain and his company from the 4th New Hampshire Infantry; their destination, St. John's River. This was changed to St. Augustine. Then, on 14 March, they were ordered to transfer the soldiers to *Isaac Smith* since her depth of ten feet, compared to *Huron*'s twelve, would give the troops a better chance for a prompt crossing of the inevitable bar. Downes was ordered to take on coal and report to the flagship, *Wabash,* at St. Augustine; and, if she was not there, to follow her to Mosquito Inlet. When this proved to be the case, *Huron* did not linger long at St. Augustine. Its population of two thousand souls were at peace with the world in general and particularly with the two or three hundred Federal soldiers posted there. Most of the five hundred civilians who had fled upon the arrival of the Union ships had returned. The women proved to be far more militant than the men, according to all Yankee comments.

Before returning to Port Royal, Stedman no doubt heard of the adventures of *Ottawa, Darlington,* and *Ellen*. While patrolling the St. John's River to Palatka and beyond, they had found the sunken hull of the famous schooner and yacht, *America*. For her speed, she had been a successful blockade runner. The Confederates had sunk her in the river hoping that the Federals would either not find her or would ignore her as a sunken hulk. Of course, the Federal Navy men raised her and declared her a prize of war. Her condition and lack of cargo could have brought little prize money for distribution among the crews of the three ships. There was, however, the sentimental thrill of the find and her preservation. English-speaking yachtsmen of the United Kingdom, Australia, and the United States continue to compete among themselves with both skills and money for the cup the little schooner won in the first international yacht race in 1851.

Flag Officer DuPont's reconnaissance in force had provided Volunteer Acting Assistant Surgeon Charles E. Stedman with no battle casualties requiring his professional expertise. Nevertheless, he had encountered the acrid odor of gunpowder fired in anger—yes, it does smell somewhat stronger than the same powder lot fired in service practice! It was also his good fortune to see the bright face of danger for his first time when it was in one of its more benevolent moods.

CHAPTER SIX On the Blockade

LONG BEFORE the end of March 1862, Doctor Stedman and his shipmates aboard *Huron* were quite certain that they were lingering in Florida waters too long, for action was to northward. Blockade running to Florida's east coast ports had ceased almost completely. All harbors, estuaries, and inlets south of Savannah had been sealed by DuPont's operations. Small Federal garrisons, supported by Union warships, had been left at Fernandina, Jacksonville, and St. Augustine.

Within DuPont's sector of operations, only two Confederate seaports, with the necessary railroad nets for assembling cargoes for export and distribution of incoming English munitions, remained to be sealed: Charleston and Savannah. The limited but effective joint land and naval operations against Fort Pulaski from Tybee Island already had practically closed Savannah to seagoing steamers. The Confederates in Savannah, however, were building a fleet of light vessels around the large, armored English blockade runner which they had renamed CSS *Atlanta*. Intelligence reports indicated that she could break the blockade by Federal wooden ships when finished. Savannah might be well in hand for the time being, but could hardly be ignored indefinitely.

Charleston was another story; the press and politi-cians from Washington to St. Paul, Minnesota, were howling for its scalp. It was there that the seditious fires of secession had been lit in 1832 and nursed into the militant conflagration of 1861. Fort Sumter had to be recaptured and the Stars and Stripes returned to its flagpole. The "Architects of Treason" had to be humbled in the very ashes of the fires they had started. Were salt plowed into the gardens of the city to preclude a second growth of sedition, such punishment would not be amiss. Passions such as these can create tactical planning myopia to the neglect of more worthy strategic objectives.

But priorities of purposes are not the concern of ship commanders and certainly not of their surgeons. If the focus of action was no longer in Florida waters, then it was to northward that *Huron* should go. She was entitled to her share of the action—and prize money, if any. Stories were circulating that there was much to be had. Moreover, first class mail from home was long overdue. There had to be a stack of letters and packages with *Huron*'s name on them back at Port Royal and Hilton Head. Letters in first class mail pouches were given a high priority, but were handled in much the same manner as other items of supply. They were delivered in bulk to each ship along with the bags of second class mail. The ship's Paymaster's men sorted them out, usually on a mess basis. A representative of each mess would make final distribution. This resulted in almost simultaneous distribution by loudly shouted names throughout the vessel.

Practically all experienced soldiers and sailors who have served outside the continental United States during a war will accept the broad assumption that there never was a mail call from which at least ten percent of a crew, company, troop, or battery did not go away disappointed and talking to himself. At times, the basic problem is epitomized with: "I may have to do something with my allotment!" Fortunately for the armed services, the millstones of time, tide, and chance usually grind away such inequities. The most joyous officer or man at one mail call can easily become the most dejected and downcast at the next. Similarly, those who had been muttering about an ill-advised allotment often emerge as the happiest of all recipients. In "Mail from the North" on page 75, the officer eagerly reaching for the mail bag bears a striking resemblance to other self caricatures by Doctor Charles Ellery Stedman. Edith had carefully dated and consecutively numbered her letters since *Huron*'s sailing from Boston. It is safe to assume, however, that at least three are not there for this mail call. They could easily appear in one of the more frequent deliveries now that *Huron* was operating much nearer the South Atlantic Squadron's Port Royal base.

During the brief period *Huron* was being resupplied and readied for a station assignment on the blockade, the crew was given shore leave on scheduled trips by the launch. Stedman illustrates such a trip in the drawing on page 77. The highlight of any shore leave was usually an alcoholic relaxation on beer, wine, or grog. Grog usually consisted of whiskey or rum cut to a major or minor degree with either plain water or fruit juice. The Army's sutlers stores were open to the sailors. Hilton Head Island was large enough for competitive games, other sports, and long walks for leg stretching exercise.

Both officers and men had ample opportunity to visit friends on other ships or ashore. Though General Sherman's force was an infantry command, each regiment had a small stable of horses and mules to use as field and staff mounts and to pull a small combat supply train. From this source, Captain Downes arranged mounts for himself and Stedman. An official friendship had gradually developed between the two men. At the Captain's invitation, they had occasionally enjoyed long walks together at Fernandina and St. Augustine. Though he was old in terms of the Navy's officer list and years of seagoing service, Downes was still a comparatively young man with a calendar age of only forty years. He was overweight and not in the best of health. As the ship's commander, he usually ate alone in his quarters and was always slow on the rise toward convivialities with others. Under such conditions, even the best of senior officers at times can become both an inconsiderate commander and a difficult patient. Doctor Stedman was rapidly learning how to cope with both, for the welfare of the man and for the good of the service.

Blockaders rolling in a calm.

OFF CHARLESTON HARBOR

Within a few days, *Huron* steamed northeasterly from Port Royal. She was to relieve one of the ten ships then attempting to seal Charleston. The mental picture of many ships grouped immediately off the conventional harbor bar, however, is utterly unrealistic. Instead, the blockaders were actually deployed from modern Folly Beach near Stono Inlet northeasterly to Bull Island, a sector of about forty miles. The cordon of ships could not be held close inshore for they had to keep themselves well to seaward of the three-fathom line (eighteen feet of water) and usually within, or on, the "deep six," or thirty-six foot line. With the gradual slope of the ocean's continental shelf what it was, a blockader's station could be miles from the nearest offshore island such as the modern Isle of Palms, then shown on the charts as just another, unromantic long island.

The gradient of the shelf also presented a never ending parade of mounting sea swells. Any one of them could almost dip a ship's lee rail under with no more than a breath of help from the usual trade winds. Surgeon Stedman recorded the offshore swells in the drawing on page 81, "Blockaders rolling in a calm." To keep the enemy confused and to make certain that unchanging ship locations did not become navigational aids to incoming and outgoing blockade runners, ships sideslipped nightly and even swapped positions on a secret schedule. One of the faster ships was always posted near the middle of the picket line, prepared to assist in close pursuit of any strange ship that failed to respond to signals or to lay to at the sound of a warning gun. The *Augusta,* a converted merchant liner, was such a vessel. Her Captain, Commander E. G. Parrott, was also the senior officer present and commanded the Charleston Flotilla except when Commander J. B. Marchand's ship was present since Marchand outranked Parrott.

Fires were banked except at dawn and throughout the evening twilight. The hour of the night's high tide called for a similar intense alert for these were the hours when something almost always happened. Steam pressures were brought to full speed capability; anchor cables were slip-stopped to facilitate getting underway as easily and as quickly as pulling the bolt in a shackle link. The cable was fastened to a marker buoy to enable the ship to return to the same compass bearings and again make fast to the undisturbed anchor and cable chain length. Such careful planning and tactics worked so well that freight rates throughout the blockade area skyrocketed to more than five hundred dollars a ton—paid in advance! Blockade running became a cat-and-mouse game for high stakes. Captain A.C. Hobart-Hampton, Royal Navy, assumed another name and began running ships through the blockade from Bermuda and Nassau. His fixed fees rose higher and higher after each successful trip. At the end of eighteen trips, he had amassed a fortune and went home to England. Captain John Wilkinson, Confederate States Navy, rivalled Hobart-Hampton's record, but never received more than the routine pay of his rank in the Confederate

U. S. Ships "Onward" and "Vandalia".

Navy.

PRIZE MONEY

To spur the capture of ships of such wary skippers as Hobart-Hampton and Wilkinson, the United States offered the traditional prize money to successful ships and crews of each squadron. This was an old English custom that the American colonists had copied and practiced during the colonial wars with France and Spain and continued during the Revolutionary War and the War of 1812. Captain Stephen Decatur and his crew of the 44-gun frigate, *United States,* for example, received $200,000 for their victory over and capture of the British *Macedonian* in 1812. In other words, blockade running was a game that both sides could play with fond hopes for a monetary bonus. A captured merchant vessel had to be sailed to a Federal port, condemned in admiralty procedures, and sold with cargo to the highest bidder. Half of the money received was retained by the government; the other half was distributed among the officers and men of the ship or ships participating in the capture. All blockading ships within the range of visual signals were considered participants. Officers and men within the prescribed distance received the distributed prize money more or less in proportion to their pay base. The flagship could be anywhere, but the squadron commander still received a thin slice from all prizes taken by any ship in the squadron. His aggregate gain, however, was not always the highest among the officers. There were many inequities in the system, but all students of naval history agree that prize money made eager beavers of all ship commanders if not all hands on all ships.

Huron got into the spirit of the game immediately. She had been on station only a few days, 12 April 1862, when a fast schooner tried running into Bull's Bay only to find USS *Onward* close inshore and athwart her course. She outsprinted *Onward* southwesterly but soon sighted *Huron* underway and on a collision course. To avoid *Huron*'s gunfire, the schooner headed inshore among the shoals and breakers and ran aground; her ten or twelve-man crew took to boats. The sea, too rough for salvage efforts, rapidly broke her up, and another prize had escaped the eager grasp of Captain Downes. It was not unusual, however, for a well-handled sailing ship to outrun a warship in a stiff breeze, especially if the latter happened to be saving coal with its fires banked.

Six days later, Dame Fortune finally smiled on *Huron.* In utter darkness, the schooner *Glide,* ". . . loaded with 100 bales of cotton, 5 tierces of rice, in bags and a quantity of flour . . ." silently tried sneaking through the blockade. She almost collided with *Huron.* Downes had a prize crew aboard before her startled skipper could collect his wits. The owner and a passenger were also aboard; and with all the crew, except the Captain and the Mate, were later put ashore as noncombatants. The *Glide*'s two officers, with the ship's papers as evidence, became witnesses in the adjudication procedures. Four seamen commanded by one of *Huron*'s master's mates formed the prize crew that sailed her to trial and condemnation.

Although she was indeed a small prize, *Glide* was much better than a larger prize which might have had to be shared with all other ships in sight. Except for DuPont's thin equity, half of her sale price belonged to Downes and his crew. The cotton alone, thanks to the fiber-hungry mills of New England, could bring about $30,000. The schooner and her additional cargo would sweeten the pot still more. John Downes could hardly be the thoroughly unlucky Jonah commander that his officers and men had occasionally whispered him to be.

Prize money was always a constant and lively topic of conversation aboard all ships on which Surgeon Stedman served. Had he been a money-hungry man whose success in life rested only upon the acquisition and conservation of dollars alone, it would have been worth the time and effort to determine when and how much he would receive from the capture of little *Glide* with her demijohns of turpentine, sacks of rice, and a hundred bales of highly priced cotton. From his letters home, there is ample evidence that Charles Ellery Stedman was not such a man. He mentions the optimism of Captain Downes and others regarding prize money, but he apparently clung to the beatitude that forecastle philosophers often quoted with solemnity worthy of the Sermon on the Mount: "Blessed is he that expecteth little or nothing, for he shall not be disappointed." Stedman's share of the condemnation and sale of *Glide* and her cargo, after the usual and lengthy delay, could have been as much as $125 for that was the portion received by another assistant surgeon on a similar warship which had made a solo capture of a blockade runner carrying 600 bales of cotton.

Although DuPont's share as squadron commander amounted to five percent of the prize money and that of Downes, as Captain to ten percent, Stedman and his shipmates did not need tabulated figures to recognize the inequities in such distributions from the fruits of their gunfire. They knew what was happening. All had heard the old, mythical story of the praying sailor aboard *Constitution* as she closed on HMS *Java* for the most spectacular battle of her career. "And what are you asking of our Lord, my good man?" asked the sympathetic chaplain. "I'm praying that He distribute the casualties aboard on the same basis as the prize monies, Sir," was the reply.

HURON CATCHES A BIG ONE

A few days after the capture of *Glide,* 19 April 1862, *Huron* was ordered to Port Royal to have her boilers scaled and her power plant overhauled. The respite from up-rolling lifts and down-rolling drops created by the never ending swells was a pleasant change for the officer who slept in bunks, but many of the warrant ranks and lower ratings, all of whom slept in hammocks, complained that the placidity of the inland waters provided none of the rhythm essential for truly restful sleep.

Before the end of the month, they were back among the swells, anchored off the north end of Folly Island and near Lawford Channel. On 1 May, a lazy schooner loafing along under a third of her sail power excited the curiosity of Captain Downes although she could easily be one of the many such vessels serving DuPont's squadron. Although she ignored signals, she hoisted an English flag. *Huron* brought her to and put an officer aboard to look at her papers which indicated she was *Albert* of most recent British registration at New Providence, Nassau Island, Bahamas. Under the name *Irene,* she had cleared her home port in New Jersey, had gone to Cuba where she was sold, complete with unbroken cargo, to a Spaniard. Apparently, it was he who had put her under the British flag. Fortunately he was aboard and the prize court commissioners could question him in New York.

The cargo manifests were innocent enough except that some cases, long enough to contain rifles, were too deep in the hold for examination. The readily available cargo was general merchandise from New York and New England. Although most was noncontraband, there were some items in great demand within the Confederacy, cotton cards for example. These were used for hand combing ginned cotton fibers for the spindles of old-fashioned spinning wheels. Many of these antique spinning wheels were coming out of attics of Confederate homes from Richmond to Houston, Texas. *Albert* was neither the first nor the last schooner with a similarly suspicious cargo. The blockade had cut off the supply of cheap, well made cloth from New England mills. Some Northern merchants and small ship owners were quite willing to traffic with the enemy when the prospective gains were more than sufficient to cover the risks involved. With so many similar schooners serving the supply needs of squadrons from the Virginia capes to Brownsville, Texas, it was hardly practical for Union ships to stop and board each and every one of them.

Most of another month rolled by before Stedman again had reason to rush topside to learn if "Beat to Quarters" was just another general quarters drill or if something was in sight. What he saw looked good. An incoming, long and lean, barkentine-rigged, screw steamer was turning on her rudderpost and making smoke for a full speed exit from Lawford Channel to the open sea. It was in dawn's early light, about 5:00 AM, 26 May, when the chase started. *Huron's* boilers were at full speed pressure, and she pretty well held her own from the beginning. A stiff norther was blowing down the coast.

Well off shore, the steamer's best chance would have been to angle northerly into the Gulf Stream and gradually to get close to the wind's eye. That would have put her on a course to safety in the neutral British waters of the Bermudas. Instead, she shook out her own sails and steered downwind for Nassau Island where HBMS *Barracouta* was patrolling. Downwind was actually the next best decision for sail power was of less value in light or falling winds near the steam speed of a vessel. Soon both ships would take in all sail, and the usually faster blockade runner could gradually step away, at least far enough to lose herself in the near darkness.

A chase before the wind.

Stedman's picture on page 87, "A chase before the wind," tells the story. Both ships have their fore-and-aft sails rigged out, wing-and-wing. In the frequent process of sending down his foremast yards and square foretop sails and further stripping his rigging to shrouds and stays for close action in inland waters and then restoring them for blockade duty, Downes had modified his foremast pattern in the way Stedman portrays. The slight angle of the funnel smoke suggests that Downes had put *Huron* into a slight yaw to starboard to bring her Parrott rifle over the port bow to bear on the steamer. It is being fired. With the help of so much sail power, *Huron* is probably doing a bit better than fourteen knots, perhaps fifteen. Early in the race, Downes sent men into the tops and had buckets of saltwater whipped up to them on halyards for constantly wetting down every thread of sail cloth. After a chase of more than four hours with the Parrott rifle in action, the blockade runner took in her sails and hove to.

The prize was found to be the *Cambria,* although Stedman remembered her as "*Cumbria.*" Her Captain blandly admitted *Cambria's* intent to run the blockade with a cargo of rifles, munitions, "hardware," and medicines. The manifest proved as much. *Cambria's* five passengers said they were enroute to New Orleans. Since Farragut had captured that city exactly a month earlier and since Major General Ben Butler's associated army troops had moved in to take over the city and the surrounding area, the nature of their business and with whom was subject to speculation. This doubt was not enough to keep the officers and men of *Huron* from viewing the passengers with dark distaste. They could be no less than gross, soulless profiteers seeking wealth from the dismemberment of the Union, the official neutral stance of Great Britain notwithstanding.

Doctor Stedman captured the thoughts of the *Huron's* crew and expressed his own sentiments in one of his best cartoons, "Party of Neutrals (?) taken on the prize," shown on page 91. The four passengers shown well represent the contemporary American concept of the entire population of the perfidious British Isles. There is the overstuffed Lancastershire manufacturer complete with small dog, gold watch chain, and top hat; the proud, arrogant Scotsman with the up-tilted nose and attired in his clan's tartan, alow and aloft; the haughty Londoner with tight headgear for the voyage, monocle, saber-tooth mustache, and the experienced traveller's musette bag. The meek little fellow with the carpet bag can be no more nor less than an aging, downtrodden, and unsuccessful Bob Crachit who had never heard a Christmas carol. George Cruikshank himself could not have better caricatured the situation.

Stedman provided no names—real, suggestive, or fictitious—for the four officers facing the passengers. The three in front, however, must be Captain Downes, Executive Officer Belknap, and Surgeon Stedman. The officer in back of Downes is most likely Paymaster Thomas T. Caswell. Because the capture of *Cambria* greatly intrigued Stedman, he undoubtedly

The "Cumbria", captured by the U.S.S. "Huron".

wrote to Edith in detail to describe the chase and its results. Unfortunately, that letter or letters did not survive the years and was not among the collection so generously provided by the Stedman family. The narrative and interpretations used herein are based upon *Huron's* logbook and the official reports of Downes and Commanders Enoch G. Parrott and J. B. Marchand. Stedman's four pictures of this period, however, tell a complete story in themselves. They most certainly embellish and supplement the essential data to be found in the *Official Records of the Union and Confederate Navies in the War of the Rebellion*.

Downes quickly learned why *Cambria* had not angled toward the Bermuda Islands and upwind when she had gained the open sea and found *Huron* in pursuit: she had insufficient coal for that distance. Like most fast steamers on the Nassau-Charleston run, *Cambria* had skimped on coal to provide more cargo space. The four hour chase at top speed with *Huron* on her heels had made heavy inroads on even that scant supply. She could not have made it upwind to the Bermuda Islands at top speed.

Banshee I, a lucky runner that had often enriched her owners, learned that lesson the hard way. Chased upwind toward Bermuda for a long, full day, she shook off her relentless pursuer in darkness and headed southwest toward Nassau. Her fuel was soon exhausted. With only stubby masts and short yards and booms like those of *Cambria,* she could not trust the light and falling airs to take her to the neutral waters of the Bahamas before a Union cruiser found her. Her masts and spars were reduced to cord-wood; the bulwarks, cabin woodwork, and furniture became planks and splinters to fuel her boiler fires. Even this provided insufficient fuel, and she was finally forced to use cotton dipped in turpentine. When she reached an island sixty miles north of Nassau, her engines were dying for charred cotton lint had choked her flues. Here, however, she was safe for England's neutrality made *Banshee I* untouchable in these waters. *Cambria's* captain had had no choice other than to sail downwind from Charleston with the hope of outsprinting *Huron*.

Captain Downes designated Lieutenant Belknap as prize master with a prize crew of twenty seamen. *Cambria's* skipper, his deck officers, and the passengers were held aboard *Huron* to prevent any conspiracy to retake *Cambria* while sailing alone under her prize crew. At about this time, *Augusta,* Commander Enoch G. Parrott, arrived. She had been twelve miles astern when *Cambria* hove to; but, being within signal distance, Parrott and his crew had a well planned and fully considered equity in the prize. Having established this claim beyond any successful reversal, Parrott returned to his blockade station to report the capture and to say that he had authorized *Huron* to escort the prize to nearby Port Royal where the latter would take on enough coal to get to New York. *Huron* would return when this mission had been fully accomplished. The Senior Officer Present, Commander J. B. Marchand of *James Adger,* was sorry to hear this for he planned that *Huron* next day would join

Party of Neutrals (!) taken in the prize.

her identical sister ships, *Ottawa, Unadilla,* and *Pembina,* in the Stono River. Instead, he would have to send *Flambeau* until *Huron* returned, although she drew too much water for that river when the tide was out. The ships were to make a reconnaissance to the point of resistance by the defenses of Charleston on the Stono; and were to be prepared to cover the landings of troops on Kiawah Island or even on the mainland as far up the Stono as Brown's Island, dependent upon hostile reactions.

Before *Huron* could return to this new assignment, Commander Marchand had signed a long letter to the Secretary of the Navy, the Honorable Gideon Welles, to report the capture of *Cambria* by *Huron.* Marchand indicated that he had authorized *Augusta* to join the pursuit; and, moreover, that the capture could not have been made without the entire cordon being off Charleston. Therefore, he was putting in a claim on *Cambria* for all ships of his flotilla in sight and signal range when *Cambria* turned in flight from Lawford Channel, including even the little flotilla in the Stono River. This meant that the prize money from sale of *Cambria* was to be divided among the crews of *James Adger, Augusta, Huron,* and ten other ships in that sector of the blockade. No doubt, the crew of *Huron* groused about it *ad infinitum.* That same rule, however, had put them in line for shares on ships captured by other members of the cordon, and would give them an equity in all future captures by the flotilla as long as *Huron* was present. Perhaps there was some equity in the distribution of prize money after all for almost everyone got something—everyone, that is, except the foot-slogging infantry, the saddle-pounding cavalry, and the powder-burnt cannoneers of the Army.

A ride on shore   28 Mar. 1862.
Fernandina

CHAPTER SEVEN Up and Down the Stono River

POWERFUL AND HISTORIC Forts Moultrie and Sumter for years had dominated the harbor entrance to Charleston. After the surrender of Fort Sumter during the first days of the Civil War, the Confederates had rebuilt its bastions, making it stronger than ever. The approaches to the harbor were also fortified. Heavy batteries were sited within earthworks on Sullivan's Island, at the upper or northern lip; and on Morris Island, on the lower or southern lip of that tight-mouthed harbor.

Union ship commanders were quite aware of these fortifications for, from the Morris Island Batteries Gregg and Wagner and from Fort Shaw, Confederate coastal gunners could reach the junction of Lawford Channel and Main Ship Channel. Their guns often growled loudly when a Union cruiser maintained hot pursuit of an incoming steamer beyond the point of reasonable caution. The cruiser was usually firing at the escaping prize for its destruction was almost as good as her capture in terms of prize money. All of the guns on Morris Island would be thundering at the pursuer using measured ranges to surveyed reference points. This was the kind of bickering no wooden cruiser could long accept.

Blockade runners had taught the Union navy that there were many channels or combinations of channels which could be used to bring cargoes into Charleston Harbor without sailing past its powerful defensive fortifications. Although Light House Inlet might be such a channel, it was sealed by Fort Shaw, at the southern tip of Morris Island, and by Fort Green, on the opposite tip of Folly Island. Furthermore, Light House Inlet was a channel from the sea into a maze of crooked creeks and bayous which seldom led anywhere other than to another creek or swamp. This could not be the passage needed for any assault on Charleston.

On the other hand, the Stono River, rather deep at high tides, could easily be that better route. Harassed blockade runners often used the Stono. The always friendly, black refugee "Contrabands" said that it was lightly held by masked batteries of field artillery which could be everywhere or nowhere; but it was impossible for a garrison to be everywhere at any one time. The Stono could be the neglected corridor most vulnerable to an amphibious thrust.

The Stono was not so much a river as it was a narrow tidal estuary. Although many freshwater creeks flowed into it, it was short and had a connecting flowage of its own with Charleston Harbor through Wappoo Creek; this was the water connection that created James Island. From the point where the Wappoo joined the Stono, Charleston's public buildings, parks, and the waterfront promenade were all within extreme range of *Huron*'s 11-inch gun. Naval gunfire could also support a land attack as far as the south bank of the Ashley River at the Charleston end of Wappoo Creek. Aware of this, Confederate General John C. Pemberton had ordered Fort Pemberton built to cover that reach of the Stono. Everyone knew about the fort, particularly the "Contrabands" who had helped build it.

Only one procedure could be used to provide accurate information about Confederate holding power on the Stono: send targets up the river to draw fire. This was the initial mission of the little Stono Inlet Task Force consisting of *Pembina, Ottawa, Unadilla,* and *Huron.* Sister ships, the four were as much alike as peas in a pod. Later, they were joined by *Pawnee,* an 1858-built heavy steam sloop twice the weight of *Huron,* mounting twelve guns, most of them 9-inch. Despite her weight, she drew only ten feet, the same as *Huron* and her sisters. *Pawnee*'s size, however, did cause some difficulties in narrow channels. Her Captain, Commander Drayton, was also in command of the task force with orders to report directly to Flag Officer DuPont which somewhat irritated Commander J. B. Marchand, commanding the Charleston Blockade Sector, for he had started the show before Drayton arrived and was enjoying it. Accompanied by little *Ellen,* Marchand had led the force up to Brown's Island, about four miles upriver, without drawing much fire. Judging that fire to have come from a float-

ing battery, Marchand had searched for the battery in nearby creeks without success.

When Drayton arrived, he left *Pawnee* below Legareville; boarded *Ottawa* and continued upstream to *Huron* and *Unadilla,* well upriver and above Paul Grimball's Plantation. Here the ground was firm enough on both banks to permit an army to make a crossing. He passed the word to his ship captains that army troops from Port Royal would soon be arriving for disembarkation on James Island on the north bank of the Stono. This would be a reconnaissance in force, perhaps an all-out offensive. The three vessels were to press on to Wappoo Creek to find out what Pemberton's batteries had to say.

They proved to be a bit talkative. When the three ships began firing on a small steamer in the bend just short of Wappoo Cut, a salvo of smoothbore cannon balls came at them, but fell short; there was no way to determine the location of the battery. Rifle projectiles, however, were nearer the target and at times were disgustingly close. Drayton, on *Ottawa,* left *Huron* and *Unadilla* still bickering with the distant battery to return to *Pawnee* and bring her upstream on the night's high tide. Her 9-inch broadside guns would give force to further argument.

With more definite information concerning the sources of hostile fire now available, the Stono River Task Force knew that the fire came from the new Fort Pemberton and possibly from some small roving guns. The Confederate batteries had been talkative but unconvincing; and the task force gave as much or

Skylarking.

more than it received. Without difficulty, the ships moved to the junction with Wappoo Creek. Dropping back downstream to the vicinity of Newton, about three miles below Fort Pemberton, Drayton reported to DuPont that the Stono was open and that the Navy could support army troops ashore up to the range of ships' guns on the river. Beyond that range, however, the troops would be on their own.

ARTIST AND SURGEON STEDMAN PONDERS THE SITUATION

Such was the condition of affairs when Surgeon Stedman found time to take pen in hand to tell Edith that all was well but not too quiet along the Stono:

> *Huron, Stono River,*
> *near Charleston*
> *2nd June, 1862*
> *No. 35. and a very stupid*
> *letter*

> *Dear Edith*
> *I take advantage of a brisk wind tearing down the windsail and through the ward-room and the consequent defeat of the flies—to do a little journalizing for your behalf and the instruction of our friends. In the letter accompanying this, I send some slight sketches which will give you some notion of the scenery of the river. I cannot give you the shadows which pass over the marshes—the water and the foliage, nor the notes of the birds that sing in the adjoining woods.*

> *These sounds are interrupted by the occasional boom of a heavy gun which will begin in tolerably smart cannonading below us where the Pawnee, the Ellen, Unadilla, Ottawa and Hale are at work. Every now & then the Pembina or the Huron will start up from repose and heave a few XI-inch or Hotchkiss shell at the batteries above, or into the woods in order to "keep up the worry" of the enemy who are at a loss to know how we fire so far and so true when we cannot see them.*

> *When it is calm, which is almost always, myriads of flies congregate in the ward room rendering it almost uninhabitable. The mus-quitoes [sic] are not yet arrived but are expected in the next boat; the noons & afternoons are cool, but the nights and mornings are hot and sultry. Sleeping is a warm and close business. My bunk is not airy, and the flies begin thier [sic] operations at an early hour. . . .*

One could hardly expect from the tone of Stedman's letter that he was on the upriver flank of a Class A landing and beachhead operation. *Ellen* and *Hale* were not a part of Drayton's flotilla, and had only recently arrived with a number of unarmed ships loaded with troops from the expeditionary force based on Hilton Head. The distance from the base to the Stono River was hardly more than a four hour coastal ferry run. Of necessity, the troops were being landed piecemeal because of the narrow waters. Nevertheless, within the incredible time of two or three days, the Navy put ashore between Brown's Island and Wright's Landing no less than fourteen regiments of infantry, one regiment each of engineers and artillery, and most of a regiment of cavalry.

Brigadier General Thomas W. Sherman, who was in command at Port Royal and Hilton Head when *Huron* had first joined the South Atlantic Squadron, had welcomed a transfer to duty in the field as a division commander in the Army of Tennessee. In March 1862, Major General David Hunter was assigned as Sherman's successor. He, however, was more than a troop commander for he was also designated as Commander of the Department of the South which included all of Florida, Georgia, and South Carolina. Had it not been for the thousands of Confederate soldiers and hundreds of gray formations within the "Department," this could have been a happy assignment, especially for an old headquarters soldier who had been a Paymaster for too much of his career. Fort Pulaski, Georgia, was about to surrender to Sherman when Hunter arrived. Its flag came down on 10 April, and Hunter accepted the honors for that victory. The main corridor to Savannah's harbor was now sealed, and Hunter could now concentrate all of his troops not tied down in coastal station duties for a move against Charleston.

Hunter planned to move out of the "beachhead," roughly from Legareville to Wright's Landing, in a thrust across James Island to capture Fort Johnson on Charleston Harbor between Fort Sumter and the city. In numbers and firepower, Hunter's force was larger than the conventional reinforced corps, the largest tactical unit in the Union armies of the Civil War. It totalled more than 12,000 men. Hunter had the means for a quick drive to his objective.

The exact resources available to the defending commander, Major General John C. Pemberton, are not so easily determined for records covering this period are not complete. However, his successor in the following September, General Pierre G. T. Beauregard, inherited a defending force of slightly less than 6,000 men—5,841, to be exact. Of these, 2,819 were assigned to garrison various defending forts and batteries, including some roving batteries of light artillery . The largest infantry commitment consisted of 1,184 officers and men on James Island. These figures, however, ignored his capability to call in police, sheriffs' posses, and a limited number of "home guard" units.

Beauregard later made one interesting comment concerning Hunter's tactics, maintaining that Hunter should have made his landings much farther up the Stono River. Had this been done, the Federal force would have been farther behind the Confederate "siege line" being prepared by Pemberton but far from complete at the time Hunter made his move. The landing cited by Beauregard also would have placed Hunter between Fort Johnson and reinforcements from Charleston.

Hunter, unfortunately, did not believe Commander Drayton's firm report that the Stono could be used at will as far as Fort Pemberton by any vessel of ten feet or less draft, and well beyond if desired. Had Drayton's report been followed, the army's advance could have been accompanied by supporting naval counter-battery fire against both the fort and any masked batteries—usually composed of light artillery only—that might appear along the river banks. Hunter preferred to believe intelligence reports that the Confederates were sowing the river with mines, "torpedoes" as they were then known. The Confederates were also believed able to put barriers in the river behind the supporting ships. Hunter chose to play it safe by landing farther downriver. Beauregard, however, insisted that the river was being navigated at will as far as Wappoo Cut when he succeeded Pemberton.

How much of this did the officers and men of *Huron* know or suspect at the time Surgeon Stedman was writing Edith? Apparently Stedman knew the Army's plans, but was not worrying about them, for his letter continues:

> *In the last letter I wrote you, I gave you an idea that we were going in to fight the batteries above, that notion is given up I believe, as the river there is so obstructed, and the advance will not be made in that direction at all perhaps. The day after Capt. Downes*

was fired at, the Ellen & Pawnee came up and the former went up abreast of the house when the riflemen poured in a volley sending one bullet through Capt. Wolsey's pantaloons. [Melancthon B. Woolsey, Lieutenant Commanding *Ellen*, had succeeded the audacious William Budd.] *The Ellen began to bang away in great rage and almost unroofed the big mansion where the rifles were hid; then the battery opened and the Ellen replied till she was hid in smoke, and a shell went right over her, covering the bow gun & her crew with water.* [Drayton later sent Woolsey word not to expose his ship or expend too much ammunition in a matter of "personal honor!"]

After a pretty lively cannonade, the Pawnee & Ellen went down the river, the former waking the echoes with her VIII-inch guns and rifled eighties. How handsome she looked, I wish you could have seen her as she dropped down the stream, shelling the woods; the woods a rich golden green, while a strip of blue water lay between her and a bright green point of marsh. We afterwards heard that Ellen landed every shell in the battery, which we learn . . . consists of 8 VIII-inch and 2 X-inch guns, not on the river as I wrote before . . . .

In the evening Paymaster May came aboard from the Unadilla; he had heard the

98   STONO RIVER

Ethiopian Serenaders.

news from Downer Court & it was very agreeable to see a body that reminded me so nearly of home.

It is a safe assumption that the news that the Paymaster from the *Unadilla* had heard "from Downer Court" concerned the birth of the Stedman's first child and only son, Ellery, on 8 May 1862. It was time for someone other than the Surgeon's wardroom messmates to hear such important news and to say something about it. Stedman continued his description of activities on the Stono:

This day Monday, 2 June is chiefly remarkable for the arrival of the troops which are landing below protected by the Pawnee at Legareville, and make it look somewhat more like business, though I suppose it will be some time yet before any movement is made, as the army always has to wait for guns, or forage or reinforcements. . . . This morning we dropped up stream so as to open the big battery & begin a fire on it, one of ours bursting in it. The contrabands tell us of one regiment having retreated from within our range—of several being killed in the different batteries, and a great confusion existing among the soldiery . . . where these fortifications are.

They can't imagine how we find them with our shells when we cant see them and never can tell where we are going to fire next. Everytime our vessels run up & engage a battery & retire after having teased them enough—they send dispatches to Charleston with the story of the repulse. So you mustnt be astonished at hearing any time of our total defeat, though you neednt believe it unless you choose . . . .

The contrabands come aboard every day & tell us just where our shot strike & where the new guns are placed; . . . The annexed diagram will give some notion of the situation which I hope will be the means of doing us some credit.—Just now 3 rifle shots were fired at the Pembina striking just below her starboard quarter; the boldest thing they have done yet. Boom goes a gun somewhere now, just to keep the ball up I suppose.

Tuesday June 3, This morning broke with a lowering sky, promising rain, a promise that has been kept at intervals throughout the day. About breakfast time sharp musketry was heard down the river where the Army is, about 3000 of whom are said to be landed from the transports we see and 5000 more of whom are expected this afternoon.

We took an officer prisoner that knew Capt. Drayton who went aboard to see him. (Drayton of the Pawnee & Bankhead of the Pembina are both South Carolinians.) The affair was partly visible from our mastheads.

This afternoon the Ottawa & Hy Andrews opened on the Folly creek fort in conjunction with the gunboats on the other side of James Island and for an hour or so a very brisk fire was kept up, the roar of the guns and screech of the shells made a sort of double barreled 4th of July, and excited our Capt. so that he began hammering the old foe above us with our XI-inch & rifle; no reply was drawn . . . either because the battery is removed or because he dont choose to waste his ammunition on us. A few shots tired us of our taciturn enemy, and I retired to write and fight flies while the rain comes steadily and silently down. . . . (Thursday, 5 1/2 pm. Some birds in our rigging are singing most sweetly. I wish you could hear em.)

Surgeon Stedman rounded out his "No. 35 and a *very* stupid letter" with comments on the most recent, though belated, news currently being circulated in the South Atlantic Squadron. They were startled by the defeat of Major General N. P. Banks in the Shenandoah Valley by a rash Confederate general named Thomas J. Jackson. The Navy men did not feel Jackson would endanger the Capital for should "Fremont & McDowell do their duty, Jackson ought to be completely cut to pieces."

Stedman, however, saw little point in speculating on "events that are past so long before you hear of them," a thoroughly sound philosophical thought. "I

hope," he added, "the whole row will put an end to the politicians' continual intermeddling, and the means of stifling that blundering ass of a Stanton." Within a year, Navy officers still hammering at the gates of Charleston Harbor were saying much the same thing of Lincoln's Secretary of the Navy, Gideon Welles, the sage-like editor from Connecticut.

VISITS TO THE INFANTRY

One personal worry was expressed to Edith in this same letter. Stedman had sent money to Frank Stedman "for four large boxes" of wine for the wardroom mess. It was to be shipped to Lieutenant George E. Belknap, U.S.S. *Huron*, via Adams Express, since Belknap was the senior officer of the mess. But Belknap had gone north as prize master of the captured blockade runner *Cambria* accompanied by a fifth of *Huron*'s crew for whom replacements had been sent. What had happened to the wine? Had communications suddenly become so efficient that the shipment was following Belknap, wherever he might be, or was it still enroute to its rightful owners aboard *Huron*? Within two or three months, Belknap was to appear again in Charleston waters as the Executive Officer of *New Ironsides*, the most advanced and best ironclad warship built by either the North or the South during the Civil War period.

It was not Downes' desire to have Belknap go north as the prize crew skipper for the captured *Cambria,* although Downes was due for reassignment himself. He had been aboard *Huron* long enough to have trained an adequate successor for Belknap. Now with his Executive Officer gone, Downes became even more supervisory over routines he had previously delegated to Belknap. Actually, Downes was a good combat commander. He saw no reason why anyone, other than a ship's doctor with an empty sick bay, should have rest or relaxation in the presence of an active and armed foe. "In case of doubt, think up something for the crew to do; a moving target is hard to hit; the best protection is a quick and effective fire power of your own; never linger in the smoke of your own broadside, it blinds your gunners and tells the foe your ship is still there." These were combat truths he had heard often from his father, the old Commodore. Downes kept his crew busy at tasks designed to make them ready for any combat emergency.

Shifting a thousand yards upsteam or downstream meant manning the capstan, shortening up against the tidal current, and lifting the anchor. The black gang had to put on enough coal to raise the steam. Nothing, however, meant more work and expense than a solid hit from a hostile heavy gun. The ship was exposed to musketry and sniper fire every hour she was in the river. Although a squad of marines was always on the alert with loaded rifles, the best cure for snipers was a round of grapeshot from one of the 24-pounders aimed right at the wisp of rifle smoke that curled from a cluster of green leaves. Smokeless powder had not yet been invented. An occasional volley of small arms also marked the source with certainty. Using grape reduced Confederate small arms

fire to a minimum; nevertheless, the mast tops were screened to provide protection. The thick, high bulwarks of the spar-deck, stuffed as they were with the hammocks of the crew, offered excellent protection to all except the gun crews who necessarily, though briefly, opened the gun ports to fire.

Although *Huron* was exposed to possible damage and casualties from enemy action every day that she was in the river and despite the fact that she was often farther up the river than any of her associated vessels, Downes had no occasion to report damage that his warrant officers—such as the carpenter and the engineers—could not correct. He did not find it necessary to evacuate any casualties, dead or wounded. But incoming, long-range projectiles and cannon balls from unidentified locations caused much concern. The defenders apparently had mounted one or more roving, heavy guns on barges which could hide in any one of several creeks emptying into the Stono. A shallow-draft tugboat tender could shift such guns in darkness. There were many near misses, but no large round made a clean hit on *Huron*.

Captain Downes was highly cooperative with the troop commanders ashore. In his eagerness to give them close support, he repeatedly had the gig manned to be rowed ashore for a conference. One small land battle took place abeam of *Huron* which was opposite the point where the Confederate main line of resistance ended on the Stono's north bank or shore line. A brigade of infantry, with cavalry support but no artillery, put pressure along the bank in preparation

Contrabands.

for a possible flanking movement. The troops quickly ran into determined resistance as well as encountering extremely difficult terrain. *Huron*'s four guns, pivoted or transferred to the engaged side, supported the effort. Before the skirmish ended, Stedman experienced a taste of land warfare. He described this in a letter dated 9 June 1862:

> *Sunday the 8th—the day . . . broke beautifully nlear with balmy airs and cool breezes, all around lay quiet as in a New England farm. I wrote my letter to you, and as I finished it, the rain began again. About 2 in the afternoon, a squad of horse appeared suddenly on the bank. . . . Downes got in his gig and went ashore . . . they wanted the woods shelled for them.*
>
> *So we opened with rifle and XI-inch, & fired like mischief for a few minutes till the requisite number of shots had been made when we ceased, and the troops moved in, two or three regiments with a few horse, slowly toward the woods. Soon dropping shots were heard, then a volley, then a roar of rifles down the line two or three times then a man was seen carried back on a litter, another with a man pickaback. Two or three, like prisoners followed.*
>
> *Another crash & roll of musketry then a heavy gun fired two or three times, and by and by a signal officer appeared and motioned us to open again, as our troops were now reappearing. Crack, bang, went our two long range guns again, and the Ellen, which had come up from Capt. Drayton to see what the row was about, joined in from her 30pd Parrotts. Whew! what a roar and screeching & bursting of shell. Soon we stopped after the troops had all been seen returning in good order; and Downes, getting into his gig, asked if I would like to go; glad of the chance I jumped in, knowing I would lose it if I stopped to shift my white socks and pumps.*

The gig pulled down river a bit and beached near a large house, obviously the regimental headquarters and field first aid station of the left flank regiment of the brigade. The house impressed Stedman almost as much as what was happening in it. "A large house, which if time allows I will try to send you a sketch. . . ." The house had only recently been completed. The rich and luxurious furniture filled him with awe: ". . . new, handsome furniture, marble-slabbed bureaus & stands, & French bedsteads still left in the chambers—the shavings from easing the drawers showed how new it was . . . as if a newly married couple had just taken the place." A shell "probably one from the *Pawnee* the other day" had passed through the building without touching "an article of the furniture."

Infantrymen and cavalrymen were around the house. "On the piazzo . . . lay one man with a part of his spleen shot away, but yet conscious." A lieutenant was "brandishing his long boot and showing where the bullet had passed through the calf of his leg." The regimental surgeon was not a Harvard man. In the middle of a sentence in his letter, Stedman drew a postage stamp size sketch of an unattractive face which he declared "looks just like him minus the dirt." The surgeon was working on a man's head wound:

> Says I, "Isn't that the ball, Sir, just be-hind the wound?" "Ya-as" said the medico, (it is a New York, Dutch regiment) "Yaas, perapsh it ish, yaw are." I believe if I hadn't pointed it out he never would have guessed it; however he did then fish it out—a rounded musket bullet. In the affair, the regiment lost about nine, killed, wounded & missing. They discovered the enemy about 1½ miles from where we are, near a church, ambushed in the woods, a rifle pit and big gun in posi-tion . . . .However they found what they wanted to, and were ordered to go no further than they did.

On the day following, Stedman went to the unen-gaged south bank to get some vegetables. This mis-sion accomplished, he returned to the ship in the midst of a fire fight beyond the north bank. *Huron* was firing everything furiously in support of the 3rd New Hampshire Infantry Regiment, reinforced by 1st Massachusetts Cavalry and a battery of Rhode Is-land artillery. Their headquarters was in the same house from which the Dutch had withdrawn. During a lull in the fighting at twilight, Stedman again accom-panied Downes to the house.

Here he immediately encountered an old Latin School classmate now serving in the 1st Massa-chusetts Cavalry. Stedman helped the New Hamp-shire surgeon with four or five wounded, taking a bullet from one man's chest and expressing the thought that a man with an arm wound offered a splendid opportunity for an elbow resection. "In a short time 4 Secesh were brought in, raw, but power-ful looking men in brown stuff with blue transverse stripes, a most unmilitary dress—and all shot thro' the chest, and belonging to the 47th Georgia." Stedman was happily proud of the New England regiments that were present in that sector, but was much saddened to hear that the 28th Massachusetts Infantry on its first contact with the enemy had taken flight, at least two companies throwing away their guns. The 8th Michi-gan Infantry, taking over their positions, had picked up the guns. The 28th Massachusetts was being re-cruited as a three year regiment from Boston and Cambridge while Stedman was waiting for orders to report for sea duty. Because of McClellan's defeats on the York Peninsula, the 28th was among the regi-ments of Hunter's command rushed to northern Vir-ginia. Here it became a part of the 1st Brigade, 1st Division of the Ninth Army Corps, Army of the Potomac. The 28th Massachusetts later distinguished itself from Antietam to Appomattox, losing fifteen officers and 236 men killed in action and one officer and 136 men who died of disease. The regiment's replacements were also recruited in Cambridge and Boston, and Stedman undoubtedly knew many of the men and officers personally.

At the house where Stedman was assisting the regimental surgeon, all was being done well: "Surgeons and hospital stewards bustled about, the fires blazed brighter and the woods grew blacker as I sauntered about this haunt of real war." He slept soundly that night though *Huron* indulged in chronic bursts of harassing fires. The next day was even better. Mail arrived from Port Royal—including the long overdue boxes of wine, "2 boat loads!" Meanwhile, a most amusing thing had taken place down river among the numerous service craft which included many schooners. A stranger moved in among them in the darkness. At dawn, she displayed her colors—the British flag. She was a blockade runner and considered herself safe at last. Had she waited until properly oriented, she could have departed quietly without hindrance for ". . . had he not been in such a hurry to run his ensign up, & waited till 8 oclk, he might have gone out as quietly as he came; no one would have thought of molesting him; they would have supposed him to be a trader." Although Stedman did not know the name of the blockade runner at the time he was telling this story, she was the *Rowena,* a schooner with an American skipper and crew, most of whom were from New Orleans.

General David Hunter's indecisive, faltering, and flawed campaign to capture Fort Johnson from the land side, thereby sealing Charleston's inner harbor and establishing a threshold base for the capture of the city, dragged itself to a dreary finish six days later. Pemberton's incomplete "Siege Line," running easterly from Dill's Landing on the Stono to the incomplete Fort Lamar east of Redoubt No. 5 and near Secessionville, had canalized Hunter's advance. His leading brigade, commanded by Brigadier General H. W. Benham, a distinguished engineer officer who had built too many forts, was funneled into the area between the Lighthouse Creek complex of stagnant water and marshes on the right and the end of the "Siege Line" on the left. Secessionville, Fort Lamar, and Redoubt No. 5 were all in his path.

The battlefield was more than two miles from Drayton's Stono River Task Force. Although *Huron*'s 11-inch could lob a shell that far, the time of flight was twelve seconds. A ten-second fuse would crack the shell before it reached its target, and it would burst over the heads of friendly troops. Although a twenty-second fuse was available, it was not as reliable as the ten-second timer. Furthermore, such extreme ranges greatly enlarged the probable error patterns in the impact area. This meant that Hunter's troops essentially would have little or no support from the ships' guns.

To defend the island, the Confederates had emplaced at least twelve guns, some of coastal defense calibers, at Fort Lamar or dug in behind redoubts. Most of the Federal casualties in the Battle of Seccessionville—85 killed in action, 472 wounded, and 128 missing—resulted from attempts to capture

The Diver and the Contrabands
Wassaw Sound, 1863.

these guns. Less than a third of the total Federal force ashore was committed during this defeat on 16 June 1862. General Hunter, however, had a quick alibi: he was not there. Benham had launched an uncoordinated attack without orders. But Hunter declined to make a second and properly coordinated attack for he maintained that the Army should stay closer to the sound of the Navy's guns. Hunter also became convinced that the most certain way of getting into the harbor was by attacking from Folly Island and Morris Island. By deciding to shift the emphasis of the Federal effort, Hunter also picked some thick forts to crack along the way: Wagner, Moultrie and Sumter. However, he did create a defensive outpost line from the Stono River, opposite Brown's Island, along the Folly River to and among the creeks and swamps to Lighthouse Inlet, thus preserving his beachhead for further operations. The long siege of Charleston had begun.

THE GUNS

Until the Stono River operations, Stedman had very little interest in *Huron*'s guns. While *Huron* was grounded off Cape Romain at low tide with her spardeck careened to a twenty degree tilt, the 16,000 pound, 11-inch, smoothbore Dahlgren Columbiad was a helpless and needless piece of junk in the thinking of a crew that breathed in fear of a violent attack by boarders. The tilt of the deck also reduced the arcs of fire of the pivoted rifle forward by at least half. During those two long days, the lighter short range howitzers, which could readily be shifted from starboard to port or vice versa, were the only two comforting pieces of ordnance aboard. Their 24-pound roundshot commanded some respect up to 1,200 yards. Although a round of grapeshot at close range could be devastating, it took forty seconds to service the piece and get it back into battery for firing. In close action such as a boarding threat, a lot could happen in forty seconds. By alternating firing the two howitzers, this dangerous time-lag for reloading could be cut in half. During the Stono River operation where *Huron* was normally beyond the army beachhead, a boarding attack by hostile troops from the always nearby vegetation was a constant possibility; this had happened to more than one careless blockader. It could happen to *Huron*! The two howitzers were important.

When Downes demonstrated the value of the forward 4-inch rifle and the 11-inch monster by using them frequently and accurately to support the troops ashore, Stedman began viewing them with increasing consideration and respect, but never with enough respect to draw an accurate picture of either one of them although Stedman could draw with admirable precision when he wanted to. Where the guns were concerned, it is quite apparent that he did not care to do so. In some of the scenes which struck his fancy, he found it necessary to include all or part of the guns. This is true of his drawing of gun drill during *Huron*'s shakedown cruise on page 67, and of his sketch "Skylarking" on page 95 which portrays the type of rumpus which can erupt in the coolness of any late afternoon when a ship is at anchor and some members of the crew want to get rid of excess energy.

Stedman did not note the day and month of the pictured bit of jousting, but it is taking place near the 11-inch big gun which is secured inboard. Because of its size and pivoting potential, there is more open space about it than anywhere else on the spar-deck. Such rough horseplay would not be possible elsewhere. The Master at Arms or "Jimmy Legs" was not light on his feet that day or the roughhousing would not have gotten as far as Stedman pictured. The men and their actions are well drawn, but the depiction of the 11-inch Dahlgren Columbiad is atrocious.

Although "Eleven Inch Gun Drill" on page 67 is a more accurate drawing of the gun, the lines of the tube continue to be out of proportion. The recoil slide is not of proper length and the tube is apparently mounted on an 1812 model carriage. About eight men of the gun crew are absent. It is unlikely that Mister Gill would have permitted that much absenteeism because each member of the eighteen-man crew was required to be competent to serve the piece in any one of four or five stations. The smoothbore tube could fire either solid shot weighing 170–180 pounds or shell averaging 136 pounds, fifteen pounds being the bursting charge. Although most fuses were accurate in time set for burning, they left a smoke trail that almost charted the flight of the projectile from gun to target. With no more than five degree elevation (some ship's ports restricted the elevation to this small amount), the Columbiad had a comparatively flat trajectory at a range of 1,700 yards, approximately one mile; and a time of flight of six seconds. The big gun's greatest weakness was its slow rate of fire. Even the best gun crews needed almost two minutes to get a round on the way. Within the restricted confines of the small turret of a monitor-type ironclad, one round in six or seven minutes was considered fast firing. Later, after being assigned to an ironclad, Stedman was to experience so much misery because of that gun and its younger brother, the 15-inch, that he can be excused for his antipathy toward it.

By contrast, the small Parrott rifled cannon pivoted on the forecastle could shoot in any direction except dead ahead through the jib-boom's standing rigging and sails. However, it could fire aft as much as the ship's hull and standing rigging would permit. This gave the Parrott an arc of fire of almost 140 degrees over either rail. Although its actual bore was 3.7 inches, it was commonly called a 4-inch rifle. The elongated cylindrical shell with a conical point weighed nineteen pounds with an added two pound bursting charge. Its range at five degrees of elevation and with a time of flight of six and a half seconds was 2,100 yards; 400 yards more than the range of the 11-inch Dahlgren Columbiad smoothbore.

Longer ranges could be obtained by increasing the elevation of the 11-inch Dahlgren or the Parrott rifle. However, accuracy decreased at longer ranges so much that targets requiring a time of flight of more than ten seconds were seldom fired upon. If either gun was fired from the still waters of a sound, harbor, or river, superb accuracy was possible up to ranges of nearly two miles. If the ship was rolling in an offshore swell or quartering across a choppy sea, hitting another ship at five hundred yards range required great skill—and a measure of good luck! Blockade runners knew the limitations of navy ordnance and generally ignored all long range shots regardless of the type of gun being used.

With a maximum broadside of only four guns plus the rifles of the small Marine detchment, *Huron* was indeed a lightly armed man-of-war. However, her guns added to those of her three sister ships and the broadsides of Commander Drayton's *Pawnee* gave the Confederates a real reason to worry. Roving guns are always bad guns, and all guns on ships are roving guns. Drayton's statement that he could provide protection all the way to Wappoo Creek was no idle promise. Even Beauregard in his postwar memoirs indicated that Hunter would have been more successful with his Stono expedition if he had followed Drayton's recommendation.

CONTRABANDS

In letters from the South Carolina coast, Stedman mentioned with increasing frequency "a contraband" or "the contrabands." This use of the word "contraband" was a new meaning for an old and honored term in international law and warfare. Early after the beginning of hostilities, belligerent powers normally publish lists of items that are not to be sold or given to the enemy. Many other items are added to these lists as a war progresses. These items are termed "contraband." During World War I, wheat bound for Germany became contraband because it gave aid and comfort to the enemy, and furthered Germany's potential for continued warfare. In France during World War II, any property or equipment belonging to the German Army was contraband and subject to confiscation by British and American forces. This included food which was usually given to the French authorities—but not the wine labelled for the Wehrmacht! When the allies moved into Germany, all firearms, binoculars, and cameras owned by private citizens were confiscated as contraband and destroyed immediately for the most part since such items were of value to snipers and underground resistence against the victorious allied forces. In the light of subsequent events, there is little wonder that contraband lists of both sides appeared and were expanded after the early recognition of the Confederacy as a "belligerent" by both France and England.

The concept that the contraband doctrine could be applied to human beings came from the fertile mind of Major General Benjamin F. Butler, a Massachusetts lawyer and citizen soldier. Although he has been much criticized by historians both North and South, the man was not always wrong. Early in the war, Butler was given command of the expanded garrison of Fortress Monroe which had not been surren-

The reprehensible want of vigilance in our Blockading Vessels. – See Daily Papers, 1862. 1863. 1864.

dered to Confederate forces. The day after his arrival at Fortress Monroe, Butler sent a Vermont regiment into and beyond the nearby village of Hampton to determine if there was any truth to the rumor that field fortifications were being built to contain any Federal advance from the small Fortress Monroe beachhead. The Vermonters drove the few armed Confederates from Hampton Village back into the field works which had been constructed largely by slave labor requisitioned from the local owners. Three of the slave laborers took advantage of the confusion to seek refuge within Butler's lines. Promptly, an agent of their owner, a Colonel Mallory, appeared before Butler and demanded that the privately owned property of a Virginia citizen be returned.

General Butler obviously needed a legal opinion. He handed one down to himself for his own guidance. He informed the agent that "according to the laws of Virginia, the slaves at issue were as much the property of Colonel Mallory as were his horses or his pistols, and as property seizable as they, as aids to warfare, and which might be used against the National Troops." Butler concluded with finality, *These men are contraband of war.* He put them to work beside his own soldiers building counter earthworks of his own; and then reported his decision and actions to Washington. The President sustained and published Butler's opinion and action.

The word "contraband" within Butler's expanded meaning at once captured the imagination of the press and the public throughout the North. Although But-

ler's concept was supplanted by the passage of the Confiscation Act of 6 August 1861, the word continued to fill the need for an appropriate term for all slaves who found refuge—and quite often employment at local and current wages—within the Federal military lines. The word and concept is still found today in literature concerning the Civil War as well as in the diaries, letters, and official records of the time.

As a field artist for *Harper's Weekly,* Winslow Homer saw far more of and became acquainted with more Contrabands than Stedman could ever have seen while on active duty. One of Homer's first exhibits after the War was his drawings of Blacks in the technical and accepted status of Contrabands. Stedman, by contrast, left only three drawings of Contrabands. In the absence of any comments in his letters, the drawings necessarily suggested their own stories.

In "Ethiopian Serenaders" on page 99, the location might be the unengaged, south bank of the Stono River where Stedman occasionally foraged for fresh vegetables. The captain's gig that put the party ashore cannot be too far away. The black children, then as now, had an unusual aptitude for making strangers feel at ease.

The locale for "Contrabands," the sketch on page 103, is clearly aboard *Huron.* Since the visitors have apparently come up the gangway, it can be assumed that the ship is at anchor. The small wave action suggests that *Huron* was in one of the many sounds back of long, offshore islands. Picking up an entire family, including the grandfather, was most unusual. That may be what prompted Stedman to draw this caricature. On one of the islands near Charleston, Rear Admiral DuPont established a small settlement to provide shelter for Contrabands until they could be placed in the custody of the Army headquarters on Hilton Head Island. This would be the ultimate destination of the group Stedman saw aboard *Huron*.

Stedman's third drawing on this theme, "The Diver and the Contrabands, Wassaw Sound, 1863" on page 107 depicts an event which occurred about a year after the Stono River operations. After a brief sojourn in Boston, Stedman was back in the same waters on a monitor-type ironclad, the historic "cheese box on a raft" class of warship. A section of the turret appears at the upper left. The overhead rigging is an awning. Because the iron hull attracted marine growth and quickly reduced the ironclad's already low speed, a diver was constantly down, scraping the hull from keel up whenever the vessel was in shallow water. The bumboat, laden with watermelon and fruit, has paused to make a sale. Attendants for the diver and his pump man could not resist hauling the diver up between the boat and the low freeboard of the ironclad. With one lead-cuffed glove on a watermelon and the other grasping the man's ankle, the diver is making the most of a hilarious apparitional situation. The officer with his hands on the safety line is Stedman; he would have regretted missing this incident. Winslow Homer might have been more sympathetic had he drawn the same scene, but he would have been equally amused.

Some Contrabands proved to be of great value. Enough competent sailors were found among them to man the small inland steamer *Darlington* which *Huron*'s green crew had almost fired upon near Fernandina before they learned she was approaching as a captured prize. Although the Department permitted DuPont to keep the vessel as an auxiliary, it neglected to provide the additional personnel needed to operate the steamer. DuPont provided two assistant engineers and three junior officers to serve as skipper and watch officers, but the remaining thirty-five crewmen were Blacks. One of the first Union Army Black infantry regiments was organized in January 1863 from Contrabands who had been assembled at Hilton Head and its vicinity.

One extremely valuable Contraband came out of Charleston. Robert Small had been a slave and pilot of a small harbor steamer, the *Planter*. While her skipper was absent, Small cast off her lines and steamed her down the harbor and into the hands of the blockaders. Small proved to be the best coastal pilot in those waters, and served as a pilot throughout the remainder of the war. During the Reconstruction period, he was elected to Congress for two or three terms.

BACK TO THE BLOCKADE

With General David Hunter's abortive land offensive against Charleston recoiling backward into a perimeter dominated by the Navy's guns, only a small holding force was required. In Virginia, McClellan, in trouble, was pulling out of the Peninsula Campaign; the capture of Richmond would have to be postponed. Over half of Hunter's regiments were rushed north to help defend Washington should the Southern armies of Lee and Jackson take the offensive.

The change in tactics in the Charleston campaign made it apparent that five ships in the Stono River no longer served any good purpose since one ship, with friendly troops aboard, could seal the river mouth. Four were therefore returned to blockade duty, a very timely move for the Northern press was yapping about the "lack of vigilance on the blockade." If this was not true, how could so many munition-laden ships get through? Successful blockade running had increased after the blockade cordons had been thinned to provide vessels to support Hunter's Stono offensive. Returning ships to blockade duty would again tighten the approaches to the city.

For home front information, Stedman drew "The Reprehensible Want of Vigilance on the Blockading Vessels" on page 111. This caricature indeed presents a reprehensible scene. This is *Huron*'s quarterdeck filled with officers, men, telescopes, and field glasses. Eyes are straining through rain and fog searching for a blockade runner that might or might not be there. The sketch well illustrates the Law of Diminishing Returns in terms of human effort as well as emphasizing the need for more ships to strengthen the thin blockading cordons.

But Stedman and his shipmates were not destined to roll in the offshore swells with few interruptions other than occasionally chasing prospective prizes. On 24 July, Commander Downes was ordered to join *Unadilla* in Ossabaw Sound where she was blockading the mouths of the Great and Little Ogeechee Rivers. Upon arrival, Downes found himself serving under Commander Charles Steedman, of *Paul Jones*. The three vessels, accompanied by an oversize armed tugboat, *Madgie,* were to "make a reconnaissance-in-force up the Great Ogeechee River" as far as the Atlantic & Gulf Railroad bridge, if practicable. The river and the adjacent railroad provided Savannah with a navigable side door that was almost as convenient for blockaders as the Stono approach was for Charleston.

Intelligence sources insisted that the fast, former commerce destroyer, CSS *Nashville,* had found refuge in the Ogeechee with a cargo of munitions from Nassau; and, now loaded with cotton, was waiting for a chance to dash to sea. These same sources indicated that the heavy guns of Confederate Fort McAllister covered the lower reach of a long and narrow oxbow bend, eight or nine steaming miles upriver. An obstructing row of piles was also said to stretch across the Great Ogeechee at that point. However, if *Nashville* could exit, perhaps Commander Steedman and his flotilla could also pass the fort.

To assume that anyone from Steedman on down was exuding enthusiasm for the effort to reach the bridge would be erroneous. *Paul Jones* was not another *Pawnee*. Fast and built for blockade duty, she

Reconnoisance of Fort McAllister, 29 July 1862.

"Paul Jones." "Huron." "Madgie."

was a double-ended sidewheeler of eight feet shallow draft. Although she had twice the tonnage of *Huron*, she carried only two 11-inch Dahlgren smoothbores, a 6.4-inch 100-pound rifle, and 24-pound howitzers. The paddle wheels made *Paul Jones* the most vulnerable target in the hastily improvised flotilla. Although the combined batteries of five 11-inch Dahlgrens, three Parrotts, and one heavy rifle plus the *Madgie's* two guns and the eight howitzers on the larger ships might give the seven gun fort a dusting off that its garrison would long remember, the ships would certainly draw all the fire the fort could muster. Knowing how much and how accurate that fire might be was important. The initial move of the flotilla would determine what the fort could do. The ships moved up river the morning of 29 July 1862.

By late evening, the flotilla was back in Ossabaw Sound and Commander Steedman was writing his report which would be left at Port Royal by *Huron* as she steamed back to her Charleston blockade station. Downes and Napoleon Collins, commanding *Unadilla*, must have been confident that the effort was going to be only a brief operation. Neither sent down their topmasts when they stripped their ships for action; this was usually done for action in narrow waters or when the ship was to move under steam alone. At 10:00, they drew fire from Fort McAllister which was situated on the high ground of the south bank of the river. Action fire ranged from a mile to two miles. The long tongue of narrow land which created the oxbow was barren except for low swamp growths;

thus three or four miles of river water beyond and upstream from the fort were visible to the ships. The *Nashville*, under her real name or any other, was not to be seen. Commander Steedman also reported that, when they came within range, "A spirited fire was kept up by both sides for an hour and a half . . . many of their shots falling near and some passing over. . . ." After an hour and a half of mutual target practice, during which it was seen that the piles did indeed stretch across the river, Steedman signalled retirement.

Huron must have had her share of water-splashing near misses, with quite a few passing overhead. Surgeon Stedman honored the episode with the sketch on page 115: "Reconnaisance of Fort McAllister, 29 July 1862, 'Paul Jones,' 'Huron,' 'Madgie.' " Most of the titles accompanying Stedman's drawings were not in his handwriting; this does explain some of the incongruities which occasionally appear, especially errors in identifying ships. *Huron* is indeed the middle ship in the sketch, and her sister ship *Unadilla* is at the left. The broad-beamed sidewheeler at the right, however, is *Paul Jones*. The small *Madgie* is not shown despite her name being included in the caption. Fort McAllister appears dimly in the distance.

In spite of Captain Downes' overemphasis on vigilance in all weather, foul or fair, the only prize money coming to *Huron's* officers and men resulted from captures made by her consorts. *Huron* had enjoyed no fun since the *Cambria* chase. Perhaps the Ogeechee expedition had changed their luck for, at 2:00 AM, 4

August, the dark shadow of an outbound schooner under full sail swept past. *Huron* immediately slipped her cable and gave hot pursuit for a capture in darkness would be another solo prize. The chase lasted an hour. By that time, the first gray light of dawn was on the eastern horizon and favoring *Huron*'s success. Her boarding party, however, had not had sufficient time to return from the prize before *Augusta,* with running lights burning, established her presence within signal range. This meant that the schooner *Aquilla,* with "no papers, logbook, nor colors," would be a joint prize of *Huron* and *Augusta. Aquilla*'s skipper said that his cargo consisted of "about 300 barrels of turpentine"—these would bring a handsome bid in New York. She was sent north with a small prize crew of older seamen whose enlistments had expired or would within a short time. Only the prize master, a junior officer, came from *Huron. Aquilla*'s skipper and crew of four men and "four contrabands" were put aboard *Sebago* which was departing for Port Royal. When they arrived, the Admiral would handle them as he saw fit. *Aquilla* was to be the last prize taken by *Huron* under Captain Downes' command.

To some of the old seadogs aboard, even worse than sharing prize money was another "last event" that was to be observed aboard *Huron* within a matter of days. On 14 July 1862, Congress enacted a law which prescribed that "the spirit ration (better known as grog) in the Navy of the United States shall forever cease, and . . . there shall be allowed and paid to each person in the Navy now entitled to the ration, five cents per day in commutation and in lieu thereof. . . ." To commemorate the last official issue of free liquor on one ship of the squadron, Surgeon Stedman drew "Splicing the Main Brace for the last time in the U.S. Navy, 3d September 1862," shown on page 119. This does not argue that no "main braces" were spliced thereafter with liquor instead of a marlin spike, but the quaint naval custom of checking a man's name from a list before he received a carefully measured drink of diluted rum, gin, or whiskey certainly perished in the ink of that statute. An unknown number of those afloat quietly welcomed the law as the abatement of a nuisance. Many of its "victims," however, undoubtedly attributed the epidemic of typhoid and malaria fevers which followed to the wanton and ill-advised legislation that had been inspired by Rear Admiral A. H. Foote, Chief of Bureau for Equipment and Recruiting in the Navy Department.

AN EPIDEMIC AFLOAT

As the long, hot summer wore on, Stedman's letters reflected a growing apprehension about his family's health. He was especially concerned about his small son, Ellery. At least one of his letters asking for information on the family was addressed to his father. Unfortunately, none of the replies to Stedman have survived; and the answers to his many questions are unknown. From his own, one-sided correspondence, it can be assumed today that Doctor Stedman, aboard *Huron*, was seeing and hearing more about typhoid fever than he had previously encountered in all of his ten years of medical education and practice.

The Crimean War, in the coastal regions of the Black Sea, had recently reminded and alerted the medical services of the Federal Army and Navy to the fact that wars breed epidemics. The Civil War had erupted so suddenly and without any prior expectations that few, if any, doctors in either service thought that the epidemic warnings inherent in the Crimean experience had any practical applications to their own duties. Indeed, with crisis facing them, neither of the two combatant governments made any serious effort to study or alleviate the potential problem. There were no massive health appropriations from the Congresses of either the Union or the Confederacy. Instead the entire problem was thrown into the lap of the medical profession: civilian and military, afloat and ashore. The only monetary aid they received came from private donations and from contributed help of organized groups such as the justly famous Sanitary Commission. Coping with epidemics, however, continued to be a problem for the medical profession.

Army doctors were soon confronted by various persistent fevers diagnosed as "camp fever," "tent fever," and "barracks or fort fever." It was no more than logical that ships at sea eventually encountered "ship fever." Naval medical history of the Civil War is not as comprehensive and all-inclusive as that of the Army, thanks to its Surgeon General Joseph K. Barnes. The ponderous, six-volume *Medical and Surgical History of the War of the Rebellion*, published by the Government Printing Office from 1870 to 1888, is the result of his inspiration and driving persistence. It is a plethora of diagnostic difficulties, quaint cures, primitive plastic surgery, and appalling statistics. Among other details is an analysis of the seasonal variations for every disease, carefully charted for each year of the war. In 1862, typhoid and malaria peaked in late September; that was the exact time that "ship fever" all but incapacitated the South Atlantic Squadron.

During the Stono River operation, sending ten or twelve thousand men and a thousand or more horses ashore and into the swamp lands and muddy creeks of James Island and other nearby islands was enough to contaminate conventional sources of drinking water. A plantation well which had been a primary source for *Huron's* fresh water was completely unuseable after a succession of regiments bivouacked in the area. It can be safely assumed that both typhoid and malaria were aboard *Huron* for both were prevalent in the Army at that time. Typhus fever, the scourge of the Crimean War, seldom appeared, if at all. The research teams Surgeon General Barnes assigned to examine thousands of disease case histories doubted if even the few reported cases of typhus were accurately diagnosed. In a report to the Navy Department later in the year, Downes diagnosed his own problem as the "North Edisto River fever." When Stedman himself was stricken, the fever ranged uncontrolled aboard *Huron*.

Splicing the main-brace for the last time in
the U.S. Navy, 30 September 1862.

HURON RETURNS HOME

Not only was *Huron* plagued with sickness, the ship herself was ailing. Bumping across the low tide shallows and constantly firing from the Stono had been costly to Commander Drayton's small flotilla. *Pawnee* was sent to her home port for a complete overhaul. *Ottawa* and *Pembina* were hardly fit for open-sea duty; *Unadilla* was but little better. A day or two prior to the capture of *Aquilla,* Downes, of necessity, had asked the Senior Officer Present for permission to kill his boiler room fires in order to work on some blown tubes. Finally, in a brief dispatch dated 7 October 1862, Captain S. W. Godon, in temporary command of the South Atlantic Squadron, reported to the Navy Department that "I have directed the *Huron* to proceed to Boston." In his opinion, the ship was useless in her condition; he also felt that the ship should be decontaminated. Commander Downes confirmed this opinion in his report to the Navy Department from Boston on 12 October: "The vessel requires a thorough breaking out, cleansing, painting, and frosting, and I would respectfully suggest that something be done to improve the ventilation below, as to the want of it I am inclined to attribute the general unsanitary condition aboard." While *Huron*'s crew was being treated by the Navy Yard's medical division, Assistant Surgeon Charles E. Stedman was regaining his health at home with Edith and little Ellery. Although he was seeing his six-months old son for the first time, Stedman left no picture of the boy at this age.

June 8. '62   Stono.

CHAPTER EIGHT The Ironclad Flotilla

THE IMMEDIATE FUTURE of *Huron* and her crew became the responsibility of the Navy Yard commander the moment that Commander Downes reported his arrival at Boston. Because of the contagious and persistent fevers aboard, the Yard Surgeon became the dominant personality in the lives of *Huron's* officers and men. He was assisted by five additional naval surgeons and a number of enlisted hospital corpsmen. The Naval Hospital was only a few miles distant at the village of Chelsea. Its professional staff was augmented by some civilian doctors and employees. The senior Doctor Stedman had been its distinguished superintendent for years; the son had been born there. Thus the fever-ridden Charles E. Stedman was right back where he had started life's journey.

In a hospital of the armed services, all men are said to be equal; but, as the old saying goes, "Some are more equal than others." Had he been ill, some such status would have been accorded Commander Downes, but his policy of always living and eating alone in his quarters had paid off for he had escaped the dreaded contagious fevers. It was he who wrote the final report concerning the contagious afflictions of *Huron*; not one word appears over the signature of the Ship's Surgeon, Charles Ellery Stedman.

How could that be? There is a professional axiom that any doctor of medicine who diagnoses his own case and publishes his prescriptions for self-cure has at least one patient who is a fool. Doctor Stedman was not in that category. Nothing appears over either his official or unofficial signature in the sources available to admit that *Huron's* Surgeon was sick at the end of that cruise or that there was an epidemic aboard at any time. These facts were reported by line officers who certainly knew when a ship was functional and when she was not. The responsibilities of these line officers superseded—and properly so—the fever-ridden thoughts of the only medical officer aboard.

Stedman, however, does provide one drawing of himself not in the best of health during his naval service. The caricature on page 123, "Sent North by medical survey 'for change of climate and medical treatment'," does not show him ill with fever but, rather, exhausted at the end of an even more arduous cruise. This is evidenced by the medicines on the sick table since these bottles suggest rest and relaxation from combat fatigue rather than treatment of persistent fevers. Further comment on this later illness will be postponed for the time being. Stedman wisely chose to offer no professional opinion or other comment as long as he was just another patient.

The wartime naval expansion had greatly increased surgical staff duties and case loads. Although additional slots for Navy Yard and hospital surgeons had been authorized, the fleets still had higher priorities. Furthermore, most surgeons wanted to be where the action was and shore-side billets were often empty and begging. Perhaps this young doctor, a local physician and near "Son of the Service," having already seen eight months of duty afloat, might be willing to accept a naval hospital billet for a while. In other words, the Navy Yard surgeons had a vested interest in getting Stedman into a convalescent status at home, cured of the fever, and ticketed for immediate duty.

RECUPERATION

Convalescing at home, Stedman quickly sensed that the Navy Yard Chief Surgeon would welcome him as a permanent member of his division as soon as he was well enough for duty. In the meantime, he was catching up on all that had happened in the city, the state, and the national news, that had not filtered down to *Huron* on her South Atlantic stations. Very few of his former classmates at Harvard College or the Medical School came to call on him. Most of them, except for "Holy Horatio" Alger, the novelist, were scattered along the far-flung Army fronts from Chesapeake Bay to the Territory of New Mexico.

Most of the war news was bad. Stedman knew nothing of what had happened while he was in feverish deliriums until he read about it at home in accumulated newspapers or in *Leslie's* and *Harper's* weeklies, and illustrated news magazines. Current news was worse than bad. Throughout the previous August, the navy's ships and the army's transports had been transferring McClellan's defeated troops northward from Harrison's Landing, down the James River from Richmond, to the defenses of Washington. Stedman may have had a feverish memory of the news of the Second Battle of Bull Run where Confederate forces under General Robert E. Lee had shattered Pope's concentration of the troops of McDowell, Fremont, and Banks. The road to Washington was again open except for the Potomac River line and the city's local, encompassing fortifications. Lee, unprepared for a siege operation, had invaded Maryland by way of Harper's Ferry to threaten Washington from the northwest. The bloody battle at Antietam had saved Washington, but McClellan's bungling regroupment and tardy battlefield tactics had permitted the Confederacy's most powerful field force to escape across the Potomac. General Ambrose E. Burnside, the victor, with naval support, at Roanoke Island, was expected to do better. But Burnside led the Army to another disastrous defeat at Fredericksburg, Virginia, on 13 December.

When Stedman first became ill, Grant's Army in the West was on the defensive south of Memphis. Two bloody battles at Iuka and Corinth, Mississippi, had given him a better grasp on his gains; but he was still on the defensive. Confederate General Braxton Bragg, with a surprisingly large force of 50,000 men,

Sent North by Medical Survey. "For change of climate and medical treatment."

had invaded Kentucky and was approaching Louisville on the Ohio River. General Don Carlos Buell had "recoiled" in front of Bragg—all the way back to the Ohio. Although it was Bragg who retreated from the Battle of Perryville on 8 October 1862, Buell failed to follow up with even a cautious pursuit. Two weeks later, President Lincoln relieved Buell; but the stalemate in the West continued throughout November and December. Along the Mississippi River, an amphibious force of ironclad river boats under Commodore David D. Porter and army troops commanded by General William T. Sherman moved southward. Sherman was roundly trounced at Chickasaw Bluffs during Christmas week by Pemberton's Vicksburg defensive force. Thus, on all fronts, the Union armies were licking their wounds as the New Year was ushered in. However, Stedman had made up his mind where and when he could best serve his country and still continue to be at peace with himself long before 1863 hove into sight.

The curative powers of home care, good food, long sleeps, rest, and no duties usually make for a brief convalescence. Stedman was no exception and was soon "In charge of the U.S. Naval Hospital at Tiadity," as shown in his sketch on page 127. Notwithstanding his usual fictitious and frivolous names for places and ships, "Tiadity" can hardly be any place other than the Chelsea Naval Hospital. The Navy Yard Chief Surgeon was obviously offering the flattering lure of being in charge of the hospital where his father had served and where he had been born. This could make a tour of shore duty even more attractive.

Stedman's caricature tells its own story about the boredom of the job. In the neat and orderly sick bay, there are only three patients with three hospital corpsmen to care for them. Surgeon Stedman has so little to do elsewhere that he has ranked the only busy corpsman out of the simple task of checking the patient's pulse. Two idle corpsmen accentuate the boredom of the scene by standing at ease near the medical chest. With all that was happening on ships and along the embattled army fronts, there is little wonder that Chelsea Naval Hospital quickly lost any initial lure it might have held for Stedman.

Moreover, Boston was not the same happy place it had been during the winter before the firing on Fort Sumter started the war. Nearly all of his friends and classmates were absent. Too many families were mourning the loss of men killed or missing in action. One or two old friends were home, but on crutches. When Stedman and Edith went out socially, he of course wore his uniform complete with gold-fringed epaulettes. But social functions were less than a pleasure. All of the other men present were much older, usually gray-headed or bald. Few, other than himself, were in uniform. A bevy of young, unattended wives always closed in on him to tell him where their men were and to ask all sorts of questions about when, where, and why. In such circumstances, Stedman felt "Blockaded" as he shows in the sketch on page 131.

There was but one avenue of escape back to what Herodotus appropriately called "the wet paths of the sea."

Stedman quickly confronted the home front with orders to sea. The sketch on page 135 shows him expressing artificial concern, exclaiming, "Matter? Matter enough! Orders to the 'Semantocook,' and she's a Monitor!" Edith and her mother probably knew as much as Stedman about the so-called *"Semantocook."* Her real name was *Nahant*; she had been launched from the South Boston shipyard of Harrison Loring on 7 October 1862, a few days before *Huron's* arrival home. It was common knowledge that Commander Downes would take her on her maiden voyage and into battle. Downes undoubtedly asked for Stedman and with Stedman's consent.

Because of the fame the first *Monitor* had brought her type, the commissioning of *Nahant* was a much more formal affair than had been *Huron's* a short year earlier. On 29 December, Captain Alfred Taylor, representing Admiral Silas H. Stringham, Commandant of the Boston Navy Yard, commissioned *Nahant* with proper ceremonies, broke out the commission pennant on the thin signal mast on the pilot house, and presented the vessel to Commander Downes and his seventy-five officers and men standing by in a rigid formation. Stedman's brief sojourn at home was almost at an end. Although water and coal were already aboard when *Nahant* was commissioned, she lingered in Boston until 3 January 1863.

NAHANT PUTS TO SEA

On that day, the watch officer, William W. Carter, certified that *Nahant* drew eleven feet, two inches forward, and eleven feet, eight inches aft. Because her low freeboard and relatively weak engines made sailing in open seas both uncomfortable and dangerous (this was true of all monitors) *Nahant* was towed south to Port Royal, not by the USS *"Opecancanaugh,"* as Stedman indicated in using another of his fictitious names in captioning the sketch on page 139, but by the chartered heavy steamer *Annie J. Lyman.* Fog and heavy weather forced them to stop at Newport, Rhode Island, until 8 January. While there, they first heard of the foundering of the original *Monitor* in heavy seas off Cape Hatteras shortly after midnight on 31 December while being towed by *Rhode Island,* an armed, large, sidewheel blockader. The foundering *Monitor,* taking tons of water through her ill-fitted hatches and under her turret, sank like a lobster pot carrying four officers and twelve men with her. Thirty-five of her crew were picked up by *Rhode Island.* Stedman's sketch clearly illustrates the problems encountered by a monitor on the open seas.

From Newport, *Annie J. Lyman* and her tow proceeded to the Brooklyn Navy Yard. *Nahant* was proving to be practically helpless at sea. Enroute to Newport, she raised no more than twenty-five pounds of steam for thirty-two revolutions of the propeller per minute. On the way to Brooklyn, there was some improvement: thirty-five revolutions per minute on twenty-five pounds of steam were required to rotate the turret to aim her guns. *Nahant*'s situation was almost as bad as that of the locomotive which brought the complaint from President Lincoln that, every time the engineer blew the whistle, the train stopped!

By the end of January, *Nahant* was at Newport News, Virginia. Here another warship bound for Port Royal took her in tow for the last leg of her coastal pilgrimage. Commander Downes reported his ship to Admiral DuPont at Port Royal on 20 February 1863 as "in good condition" after "three days, fifteen and two-thirds hours from Cape Henry," Virginia. From there to Cape Fear, there had been "rough and boisterous weather." The "forward overhang had thumped heavily on the head seas . . . shaking the vessel very much. The decks leaked badly, and considerable water forced its way under the turret, wetting the belts and blowers, causing the belts to stretch and break or tear out their lacings, putting everybody to serious inconvenience for want of air below, besides causing constant instant depression of steam by stopping draft of the furnaces by constantly necessitating the stoppage of the blowers to repair damages to the belting." In other words, with the exception of being leaky and incapable of mobility at sea on her own power, *Nahant* was "in good condition." However, if *Nahant* was compared to her sister ironclads being assembled at Port Royal, Downes was correct about his ship for all were in essentially the same condition.

At the same time, all was hurry and scurry among the ships at the Port Royal base. *Nahant*'s surgeon sensed the situation in the drawing on page 143. The large, 40-gun steam frigate at center is DuPont's flagship, *Wabash*. The strings of objects above the smoke stack are not flags; they are hand washed hammocks, blankets, and clothing hoisted high to dry. Should a thoughtless fireman stoke the sleeping and banked fires, there could be hell to pay! The much larger sail ship at right is the obsolete, 86-gun, ship-of-the-line, *Vermont*. Her protruding guns are as obsolete as the ship. DuPont used her as a store ship. She is so high in the water that Stedman's drawing sustains DuPont's complaint to Secretary Welles that he was so short of supplies that his men were required "to live off the Army." But winds of change were blowing from across the far-off Potomac River.

NEW SHIPS, NEW PLANS

Rear Admiral DuPont, at heart a high seas sailor, was justifiably suspicious of ships that were underpowered even for inland waters. The Admiral knew, however, that Secretary Gideon Welles was in technical matters completely under the influence of Assistant Secretary Gustavus Vasa Fox and the Swedish naval inventor and designer, John Ericsson. The strategic victory won by Ericsson's hastily-built *Monitor* was complete proof to the Navy Department of that type's capability to win any sort of naval battle with ships of the Confederacy. Since most of such operations would be on inland waters, nothing more

In charge of the U. S. Naval Hospital at Tiadity.

was needed than an unsinkable platform for two of the heaviest pieces of naval ordnance in existence at the time.

The South was known to be building several *Virginia*-type ironclads: *Tennessee* at Mobile, Alabama; *Atlanta* near Savannah, Georgia; and *Albemarle* at Elizabeth City, North Carolina. Two other ironclads, *Palmetto State* and *Chicora,* were nearing completion at Charleston, South Carolina. The initial thought in the North was to build enough monitor-type ironclads to checkmate each of these Southern vessels with at least one monitor such as *Nahant,* which had some improvements made based upon the experience of the original *Monitor.* Because her two 11-inch guns had proven inadequate for cracking *Virginia*'s armor at gun-muzzle range, *Nahant* and her sister ships would be armed with one 11-inch and one 15-inch Dahlgren smoothbore, both in the same turret. The latter's 420-pound, solid shot or 385-pound shell, including its bursting charge, should be able to do the job of cracking Confederate ironclad armor. The only other difference from *Monitor* was in length, width, and tonnage: *Monitor* weighed 987 tons and was 172 feet long, 42½ feet wide; *Nahant,* 1,875 tons with a length of 200 feet and width of 46 feet. In executing this plan for posting these inadequately powered steam vessels as checkmates all the way from Roanoke Island, North Carolina, to Mobile, Alabama, Admiral DuPont would have been satisfied to have had only three: two for the Charleston ironclads and one for Wassaw Sound's *Atlanta.* Since some of

the Confederate ironclad threats to wooden blockade ships were far from complete, dispersal of an entire flotilla of powerful monitors was hardly justifiable to someone in the Navy Department, possibly "Mister" Fox, as the Assistant Secretary was referred to by career officers because of his service from 1838 to 1856 as a midshipman and passed midshipman.

Since DuPont was reluctant to sail his wooden ships past Forts Sumter and Moultrie and up to Charleston City in the same manner that Farragut had sailed his ships up to New Orleans, why not give this flotilla of invulnerable ironclads to DuPont? He could sail them up to the Charleston waterfront and duplicate Farragut's feat at New Orleans by receiving the surrender of the city. This was plausible in Washington but appeared somewhat asinine to many officers on the scene of action who had been with Farragut and were now with DuPont.

Below New Orleans, it had been utterly impossible to block the deep, wide, and mighty Mississippi with beached obstructions and piles. Gigantic chains, held at water level by anchored barges and hulks, were the best obstruction the Confederates could devise. Under the cover of darkness and just prior to the advance of Farragut's squadron, two *Huron*-class vessels created a gap in the barrier and Farragut sailed past Forts Jackson and St. Philip to force the surrender of New Orleans.

By contrast, the natural and well-defined channels in all of the coastal rivers, estuaries, sounds, bays, and harbors south of Cape Henry could be blocked by driving piles into their shallow bottoms. That is what the defenders of Richmond did to block the James River channel just below Drewry's Bluff, within sound of Richmond's church bells. It was not the Confederate guns on Drewry's Bluff that turned back Commander Rodgers' James River Squadron led by *Monitor* and the armored *Galena*; it was the driven piles and sunken barges blocking the channel. But for these, Rodgers would have had Richmond under his guns in the Farragut style. Indeed, had Flag Officer Goldsborough, in command at Hampton Roads, been more imaginative and aggressive and less dependent upon the Navy Department completing the building of *Monitor* before *Virginia* could sally forth from Norfolk, he would have similarly blocked the Elizabeth River channel out of Norfolk and into Hampton Roads. This action would have left the heavily armored and deep draft *Virginia* completely impotent, and the first battle between ironclad ships of war would have taken place later and elsewhere. But good sailors are as reluctant to block a channel they hope to use, as good soldiers are to blow a bridge that may provide a crossing in future planned advances.

In reality, for Secretary Welles to listen to adverse comparisons of DuPont to Farragut from his "technicians," Ericsson and Fox, was no less than folly. Welles should have told them to quit trying to compare incomparables and to concentrate instead on logistical support of the squadrons. Instead, he instructed them to give DuPont a flotilla of these new, indestructible, floating engines of destruction to see what he could do with them.

TEST FIRING

Now that DuPont was getting more monitors than he had any reason to expect, it was up to him to use them to the limit of both their numbers and their individual capabilities. First to arrive was *Montauk,* an identical ship to *Nahant* although built in a different yard. *Montauk* was commanded by Commander John L. Worden who had fought *Monitor* against *Virginia.* Although he had begun that fight, his Executive Officer finished the engagement after Worden was temporarily blinded by face wounds. Worden wanted an opportunity to command in an engagement which he could finish; DuPont was happy to oblige him.

The former commerce raider, CSS *Nashville,* was still in the Ogeechee River, upsteam in the oxbow bend above Fort McAllister, clearly visible across the point of low land which created the bend. *Montuak* was teamed with two *Huron*-class ships and an armed, light-draft tug; they could help *Montauk* if she got into trouble. *Montauk* would accept all the fire the fort could offer by moving up close to the pile obstructions near the fort, within 1,200 yards range of *Nashville*, across the point.

All worked as planned. At dawn on 28 February, the attackers advanced to their predesignated position. Staff officers stood with watches ready to clock the rate of fire from each gun on each ship, especially *Montauk*'s two-gun battery. Other officers were to do the same for the seven guns in the fort. Intelligence sources had already revealed their calibers and other characteristics. While the wooden ships stood back to engage the fort, *Montauk* moved to her position, anchored, and at 7:07 AM fired her first 15-inch round at *Nashville*, grounded in low water 1,400 yards away. She had no choice other than to absorb the punishment coming from *Montauk*'s guns. By 7:57 AM, *Nashville* was on fire and her crew was abandoning ship. Ground fog ended target practice for both sides from 8:13 to 8:40. When the fog lifted, it could be seen that *Nashville* was wrapped in flames from stem to stern. *Montauk* had not fired a single round at the fort. Both her pilot house and turret had been hit but without serious damage. The Confederate commander reported almost as little damage to his defenses: the barracks of the attached rifle company had been hit and the grass on the parade ground had been messed up. He was certain that his rifled gun had hit one or more of the wooden ships before they withdrew, as well as causing possible damage to the ironclad. With regret, he reported that the retiring monitor had plowed right through his mine field but nothing had happened. Mission accomplished by both sides.

Montauk's rate of fire, however, had not been impressive. During the engagement, her 11-inch gun had fired only seven rounds at the best target any gunner could ever hope to see. The 15-inch gun had expended only eight rounds. The shot-fall patterns were tight; but, had *Nashville* not been grounded, she would have disappeared upstream and around the next bend. Within the same two hours and five minutes, the fort had fired about fifty rounds at *Montauk* alone. Her low silhouette made her a difficult target and there were no hits on the low 11-inch freeboard. There were deck hits, but these glanced off harmlessly. More serious, however, was damage incurred when the *Montauk* struck and detonated a torpedo, or mine, as she retired down river. The detonation sounded like a double explosion and fractured the hull under the port boiler. *Montauk* took water rapidly, but the ship's pumps soon brought the inflow under control. A rib section had been pushed upward and a hull seam opened. *Montauk* spent ten days undergoing repairs after her return to Port Royal. The incident was truly bad news for previous reports of underwater explosives had not proven true. Now, however, torpedoes, or mines, were actually known to exist; future reports had to be taken seriously.

Because *Montauk* had ignored the fort while sinking *Nashville*, which DuPont had been blockading for eight months, the Admiral still had no idea of the impact of the heavier guns of the new monitors on hostile land batteries and forts. He only knew that *Montauk*'s guns had been dreadfully slow on the trigger. Perhaps a flotilla working as a team would do better. DuPont decided to send the next three newly arriving monitors up the same river with the sole objective of firing at Fort McAllister. Three mortar schooners, two *Huron*-class ships, and a heavy tug would stand by downstream. With no restraint on its firing elevation, each mortar (there was only one mor-

Blockaded.

tar on each anchored schooner) could lob a 200-pound shell almost three miles from an angle of forty-five degrees. The average rate of fire for a mortar was one round every ten minutes. Thus it could be expected that one timed shell could burst over the enemy's parapeted guns every three and a half minutes. Of course, a good mortar commander would never signal a schedule, but this was the firing capability for the three schooners.

The monitor flotilla consisted of *Passaic*, Captain Percival Drayton commanded her as well as the entire operation; *Patapsco,* Commander Daniel Ammen; and *Nahant.* The three were identical ships though built at different yards. There was one slight difference: because no 11-inch Dahlgren smoothbore was available for *Patapsco,* an 8-inch, 150-pounder rifle had been substituted. This can be compared to putting a three year old gelding thoroughbred in the same stable with a Clydesdale draft horse. To add to the problem, neither gun worked well in battle.

Under cover of darkness, Captain Drayton sent small boats to sweep the channel for mines. At dawn on 3 March, he led his ironclads to within a thousand yards of the fort, somewhat closer than Worden had taken *Montauk* to engage *Nashville. Nahant,* at the end of the column, was almost in the same position which *Montauk* had occupied. Stedman most likely stayed with the Captain in the pilot house on top of the turret until the guns began to roar. He would then go to his sick bay and stand by for casualties. That had been Stedman's practice in other operations. It is possible that the habit started at McAllister. To both Downes and Stedman, the current operation must have seemed like a repetition of the same song and dance encountered by *Huron* with Commander Steedman's flotilla of *Paul Jones, Unadilla,* and *Madgie.*

The monitor operation, however, turned out to be a longer show. There would be hours of hammer-and-tongs artillery exchange with the fort. The anchored ships were as stationary as the fort. There would be no time out for the noon meal. Although the Confederate gunners practically ignored *Nahant* and gave *Patapsco* only a courtesy hit which may have been intended for *Passaic,* they hit *Passaic* with every one of their eight weapons, including a recently acquired 10-inch mortar concealed in a nearby wooded area. One of the mortar shells ". . . fell on the deck over the bread room which undoubtedly would have gone through had it not struck a beam." As it was, it opened "quite a hole." Had the shell been "loaded with powder instead of sand . . . it might have set the vessel on fire." This was Drayton's analysis. *Passaic* was hit at least thirty-four times; nine hits on the narrow side armor, thirteen on the deck, five on the turret, one on the roof of the turret, one through the smoke stack, two on the outrigger and boat spar.

At no time during the six hour engagement were the guns or the fort appreciably silenced nor was their fire diminished although one enemy gun may have been put out of action. The range of the schooner mortars often had been unnecessarily short. The almost flat trajectory of the monitors' guns caused little or no damage to the defensive earthworks. The rate of fire of the turret guns was not as fast as *Montauk*'s had been. She, however, had been in action for only an hour; Drayton's flotilla engaged for six hours and stood at battle stations all day. All three monitors incurred damaged gun mounts and recoil slides, particularly to their 15-inch guns. *Nahant* fired thirty-two 15-inch shells and thirty-nine 11-inch. *Patapsco* got only fourteen rounds out of her 15-inch gun, but fired forty-six from the Parrott rifle. *Passaic* did not report her ammunition expenditure. All three ships had at least one gun out of action during part of the engagement.

Although the expedition had not succeeded in neutralizing Fort McAllister, it had learned a valuable lesson. Every officer and most of the men in the ironclad flotilla realized that the design of their ships limited their ability to attack land targets located on bluffs or other high elevations. They knew that they had good ships for fighting other ironclads if the opponents stayed in smooth, inland waters and could not steam at more than six knots. The monitor turrets, although providing good protection for the gun crews, were too small for fast and accurate service and firing of the two large guns. The great size and added equipment for the new and untested 15-inch gun was the last touch toward crowded inefficiency. The same housing which provided protection for the crews also destroyed the versatility that the guns might have had for targets requiring anything other than low, almost flat trajectory rounds. Firing their guns at such low elevations also deprived them of the longer ranges which could be obtained at higher elevations.

Captain Drayton, in his report to Admiral DuPont, regretted frankly that his flotilla had failed in its mission. The failure was against a fort which had only seven guns, four of them mere 32-pounders, and one mortar. Notwithstanding this sagging confidence in the ability of their ships to end the war or even to capture Charleston as Farragut had captured New Orleans, the fact that *Passaic* had taken such a pounding without a single casualty was somewhat comforting. Hearts could be light and gay as a result. But the day would come when Stedman would be echoing complaints that there seemed to be an Ericsson lobby in Washington that was more interested in selling Ericsson ships than in providing the squadrons with their actual needs.

LULL BEFORE THE STORM

Other than Downes and Stedman, none of the officers aboard *Nahant* had served aboard *Huron* on her last cruise. If there were any shipmates among the crew, Stedman did not mention them in his letters to Edith. Because of his high seniority on the old promotion list, Downes had become a commander. Through lack of seniority on that same old list, George E. Belknap, now aboard *New Ironsides*, had been promoted to lieutenant commander. *Nahant*'s Executive Officer was Lieutenant Commander David B. Harmony, a classmate of Belknap's at the Naval

Academy. Stedman quickly transferred the warmth and affection he had felt for Belknap to the pleasant and affable Harmony. In time, Stedman would decide that Harmony was an even better buffer between the taciturn and driving Downes and his junior officers and men than Belknap had been on *Huron*. Harmony was more than just a buffer; he was a seasoned, combat veteran. When the war began, he was a lieutenant and watch officer aboard *Iroquois,* a handsome, heavy, wooden sloop-of-war. As a part of Farragut's West Gulf Squadron, *Iroquois* had taken her share of the maulings administered to Farragut's Squadron both in passing Forts Jackson and St. Philip and in fighting the improvised Confederate fleet between the chain barrier and New Orleans. She had run the batteries at Port Hudson; had helped in the capture of Grand Gulf, and had been exchanging shots with the bluff batteries at Vicksburg when the Confederate ironclad *Arkansas* successfully shot her way through both the Union ironclad riverboat squadron and the wooden, saltwater ships. Harmony brought a wealth of recent combat experience to *Nahant*.

During March, additional warships arrived at Port Royal. There was much visiting among ships as old friendships were renewed. Living an ironbound life below the waterline of an artificially ventilated vessel in a season and in latitudes where outer temperatures could fluctuate between forty and eighty degrees gave Stedman more sick bay traffic than usual. He resented the Navy's paperwork more than any other task required. All hands agreed that the monitors were nothing more or less than fighting machines; as habitations for hard working men, they were fit for neither man nor beast.

There were always minor tragedies caused by the cramped living quarters. Stedman permitted the storage of a ". . . dozen bottles of cooking wine in my lower drawer which was empty save for a pair of pumps and some wrapping paper." When the wardroom steward needed some wine, he found that the drawer was stuck and had to haul the bottles out through the drawer above. ". . . he then discovered that the corks had come out of nearly all the bottles & their contents had expended themselves in my shoes principally. You can fancy how absurd the bottles looked just half full, & what a peculiar smell the operation imparted to my pumps."

In the same long letter dated 30 March, Stedman noted the sudden increase of soldiers on the beachhead General Hunter had preserved when he backed away from a showdown battle for James Island and the capture of Fort Johnson. Sam Green, from Harvard College days and now assigned to the 24th Massachusetts Infantry Regiment, came aboard for a visit. His impedimentia had not arrived and he had ". . . spent night before last under the shelter of a barrel which he knocked to pieces, & having made a fire, tried to make himself comfortable . . . the only time he had been warm for 48 hours was when he went aboard a schooner to see a sick man and warmed himself at the stove for two hours."

Supply schooners for both the warships and the

"Matter? Matter enough! Orders to the 'Semantocook,' and she's a Monitor!"

regiments were more and more in evidence. Supplies and ammunition were being stockpiled but not necessarily being put ashore. At least fifteen schooners with special markings carried ammunition intended exclusively for the ironclads which had been augmented by the arrival of *Galena*. Although a well-armored conventional ship, she was not tough enough to accept the plunging fire she had received from fortifications on Drewry's Bluff on the James River near Richmond. In this engagement, *Galena* had suffered twenty-five casualties, twelve of whom died. Her Commander, John Rodgers, opted for command of a monitor.

In contrast to the cramped quarters aboard the monitors, the reverse was true of *New Ironsides* for she was the largest and most advanced ironclad of her time. Stedman visited her often to see Belknap. To Stedman she was a dirty ship; but in his thinking, all iron ships were dirty. In addition to the initial monitor flotilla at Port Royal, there were other monitor arrivals already present or expected shortly. These included *Weehawken*, Captain John Rodgers; *Catskill*, Commander George W. Rodgers; *Nantucket*, Commander Donald McN. Fairfax; and *Keokuk*, Commander Alexander C. Rhind. *Keokuk* was an experimental vessel. Her low, armored whaleback deck made her look like a monitor. She had two turrets, one armed with an 11-inch Dahlgren. Installation of the other turret was incomplete. She had a speed of nine knots, a shallow draft, and handled handsomely both at sea and in inland waters. High hopes were

held for her. Stedman, like all other monitor men, was greatly intrigued by *Keokuk*. He sketched a tiny silhouette of her in one of his letters to Edith.

Stedman also described more of his visits with "the sojers" and some of his long walks ashore with Commander Downes. He called on the 24th Massachusetts Infantry to see Sam Green who had even more information about their classmates. He met Colonel Francis Osborn, the regimental commander, and ". . . had a little stroll along the wood, under beautiful mossy vales—& along the hard beach by the uprooted trees, gathered some jasmine to wreath round your portrait, and returned to the ship." The next day he was again on shore and asked an officer of a Connecticut regiment "what our troops had come here for, & he replied 'to protect the fleet'." At the time, most of the monitor flotilla was in the Stono River.

Early in April, Downes asked Stedman to join him on another of their long walks. They stopped at the headquarters of Brigadier General Thomas Greely Stevenson, a former commander of the 24th Massachusetts Infantry and a prominent citizen soldier in Boston's volunteer militia before the war. Stevenson introduced them to his staff, most of whom were Bostonians. Downes and Stedman wanted to have a look at the "Rebs" from the forward line of pickets:

> *The grassy road wound under the stately oaks with their long streamers of gray moss floating from their gnarled arms; the great old pines shed forth their aroma, the laurel*

and oaken underbrush glistened in the sun, and once in a while the pipes of the robin or the caw of the crow would break the stillness. Then suddenly the roar of a XV-inch gun . . . would be echoed by the report of the [bursting] shell, and all would be quiet again. . . .

After a walk of perhaps two or three miles, we came up with the advanced picket, where all hands looked as if they were on the alert. The officer & two or three men standing out at the edge of the trees & looking towards the plantation where the rebs were lodged in a mansion house; out of rifle shot, across a field. Yesterday morning one of our companies was picketed in their house & the rebs this morning made a dash on it and surrounded it with some 600 cavalry and infantry; but Stevenson had been too sharp to leave his men there and had withdrawn them the night before. . . .

The Capt brought off Sam Green in the gig with us, & he dined in the wardroom, after which Skipper made Sam & me come and drink tea with him. . . .

On the eve of so great a fight as we are to be engaged in, I suppose I ought to have some interesting feelings but I haven't. —10 p.m. Harmony has been visiting and returned saying that the attack will not be made for 8 days; you can't fancy how disgusting these delays are after your mind is made up. . . .

Good night darling Edie and God bless you and the little boy. Your affectionate Husband Cellery [sic] Stedman

General war news and local rumors were running a neck-and-neck race. Rhind, skipper of *Keokuk*, was certain that the reported loss of the Mississippi River was a hoax: ". . . that Farragut had run past Port Hudson, Dave Porter got in the rear of Vicksburg,—all of which we are determined to believe for 2 or 3 days at least, by way of variety."

Returning from transferring some patients to *Sebago,* Stedman had the boat crew pull him back by way of *James Adger,* still senior ship for the Charleston blockaders, ". . . & here I found many of her old officers—the doctor, purser & others . . . in the wardroom besides Capt. Worden, the flag lieut, & the signal officer who was instructing the signal officers of the vessel; with wine & ale on the table & cigars going around." There Stedman met the Admiral's pilot, "who said the *Keokuk* and *Bibb* were going out tonight or tomorrow—to carry and place the buoys, so that the *Ironsides* could go over the bar on Saturday—the highest tide. This looked like business. . . ."

Back aboard *Nahant,* Sam Green was waiting for another pleasant visit. The following Saturday evening, the day before Easter, Stedman reported a "tremendous row" in the cabin country of *Nahant* "ever since dinner, when Gen. Stevenson dined with the Capt. after which a lot of Ironclad Skippers have been drinking wine, & making a noise which has prevented my writing as I wished, but there is little to say except that it has blown hard from the N.W.West, bright & cool. . . ." He complained that they had not yet gone into action, ". . . & we have all been surprised that we have not gone to sea & cannot imagine the reason." Rumors and delays were wearing down Stedman and others as well, including the noisy monitor captains in the wardroom.

The pilot whom Stedman had met on *James Adger* proved to be a reliable transfer agent for first class rumors, missing by no more than twenty-four hours his predicted departure date for *Keokuk* and *Bibb* to sally forth to mark the channel with buoys. On Easter Sunday, *Keokuk* arrived from the Edisto River to join *Bibb* in marking the channel. On Monday, *Keokuk*, because of her power, shallow draft, and ease of handling, led the other ironclads over the bar into the Charleston Main Channel which in those days paralleled Morris Island though modern engineering has since modified this approach. By 9:00 AM, all ironclads, including *New Ironsides* to which DuPont had moved his flag, were anchored in line ahead above the bar to await the tide and the clearing of the heavy haze which brought dubious outlines to normally easily recognized landmarks, while obscuring some completely. Logbooks are in agreement about the haze which hung over the entire harbor area; this was the reason that DuPont did not proceed farther that day.

Tuesday, 7 April, the wind was moderate, northward and eastward; the weather clear. "Enemy oc-cupied in transporting guns down Morris Island beach, having observed our troops signaling from north point of Folly Island," was the report in *Keokuk*'s logbook. Through Stedman's eyes from *Nahant's* deck:

> *We could see the rebs very busy on the beach & sand bluffs companies marching up and down, "four-horse mule teams" as one of our engineers called them, driven briskly along, and parties busy apparently in hauling up big guns & mounting them; tho some of the pieces we thought were Quakers. At any rate Secesh was uncommonly lively, & seemingly puzzled at our movements. I think they fancied we were going to land troops.*

The Confederates indeed feared a coordinated sea and land attack, initially thinking it might come from Folly Island. Their infantry and light artillery, which had been placed to defend the coast artillery from land attack, were being moved to positions for containment. General Hunter did not make their fears come true for he had changed his mind again. He did not think Charleston was worth the price its capture would cost and he soon wrote the same to President Lincoln. Major General Quincy A. Gillmore was sent to relieve Hunter.

By 12:30 PM, the tide was right and the ironclad flotilla moved in. They were advancing in line ahead when *New Ironsides* hoisted the stop signal. The col-

Towed South by the U. S. S. "Opecanchanough".

umn leader, *Weehawken*, was pushing a heavy raft with a V-shape stern into which the monitor's bow was fitted and held by lines from the starboard and port bitts to ringbolts abaft the point of the V. At the front end of the raft were grapnels for picking up hostile torpedoes. Among these grapnels were friendly torpedoes intended to demolish underwater obstructions in the channel. This was another of Ericsson's inventions. Captain Rodgers considered it more dangerous to his ship than to anything the Confederates had used to bar the channel. Assistant Secretary Fox had insisted that it be tried. Rodgers, however, removed the torpedoes although he was willing to give the grapnels a trial run. The raft was a failure. Because of wave action, it alternately tried to climb aboard over *Weehawken*'s low, abbreviated bow, and then to crawl under the overhang to battle the recessed hull below. There its lines became fouled with the anchor which dangled from the hull. The advance of the entire column was delayed until Rodgers disengaged the invention that had already caused a bow leak. The rising tide swept the raft onward and into Confederate hands. Ericsson's invention became an unintended gift to the Confederate cause.

THE BATTLE IN CHARLESTON HARBOR

The advance was continued until *New Ironsides* signalled "ignore actions of the flagship" and dropped her anchor. There was less than a foot of water under her keel. Rodgers led the monitors into position for bombardment of Fort Sumter. Confederate batteries were relatively quiet until the monitors were a thousand yards from Sumter. Some moved closer; others stopped.

At that moment, cannonballs and rifle bolts were rained upon them from Morris Island, Sullivan's Island, Fort Moultrie, and Fort Sumter. *Weehawken* was leading, followed by *Passaic*, *Montauk*, *Patapsco*, *Catskill*, *Nantucket*, *Nahant*, and *Keokuk*. *New Ironsides* was unable to close to the range Rodgers wanted for firing on Sumter. Confederate gunners tested her with a number of hits only to see their rounds bounce away from her sides. Thereafter the monitors received the undivided attention of the Confederate batteries with most attention paid to the leader of the column and the tail of the formation, depending which was in better range for the battery choosing its mission. *Weehawken*, at the head of the column, was able to take the rain of iron. *Keokuk*, at the tail, lacked heavy armor and came out of the engagement looking like two inverted colanders on a raft; cannonballs and heavy rifle projectiles had punched that many holes in her two turrets. She came out of action with only two dangerously wounded, two severely wounded, and eleven "slightly wounded," including Commander Rhind. *Keokuk* was forced to pass between *Nahant* and her targets before making a U-turn into the channel and going out of action. Next day, at the end of a towline, *Keokuk* sank off Morris Island when her crew was unable to save her. Fortunately, tug *Dandelion* rescued the crew.

Nahant inherited all of the metallic abuse previously heaped upon unhappy *Keokuk,* for *Nahant* was now at the tail of the column. The records reveal that she was pushing up to within 500 yards of Sumter when *Keokuk* withdrew. "We soon began to suffer from the effects of the terrible and I believe unprecedented fire to which we were exposed, and at about 4:30 PM, the turret refused to turn, having become jammed from the effects of three blows from heavy shot," Downes wrote in his after-action report. "One of them put a dent in the base of the turret and two others on the pilot house on top of the turret, which killed the Quarter-master; incapacitated others, and disarranged the steering gear in its course." Downes was also wounded, but he carried on alone in the pilot house.

Surgeon Stedman saw little of this for his battle station was below the waterline, which itself was only eleven inches below the iron plates of the "weather deck." He had remained in the pilot house until 2:45 PM when "... a burst of white smoke ... near the *Weehawken,* [was] followed by volleys from the forts on Sullivan's Island and shot falling thick and fast churning up the water around the leading vessels." Downes sent him below to the wardroom where his equipment was in readiness. Stedman continued his description of the engagement:

> *I could hear the faint reports of the enemies* [sic] *guns from my air tight den. Pretty soon a shot struck up, just over Severing's head in the engineers store room knocking him off his stool to his great delight, and*

after that the balls & shells & bolts rattled like hail upon us; every little while showers of water would fall upon us and down the turret, thrown up by shot striking alongside.

> *"Here comes a wounded man" cried one of the boys, & who should it be but the poor pilot. "Open the door for another" and the old Signal Quartermaster, was brought in with his head stove in. "Stand by boys, make room for McCallister—g—d—we're catching it now." I found that the pilot on recovering from his swoon was only severely bruised in the neck and shoulder, & McCallister was stunned only, but poor old Cobb, the quartermaster, who had been thirty years in the service was past surgery & died in the night....*

The two quick, successive hits almost in the same place had sent lethal iron splinters, broken bolts, and sheared nuts flying about the interior of the pilot house. A long 78-pound iron fragment killed the quartermaster. The same fragment painfully injured Commander Downes' foot. Had the fragment's impetus not been checked by the steering gear and wheel, Stedman would have necessarily had to amputate the Captain's leg. Downes did not even mention his injury in his official report. Sheared nuts and bolts also hit several men serving the guns in the turret.

"Of the men struck by flying bolts not one left his station at the gun voluntarily, and only one at all, and he remained until he fell senseless and was carried below," Downes officially reported six days after the battle. He also cited Acting Ensign Clark who commanded the gun division in the turret "under the general supervision of Lieutenant Commander Harmony." Unlike some of the other monitor commanders, Downes did not anchor at any time during the engagement, and held most of his fire for the shorter ranges. *Nahant* fired only seven 15-inch rounds and eight 11-inch rounds. Downes broke off his share of the battle when his guns were frozen in position by the damaged turret.

> *We were within 500 yards of Fort Sumter, unmanageable and under the concentrated fire of, I think, 100 guns at short range, and the obstructions close aboard, but fortunately we got the preventer steering gear in working order in time to prevent disastrous result and getting my vessel once more under command, I endeavored to renew the action, but after repeated futile efforts to turn the guns onto the fort, I concluded to retire, for a time, from close action and endeavor to repair damages.*

About this time, Admiral DuPont aboard *New Ironsides* considered the problems caused by passing time and changing tide. He could not afford to have his ships become frozen in position with their keels in the mud of a low tide. The withdrawal signal for all ships was hoisted. From DuPont's viewpoint, other than *Keokuk,* all ships appeared to be fully functional though the rates of fire from some had slackened. That was to be expected for they were not rapid fire artillery even at their best. As soon as the ironclad flotilla had reassembled out of action, the Admiral called his captains aboard the flagship. Excepting Rhind and Downes, none had experienced personal pain or injury. All, however, were unanimous in indicating that their respective ships were in need of repair before again entering the triangle of fire the harbor defenses had so conspicuously unveiled.

The reports of the captains indicated that the nine ironclads had fired only 139 rounds during the attack period of an hour and a half, an average of only slightly more than fifteen rounds per ship. Most of the ships had experienced jammed turrets, faulty gun mounts, or both. Some minor though dangerous leaks had occurred. None of the monitors could afford another deck or turret hit in the dents of a previous blow, especially on the hull side plates, the turret, or the pilot house. In contrast to their own damages, none of the captains believed that Fort Sumter had been materially damaged. Admiral DuPont listened to their reports without comment, left orders to his staff unchanged, excused himself, and went to bed. At dawn, a signal from the flagship cancelled further ironclad operations pending repairs. To the Navy Department, DuPont reported that he was thankful that the battle had been "a failure but not a disaster."

As usual, the first news of the battle to reach the North came from Confederate newspapers. The South claimed a great victory for General Beauregard

Port Royal Harbor, S.C., 1863.

and an appalling defeat for the ironclads. John Ericsson was greatly disturbed. He rushed word to Admiral DuPont that if the Admiral needed another torpedo-sweeping, obstruction-demolishing raft, he had one in reserve. "Mister" Fox was also deeply concerned. He considered transferring the monitors to Farragut below Vicksburg for Farragut would know how to use them. That unpopular rumor immediately spread and was mentioned in Stedman's letters to Edith; it had considerable basis in fact. However, ships so slow that they could hardly breast the main current of the Mississippi and with guns restricted to an elevation of five or six degrees were the last things Farragut could use for counter-battery fire against the fortifications on the high bluffs at Vicksburg. No one knew this better than Farragut; the monitors were not sent.

After the engagement, Assistant Surgeon Charles E. Stedman, U.S.N., wrote and filed the only document that appears over his signature in the *Official Records*:

U.S. Ironclad Nahant
Off Charleston, April 7, 1863

Sir: I have to report the following casualties in the action of today:

Commander John Downes, Massachusetts, slight contusion of foot from a piece of iron loosened from pilot house.

Pilot Isaac Sofield, New Jersey, severe contusion of neck and shoulder from flying bolt in pilot house; is doing well.

Quartermaster Edward Cobb, Massachusetts, compound comminuted fracture of skull from flying bolt in pilot house; has since died.

John McAllister, seaman, Canada, concussion of brain from flying bolt in turret striking him on head; is doing well.

John Jackson, seaman, Massachusetts; Roland Martin, seaman, Massachusetts; James Murray, seaman, Massachusetts, were slightly injured by falling bolts in turret, not disabling to any of them.

Very respectfully, your obedient servant,

C. Ellery Stedman
Assistant Surgeon, U.S. Navy

Stedman had gone into the battle somewhat miffed at his Captain. Late in the afternoon of Easter Sunday, as the ironclads were lining up to cross the bar into the harbor channel, *New Ironsides* had passed *Nahant* and splashed her anchor down nearby. Belknap promptly sent a boat to bring Stedman aboard for a friendly visit. When Stedman asked the Captain for permission to leave the ship, Downes had said no, and the boat returned without Stedman. After the battle, however, Stedman was filled with admiration for Downes:

We went farther up than any but the Keokuk . . . & had all been as gallant and as cool as John Downes the result might have been kept off a while longer. I always said he'd fight, & he has won the admiration of his officers and crew. . . . This morning the Keokuk sunk on the beach where she was *towed by two of our tugs; I saw her go down and a melancholy sight it was . . . . I suppose they can repair us at Port Royal, but what good we can do is yet to be seen; ironclad stock is down.*

God bless you and the boy. Give my love to all.

Your affectionate Charley

How dear those letters were!

Port Royal Harbor

CHAPTER NINE Ironclad Stock Is Down

WHEN THE MONITORS were unable to resume the battle on the day following their repulse by the Charleston forts, Stedman experienced the bitter feelings of a man filled with the pangs of defeat in his first battle. Blame for the defeat could not be attributed to the ships' commanders nor to their men for all had performed their duties with the calm coolness of a dress rehearsal drill and at an enduring pace that had surprised Stedman. Any reason for failure had to be in the ships themselves and because of the slow rate of fire of their guns. These same guns, however, were constantly fired at a faster rate and at greater ranges from the decks of more conventional ships: the fault, therefore, must be the design and construction of the monitors. That fact clearly exonerated all of the commanders and their crews on every count. Furthermore, the orders to do a Farragut past the forts had come from Washington; that cleared the squadron's high command of any responsibility for the tactical error, if such it was. The piles across the channel, clearly seen from *Nahant*'s pilot house only five hundred yards away, made it even more evident that the order was an error directed by distant, unrealistic bureaucrats.

Although the press might echo DuPont's report that the attack was not a defeat but merely a "failure without disaster," it was also easy for Stedman to rationalize that the public should also know that the Confederates were even more unhappy about the affair. Their guns had sunk only one experimental "tinclad"; yet Sumter was damaged far more than it had appeared to be through the smoke of battle. More of its guns had been silenced than the unfortunate *Keokuk* had carried in her turrets. Any sensible man had to concede that there had been no defeat; it was just another inconclusive, "drawn battle."

In that spirit, Stedman drew "The Monitors 'Otternel' and 'Semantecook' with 'Ironsides,' in action," shown on page 149. The sketch merits far more than a casual glance. Though Stedman failed to give *New Ironsides* her full name and though he continued his confusing practice of giving fictional names to some ships, this was not true in his letters home. Here, he correctly recorded the order of battle for all of the ironclad flotilla. *"Ironsides,"* however, was never *"New"* in either his letters or sketches.

The high silhouette vessel in the background is *New Ironsides,* frequently used as a combat flagship by both Admirals DuPont and Dahlgren. This is not a good representation of the ironclad. She was an ugly vessel, but probably was the most powerful warship of her era in either Europe or America, prior to the replacement of iron with steel plates in 1885. Decommissioned in the summer of 1865, *New Ironsides* was "put in ordinary" at the League Island Navy Yard with only a caretaking detail aboard. She was completely destroyed by fire on 16 December 1865. There are few pictures of the vessel; none are flattering.

Stedman's "Otternel" was actually Commander Fairfax's *Nantucket*; she is shown firing at Fort Sumter. *Nahant* is coming into the picture at the right, completely stripped for action. The peculiar lines of *New Ironsides* detract little from *Nantucket*'s entire silhouette, and the turret with the pilot house on top, the thin signal mast with the commission pennant flying are excellently drawn. The heavy horizontal bars across the dimly pictured square ports of *Nantucket*'s pilot house gave additional protection against unchecked, direct entry by a hostile projectile.

While the guns were being serviced, the turret's gunports were turned away from the enemy. This provided a warning to the enemy. The moment the "two eyes" of the turret looked directly at them, hostile gunners at the target prepared to jump for cover in a bomb proof. With two to five seconds at their disposal following the muzzle flash which accompanied the firing of the ship's guns, most of the fort's gun crewmen could jump with time to spare. The large, slow cannonballs could be seen approaching in flight—something like a baseball in a hot line drive just over the second baseman's head and deep into center field. The fort usually made a clean catch, but there was never an umpire there to signal an "out." Ironclad skippers knew full well what was happening each time they prepared to fire. They tried to camouflage the gunports, and attempted to confuse the enemy by painting pairs of "Quaker gunports" on the side of the turret directly opposite the gunports. None of their efforts, however, proved to be worth the trouble involved; and the games continued to be played under the original rules.

With the ironclad flotilla still inside the channel bar but out of effective range of fort and shore batteries, the post mortems were as immediate, analytical, and militant as those at any bridge table following a badly bid and poorly played hand. Stedman was a good listener although probably not a full-throated participant. In a letter home dated 9 April, he recorded his own thoughts:

> *I was wrong in thinking that we did not damage the fort: nineteen shotholes are visable in it and the Weehawken's people say that Nahant knocked over the lookout-bastion.— Had our vessels had broadsides & had been able to maintain their position together under fire we could have broken down that curtain of the fort—but these ifs. Hunter & DuPont both knew that a purely naval battle at Charleston could have no decisive result . . . but orders must be obeyed; and yet the President's secretary—Hay—was here yesterday & said that Mr. Lincoln was prepared to hear of a repulse! Just think, we went within*

500 yards of Fort Sumter! What would have been the result, if all the vessels had passed on as far as the rear division, of which Keokuk and Nahant were the last—and went farther- erest [sic]—cannot be told.... We shall prob- ably not get credit for this, as there is a strong Ericsson Party which controls all of the news- papers in New York bound to maintain the invulnerability of their monitors....

We were hit 8 times on the pilot house by 10- & 11-inch & 3 more would have knocked it into the river; The steering gear was en- tirely disarranged & we had to use the pre- venter wheel in the turret chamber. In the turret are nine shot marks, fifty-six bolts bro- ken: One shot struck upper part and broke through all the plates; some of them in two places. Another shot down off the "Apron" inside that supports the gunrail & interferred with turret-turning-lever. Flagstaff carried away: Jack-staff seared, Steam Whistle shot away. Upper part of smoke stack—seven large shot holes & seven small ones (from fragments of shell): smoke stack Armour—3 shot marks. One pierced through the armour, making a hole 15 inches long and 9 broad, displaced grating inside and broke 7 bolts; Deck struck 14 times, twice seriously. One shot broke the plates badly and starting up 25 bolts; another started the plate & 20 bolts.—In the hull ar- mour 8 marks; armour badly broken in sev-

eral places and plates started from the side & deck & etc.

The above is from Harmony's report....

Lieutenant Commander Harmony had had greater opportunity to analyze the damage than had Downes in making his earlier report to DuPont. The hits were more numerous and more severe, as Stedman indi- cated in the passages of his letter lifted from Har- mony's report. While Harmony was making this analysis, Belknap came aboard *Nahant* to take Sted- man to his belated visit to the combat flagship, *New Ironsides.* Apparently it was here that Stedman picked up the rumor that all ironclads but two, *Passaic* and *Montauk,* were to be ordered to the Mississippi to support the capture of Vicksburg by Farragut, Porter, and Grant. Stedman not only reflected the line offi- cers' views of such folly—"... was there ever such imbecility as that which orders us there..."—but he also took a dim view of the health hazards in that climate with the crew constantly kept from light and fresh air by small arms' fire. He was deeply concerned about

... the general effect on our health while we live during the summer in such a craft as this invention ... is. One thing is certain, they will need a Doctor—& I shall be of some use there, & I wouldn't apply to be detached for it seems to me that would be like a line officer trying to get from under fire. The hardest thing to bear will be the length of time be-

The Monitors "Otternel" and "Semantocook with
the "Ironsides", in action.

tween the mails. . . . Kiss Elly whom I do so long to see again.

Stedman's opinion a few days after the battle that "Ironclad stock is down" proved to be the understatement of the season. Within the Atlantic squadrons there were no bidders, and the morale of the ironclad captains was lower than the Deep Six. With the possible exception of Captain John Rodgers of *Weehawken*, each and every one of the monitor commanders would have welcomed transfer to a wooden, third rate, paddle wheel blockader. Commander Rhind was given such as assignment after *Keokuk* was shot from under him.

Six weeks after the battle, the monitors were either still undergoing major repairs at Port Royal or licking their wounds in the comfortable estuary of the Edisto River about midway between Port Royal and Charleston. *New Ironsides* had been left at Charleston to counter any possible Confederate sortie by either or both *Palmetto State* and *Chicora*. Because *New Ironsides* also needed a major overhaul, Admiral DuPont wanted to know which one or two of the five monitors languishing in the Edisto was most prepared to take the place of *New Ironsides*. The collective answer of the monitor captains was: "None of us!" Their official analysis jolted the technicians in the Navy Department:

North Edisto, S.C., May 25, 1863

Sir: Having understood that when it shall be necessary to withdraw the New Ironsides from the blockade . . . that vessels of this class may be regarded as necessary and fit to take her place, we beg leave to express our opinion on that point.

The hatches would have to be battened down during the whole time and the vessels could not fail to be disabled from loss of health to the crew.

The loss of speed from foulness of bottom, now amounting to one half of what they had when put in commission, would put it out of their power to chase effectively or to get offshore in a gale of wind even with the assistance of an ordinary steamer.

The extreme sluggishness of the compass would make it impossible to make any given course of a cloudy night. If clear, setting the course by a star and giving time for the compass to traverse would make its use possible.

The ground tackle in a heavy seaway would, in our opinion, be inadequate to hold her.

In short, we think these vessels are entirely inadequate to maintain a blockade at sea.

Very respectfully, your obedient servants,
John Rodgers, Captain
Danl. Ammen, Commander
Geo. W. Rodgers, Commander
D. M. Fairfax, Commander
John Downes, Commander

A NEW ADMIRAL FOR NEW SHIPS

On 6 June, Admiral DuPont received an echo from the state of affairs within the ironclad flotilla. The communication came over the signature of Navy Secretary Gideon Wells: "Sir: On being relieved by Rear Admiral Foote, you will please turn over to him such instructions, or furnish him with copies. . . ."

That Admiral Foote was a man of sterling qualities, of great moral and physical courage, afloat and ashore, and that he was most deserving of a high command, all at that time and since have agreed. He had strong religious convictions, and had denounced slavery long before the Abolitionists had made it a militant issue. In 1841, while second in command of *Cumberland,* he had organized the first ship's Temperance Society in the history of the Navy; he and that society weaned the crew from the grog ration for the remainder of the cruise. Foote's antipathy toward liquor had resulted in the legislation which stopped "splicing the main brace" for all time the previous year. It seems ironic that his terminal affliction was diagnosed as Bright's Disease, in that era said to be the grim destiny of wine bibbers and alcoholics. Foote died in a New York hospital on 26 June 1863, "enroute to Port Royal." The publicized assignment to a major command must have made his deathbed a bit more comfortable to that dynamic sailor. Had Foote been in good health and been able to appear aboard *Wabash* with his flag staff, they would have been heartily welcomed throughout the Squadron.

However, the Captain waiting in the wings prepared to accept the temporary rank of acting rear admiral and to play the leading role in the Charleston naval drama had credentials vastly different from those of Foote. Captain John Adolphus Bernard Dahlgren was endowed with a Renaissance mind of great curiosity equally adaptable to all forms of learning whether it be literature, law, mathematics, a field of science, or medicine. The guns previously mentioned and the processes for manufacturing them were the products of his imagination, mathematical abilities, and technical skills. The Navy had used his unique talents to its own great advantage—and at times to his private prosperity. Following his last tour of sea duty in 1847, he had invented, tested, and patented a percussion lock for firing a cannon. By 1850, he had also designed and patented a light boat howitzer; it found a good market in Europe and at home. As ordnance officer for the Washington Navy Yard, he established a gun factory and pioneered the beginnings of a Naval Ordnance Bureau. Although the distinctive outlines of his guns appeared in the large 15-inch gun and in conventional pieces of smaller bores and lengths, the 11-inch smoothbore was his masterpiece.

Dahlgren had become a Lincoln favorite during his service at the Washington Navy Yard. This friendship had brought him command of the Navy Yard despite the fact that he was only a commander. His lack of seniority was ignored when he was promoted to Captain in 1862. Now—and worst of all in the thinking of the seagoing gentry of the Navy—the "palace sailor" had asked for and been given DuPont's command. The shoreside "technicians," headed by "Mister" Fox and that impractical inventor, Ericsson, had sent out one of their own breed to tell the fighting captains how their equipment should be handled. Dahlgren hoisted his flag to the main truck of *Wabash* on 6 July.

Throughout the intervening weeks of the changes of command for both the army command ashore and the squadron on the Charleston front, everything at Stedman's level was in a state of suspended animation. "As long as we don't go further south I don't care what they do with us; and the Capt. doesn't seem to think we shall." Stedman predicted a great "row between Ericsson & the Ironclad skippers." The rumor was being circulated that the inventor "prides himself on never having visited one of his Monitors, and tries to impress the world with the superiority of theory over practice." Stedman viewed the coming summer with concern: "I have sent some 15 men to the hospital . . . & when hot weather sets in, few of the old crew will be left." The number hospitalized was twenty percent of *Nahant*'s crew strength. Her logbook reveals that forty-one seamen, ordinary seamen, and landsmen came aboard as replacements on 19 July. The replacements were not the result of combat casualties but were required because of losses from sickness or the expiration of some enlistment periods. This large percentage of replacements supported the complaints of Stedman and others regarding the poor health conditions on the monitors. However, the medical records of wooden ships the previous summer were far from flattering.

During the change-of-command interlude, *Nahant* did participate in a small but highly publicized naval battle. Intelligence sources had indicated that the Confederate ironclad, *Atlanta,* was combat loaded and prepared to make a sortie from the Wilmington River, a tidal exit from the Savannah River, into Wassaw Sound. There was little doubt that she could brush aside the usual two wooden vessels on blockade duty at that station, and would then be able to proceed to the high seas. It was equally certain that she could outrun the monitors for she had a speed of ten knots. *Atlanta* had to be sunk or captured at the exit from the river or not at all. For this mission, Admiral DuPont ordered Captain John Rodgers to Wassaw Sound with his *Weehawken* reinforced by *Nahant.*

BATTLE WITH *CSS ATLANTA*

For a time, it appeared to be only another rumor, and the two monitors seemed to be taking part in a fruitless waiting game. Early each morning, a small enemy steamer would appear at the head of the sound, take a look to see if the ironclads were still there, and then disappear back upriver. However, in dawn's first light on 17 June, a ship appeared that kept coming. She was the *Atlanta*; two armed steamers followed in her wake. The drums on both monitors rumbled the "Beat to Quarters." Stedman turned out, wondering if it was only a drill, a false alarm, or the real thing.

Capture of the Confederate iron-clad "Atlanta"
by the Monitors "Weehawken" and "Nahant."

The pilot for these waters was with the senior officer present, Rodgers, on *Weehawken*. *Nahant*, of necessity, had to follow in her wake despite the indication that *Atlanta*'s course showed a desire to run past *Weehawken* to engage *Nahant*. Her opening shot was at *Nahant* and a near miss which cut the lines to the long boat she was towing, setting it adrift. Her few subsequent rounds were all fired at *Nahant*. Because of his slow loading guns, Rodgers was risking no misses: *Weehawken* closed to 300 yards, and opened fire. *Nahant*, with loaded guns, maintained a collision course with *Atlanta*, while *Weehawken* got off five rounds. Downes' plan was to ram and fire; but, just as he was about to foreclose the mortgage on *Atlanta*, she ran aground and hoisted the white flag. *Nahant* could not stop in time to avoid giving *Atlanta* a less than gentle nudge which cracked or bent a lower armor plate or two. Lieutenant Commander Harmony was aboard *Atlanta* in a matter of seconds. Captain W. A. Webb, C.S.N., offered his sword to Harmony in token of surrender. Harmony, who had known Webb in the Old Navy, refused the offer, for it was Webb's privilege to surrender to the senior officer present, Captain Rodgers.

Most of this happened while Stedman was below. When *Atlanta*'s first round whined overhead, he had "returned to my duty in the wardroom with much dignity: the way the men skedaddled that were clearing the ship for action was a caution." Ensign Clark, in the turret, passed the word downward regarding the progress of the battle. His remarks were accentuated by the shrill noise of incoming projectiles from *Atlanta*'s Brooke rifles intermingled with the heavy roar of *Weehawken*'s Dahlgrens. The clang of four bells came from the engineroom below when Downes in the pilot house called for more pressure and more speed for his intentional ramming. It was in the midst of this clamor that young Clark suddenly shouted that *Atlanta* had surrendered:

> *I was very angry with Clark who told me she had raised the white flag thinking he was chaffing me but it was so! . . . Harmony was sent to take charge—& soon after I was sent aboard to help attend to the wounded. I found 1 dead and 10 or 12 wounded; we amputated one arm & another leg was needing it, but the steamer Island City out from Fort Pulaski had come around & we placed the wounded & prisoners aboard. . . .*
>
> *The officers were all nice fellows & we had a number to a late breakfast and lunch, though the news they brought was not pleasing—the defeat of Grant at Vicksburg and Banks at Port Hudson* [This "news" concerning defeats for the Union's Mississippi River forces was erroneous. On 4 July, seventeen days after the capture of *Atlanta*, Vicksburg surrendered to Grant; and Port Hudson surrendered to Banks on 9 July.] *Capt. Webb and Lieuts. Alexander and Barbot were known to Downes*

Stedman formed a very favorable opinion of the two Confederate surgeons, Doctors Freeman and Gibbs. "The Capt. appeared to be a nice fellow, but the 1st & 2d lieutenants were very drunk by noontime. . . . The middies were very pleasant little gentlemen & the Purser was a brick. One mid gave me a secesh navy button, very pretty." The friendly, enemy officers explained why they had fired at *Nahant* instead of *Weehawken*: because *Nahant* had a white awning over the weather deck aft of the turret; the *Atlanta* thought that the officers slept under it and that they were still in bed.

One odd aspect of the engagement was not mentioned by most participants although perhaps seen by all. After *Atlanta* went into action, her two armed, auxiliary consorts retired; but two other distant vessels remained. They were commercial steamers, loaded with ladies and gentlemen who had bought tickets to watch the battle. Naturally, their hopes had ridden with *Atlanta*. What amused Stedman most about these two "excursion" steamers was the reaction of his own Captain. Downes had not fired a gun during the battle. He was, according to Stedman, a most

> *. . . astonished & disgusted man when she ran up her white flag. Then he turned to the steamers above, that were filled with people from Savannah to see us captured or sunk—took off his hat and sings out—'Oh you Secesh devils—you came to see us threshed did you; & be d____d! Now go back where you belong.' It was very absurd, considering that the fellows were 3 miles off.*

Captain Webb's account of the battle was little different from the victors'. All the way down the sound, he had had trouble steering because of occasional contacts with the bottom and the currents of the incoming tide. He had not laid to while awaiting the attack, as Rodgers had thought, but was actually aground and waiting for the tide to lift him clear. Webb could only bring one or two of his guns to bear on the closing monitors. The four hits from *Weehawken* had caved in his armor, creating lethal splinters from the timber backing the armor as well as sending iron splinters flying about. His pilots had been wounded. Webb felt that not striking his colors would have been a criminal and needless sacrifice of men.

The loudest voice of discontent came from John Downes who was certain that Captain John Rodgers had not given *Nahant* the credit she deserved. When Secretary Welles sent a letter of commendation to Rodgers, Downes protested. Then someone in Washington wanted to know what had happened to possible trophies, souvenirs, and the swords captured with the ship. It turned out that Rodgers had insisted that the Confederate officers keep their swords when they surrendered to him. Although Downes and his crew received the same share of prize money as *Weehawken*, the same was true for the two wooden ships on blockade station, standing by to help if one or both of the monitors had a jammed turret, became grounded, or was otherwise unable to continue. Rodgers had not even mentioned these two ships; why should he. The records showed that they were there. Downes basic complaint, however, rested upon the fact that *Weehawken* was getting all of the publicity although all of the hostile shots had been fired at his *Nahant,* and despite *Nahant*'s closing with and ramming *Atlanta.* Perhaps Downes might have been coming down with "monitor fever." He was the type, however, who always saw the hole in the doughnut but, in doing so, often failed to see the doughnut.

"Monitor fever," an ironclad-form of the more conventional "ships' fever" of the preceding year, was incipient aboard *Nahant.* At the end of the day following the battle, Stedman recorded his only complaint about his own health made during his first two years of commissioned service: "My exposure to the hot sun yesterday morning—the excitement and fatigue brought on pains in the limbs & chill, last night; all of which has gone this morning and I feel very well. . . ."

More serious was the loss of David B. Harmony as Executive Officer of *Nahant.* He had been detached to command *Atlanta* and her prize crew on the journey north to condemnation proceedings and induction into the United States Navy. It was thought that he might command her in that new role. Harmony, however, did not want to stay ashore long enough to transform *Atlanta* into a Union warship for there was

a war in progress; he returned to *Nahant* after a short leave. While clearing from *Atlanta* after her surrender, *Nahant* had bumped *Weehawken* slightly "because she failed to get out of the way," but even the slight bump had opened a seam. Rodgers went to Port Royal to check the damage leaving Downes in command at Wassaw Sounds. "Rodgers being gone," Stedman reported, "J[ohn] D[ownes] is senior officer & makes himself very disagreeable in that position. I wish Harmony would come back, for he keeps him in tolerable order."

Stedman's memory of *Atlanta*'s surrender is well pictured on page 153, "Capture of the Confederate iron-clad 'Atlanta' by the monitors 'Weehawken' and 'Nahant'. " For reasons known only to him, Stedman this time saw fit to identify his own ship by its correct name. The drawing is a good action picture of the two sluggish monitors trying to beat one another to the prize. It correctly supports *Nahant*'s being nearer the enemy and ahead of *Weehawken* to receive the surrender and put the prize crew aboard. Stedman's drawing, however, could have contributed nothing more to the pros and cons of his commander's unseemly contentions, all of which Captain Rodgers had cavalierly ignored. Had Stedman been willing to become involved in the argument, he might well have drawn a closeup of Lieutenant Commander Harmony of *Nahant* declining the abjectly offered sword of *Atlanta*'s commander. To the contrary, even Stedman's letters reflect a higher esteem for Captain John Rodgers and his cousin, George W. Rodgers, com-

Pleasures of letter-writing: mercury 98° F.

manding the monitor *Catskill,* than for Downes. Doctor Stedman became increasingly convinced that Downes' worsening health was due to service in a debilitating climate and the insufferable living conditions aboard a monitor.

BENEATH THE ARMORED HATCHES

Life below the waterline of a monitor was well depicted by Stedman in "Pleasures of letter-writing, mercury 98° F." on page 157. The scene is the wardroom of *Nahant.* The date was toward the end of June or early July 1863. The turnover of officers by that time had been sufficient to make identification impossible. The self-pictured Doctor Stedman is just right of center, mopping his brow. The overly-stout

No wonder. "Why Captain Gunnell – I did not recognize you."

officer at the center could not be Captain Downes for, with his own more spacious quarters, he would never have gone elsewhere to write his personal letters. Actually, the ship's writer would probably have handled all but his most personal correspondence. Downes would never have carried his to the common table for all officers aboard. On 11 July, Stedman wrote:

> *How can I write all I want to, which would be about 40 pages of foolscap, in a temperature of 98° I cannot see. If I could do so, I should tell you of exciting scenes, which could not have surprised the rebels as much as this whole movement has surprised me. I have been through a deal of danger out of which, so far, I have, thro' God's mercy, come safely. Whatever the result of this attack is, it must be ranked, for brilliance of conception as second only to Grant's maneuvers, which we learn today from prisoners, have resulted in the fall of Vicksburg; those who were in the least ailing when we left were the first to cave in.*

The "excitement" cited by Stedman in this letter was the first coordinated land and sea attack against the Morris Island defenses of Charleston Harbor. The three day battle, which began at 5:00 AM, 9 July, came as the result of orders from the White House to both Dahlgren, the new commander afloat, and to Major General Quincy A. Gillmore, the new commander ashore, to get going, something had to happen soon and without delay. Gillmore's battle plan was simple: he would capture Morris Island if the Navy would properly reinforce his own artillery support fires from the massive concentration of heavy guns he had secretly emplaced at the adjacent end of Folly Island. While the heavy artillery was being moved there, he ostentatiously massed his men and supplies on the Stono River, giving every appearance of being about to resume Hunter's old effort to cross James Island to capture Fort Johnson on Charleston's inner harbor. To add to this ruse, a brigade would vigorously attack from Grimball's Landing toward Secessionville, the point at which Hunter had prematurely broken off his offensive. Having thus drawn Beauregard's mobile reserves to that area, the secretly emplaced artillery and the main body of infantry and engineers could attack across Light House Inlet for a quick capture of Battery Purvience and Fort Shaw with their associated earthworks and other light artillery emplacements. The infantry could then push rapidly northward to capture Battery Wagner. Its heavy guns could be turned on Sumter and Moultrie while the same operation continued on to Battery Gregg on Cumming's Point. General Gillmore expected the Navy to support strongly with naval gunfire both the vigorous feint from the Stono and all resistance points on Morris Island from Light House Inlet to Cumming's Point. And this Admiral Dahlgren would most certainly do for President Lincoln had written identical letters to each telling them to cooperate or else!

Dahlgren promptly brought up monitors *Catskill*—to which he transferred his flag, *Nahant, Weehawken,* and *Montauk.* Although all were still undergoing repairs, they looked good enough to fight. Wooden blockade ships, with twenty degree elevations possible for their deck-mounted 11-inch guns, would line up farther offshore and, by firing over the monitors, would further reinforce the bombardments from land and sea. The guns of the wooden ships had three times the range of the same guns mounted in the turrets of the monitors, and they could be fired at a faster rate.

THE BATTLE FOR MORRIS ISLAND

The first day of the attack, *Nahant* provided the otherwise idle Surgeon Stedman with a ringside view of a narrow-front land battle that was a textbook demonstration of coordinated fire and movement. Few have ever been privileged to see such a battle from such a favorable vantage point. In his narrative description of the battle written to Edith, Stedman opens with:

> *As we were moving in, exactly at 5, boom! went the first gun from Gilmore's [sic] batteries followed in rapid succession by thirty more. The rebs knew we had four guns in position on Folly Is'd, but they seemed taken by surprise.... Such a splendid sight; the flashes of the guns—the shells bursting far up Morris Island—the sun just rising and tinging the dense clouds of smoke as they rolled off to leeward—the rebel batteries replying but*

faintly to the roar of our guns; it was worth while to have seen that. But when the monitors opened on Morris Island with their flanking fire, spitting their enormous shells & shrapnel exactly into the enemy's batteries, it was too much for Johnny Secesh. . . .

The initial targets for the monitor and the heavy cannonade from the north end of Folly Island were Confederate Battery Purvience, Fort Shaw, and their associated earthworks on the south end of Morris Island. General Gillmore's assault regiments had already crossed the inlet under cover of darkness, and were concealed in the high swamp grass and brush. The artillery preparation on the hostile positions was to last for two hours. At their sudden silence at 7:00 AM, the infantry assault formations were to move forward. Stedman continued his description:

Soon the cessation of noise told me that something was up & I rushed on deck again, . . . & there were our troops deploying on the beach with the old flag flaunting over them, scrambling into the works, or bagging their prisoners, whom we saw walked off to the rear. The Weehawken burst a shell right on the parapet of the most northerly battery, the Secesh retired & in five minutes our men had it & had turned a gun on its former owners and were blazing away . . . & soon our people were in possession of one third of Morris Island.

The soldiers had actually done much better than getting a third of the way up to Battery Wagner, their primary objective, for they were within rifle range of the fort's redoubts that night. Not shown on their obsolete charts was a tide-washed gully across the island just short of the frontage of the redoubts; this all but cut the island in two. To cross it, the troops had to use a mere strip of dry land, two feet higher than the marsh on the left and the tidal waters on the right, a strip only a hundred feet wide. The passage could be raked with grapeshot from field guns in the Wagner works; the ranges had undoubtedly been measured carefully and orientation points established by the defenders. Gillmore, however, was determined to have a go at it with a dawn assault the next day. In such close work, distant naval support fires could be more hazardous than helpful. Since the Confederate guns from Forts Sumter, Johnson, Moultrie, and Sullivan's Island were hammering his own lines of communication from the intervening gully to the rear, Gillmore asked the Navy if its guns could attract some of those fires.

After a miserable night below the hot, battened down hatches of *Nahant*, her crew was turned out to clear the ship for action. In the swells, water constantly sloshed the length of the weather deck. By ten o'clock nothing had happened, although all hands were standing by at battle stations. Stationed with his surgical layout in the wardroom, Surgeon Stedman was miserable in body and in mind:

After a set-to with Wagner.

We were routed out at five this morning, & now about 10 I am seated in the wardroom with the temperature about 93° to write a letter; early in the morning the Admiral signalized to be in readiness for action & our ventilators were taken off—I have our air-port open tho' expecting every moment a sea will wash down. I have had a shave & my head rubbed which has refreshed me immensely. How long I can stand this I don't know—I wish I had a gallon of whiskey. . . . I think 3 or 4 more days will lay me up. . . . (There's sea down the air-port) But let me get back to where I left matters last night. (the wretches are bursting a shell right over my air-port now.)

The monitors, still led by *Catskill* with Dahlgren aboard, were moving in the Main Ship Channel to abeam of Battery Wagner; and were beginning to draw fire from her coastal battery of 8, 10, and 11-inch smoothbores and rifles. They were also drawing fire from Sumter, Moultrie, and Sullivan's Island. It was *Catskill,* however, which was attracting most attention from all directions.

On the land side, Wagner's garrison had saved their fortifications, magazines, and bombproofs by giving Gillmore's dawn assault a bloody repulse. There now was no reason why the monitors and their longer-range wooden ship consorts should not teach Wagner to be more polite toward visitors from the North. At the same time, the monitors did not crowd up to Wagner the way they had to Sumter in the earlier attack. Considering a mile to be a satisfactory range, *Catskill* called the tune for their efforts. By afternoon, Stedman waxed tired and weary of it all:

I got sick of the heat & smoke & foul air in the wardroom & went into the turret chamber, where the noise from the guns, the blowers, & the officers was terrible—"go ahead fast," "Starboard," "ready, fire, bang," "15-inch shell," "11-inch shrapnel" &c &c. By & bye I crept into the turret, & watched the firing which was very exciting & interesting. Pretty soon H. [Harmony] asked me if I didn't want to fire the 15 inch gun, which I did, and the shell split right in the corner of the parapet—flash—flash—clouds of smoke & dust, bang goes the shell.

At six we returned to our anchorage; the heat excessive & 2 or 3 more men beat up, including the engineer from the Ironsides.

For the participating naval vessels, the third day was much the same as the second with emphasis of their fires directed on Fort Wagner. The monitors received occasional attention not only from Wagner's coastal guns, but also from more distant Confederate batteries. *Catskill* did not lead them close in, but maintained ranges of about a mile, moving about to prevent the Confederate gunners from using repetitious ranges. All hostile fire concentrated on *Catskill* until *Nahant* ran afoul of shoals and had to drop her anchor. Something fouled both the anchor and the propellor. The Wagner gunners quickly detected her stationary status, made range adjustments by observed shot falls. *Nahant* took six hits, three of them more damaging than any received at closer range from Sumter in the previous battle. Fortunately, no one aboard was injured sufficiently to merit casualty reports. The monitors withdrew, leaving the wooden cruisers to indulge in their extremely long range, harassing fire on the Morris Island targets. The "1 & 200 pd rifles seem to carry as far as you want them to," Stedman observed in passing, but it was "very exciting & oh terribly, terribly hot.—Grand news from Meade & Vicksburg—the latter from the rebels."

In his diary covering the three-day operation, Dahlgren aboard *Catskill* reported sixty hits on that vessel, six on the second-in-line *Nahant*, and two on *Montauk* and none on *Weehawken*. *Nahant*'s logbook, however, records a total of twenty-three hits: six the first day, eleven the second, and six the third. *Nahant* appears to have suffered the most damage of all. The Admiral took his shot-torn flag back to his little flagship, *Augusta Dinsmore*, a fast, well-appointed steamer armed with two 12-pounder rifles. Dahlgren took her into Light House Inlet for closer deliberations with General Gillmore. That Admiral Dahlgren—the chairborne, drawing board admiral who had not done a ship's cruise since 1847—was more than willing to ride into action with the big, slow-firing guns was

noted and often mentioned by all ranks and ratings in the South Atlantic Squadron. Stedman was no exception. To Edith, he confided: "There is no doubt about Dahlgren's pluck but he goes off & refreshes himself with ice & claret & turkeys aboard his flagship, the *A. Dinsmore*."

In the early afternoon of *Nahant*'s fourth day off Morris Island, she was ordered to sally forth to observe and report the effects of the long range firing by the offshore wooden cruisers. Were they doing any damage? Were they keeping the battery from being reinforced or resupplied with food and munitions? *Nahant* picked up six more hits on that warm afternoon. Three 10-inch rifle projectiles put as many dents in her turret; another crushed in the armor near the stern ". . . and opened a seam like a fish's mouth," according to Stedman. While Downes went to *Augusta Dinsmore* to report his findings on the results of fire missions of the wooden cruisers and the additional damage received by *Nahant*, Stedman was worrying about the ship's casualties that were not results of enemy action, but which came purely from the bitter business of working and living on an unseaworthy pigboat:

> *I forgot to say I believe that Bordley, 2nd Assistant Engineer, had been surveyed and sent home, and now we have two volunteer engineers aboard, exclusive of the one from Ironsides whom we busted up in about 24 hours. We have sent away 7 or 8 people done up. Neal came back yesterday evening saying*

he was well (which he isnt) he stood it on Powhatan as long as he could but had to come back & help us fight the rebs.

When Captain Downes returned from the flagship, he was less secretive than usual. *Nahant* was to leave for Port Royal without delay. Here they would pick up all personal property left there, retrieve any of their own men who had been left with the Surgeon on the shoreship *Vermont,* and pick up any needed replacements that might be available. Then they would proceed to Wassaw Sound, Georgia, right where they had captured CSS *Atlanta.* Reliable intelligence sources indicated that another ram or ironclad was secretly being completed in Savannah waters. A damaged and leaky *Nahant* would still be able to contain the rumor by putting command minds at ease, and at the same time could meet any craft the Confederates might produce.

In the quiet waters of Wassaw Sound, Downes could think of nothing better for keeping the crew busy than to have all watches kept to avoid a night surprise, and, during daylight hours, to have the crew scrape marine growths from the ship's hull, tighten nuts, rethread bolts, and hammer out the dents in *Nahant*'s armor. This was the subject of Stedman's drawing, "After a set-to with Wagner," on page 161.

Stedman's letters at this time revealed much unhappiness caused by news from the home front and by the trend of affairs at Charleston. The anti-draft riots in New York were disgraceful; the handling of them by the civil authorities, especially in New York, was even worse. On Morris Island, Gillmore had decided to capture Wagner Battery the long, slow way using parallels, traverse, and saps: trench warfare and victory by attrition. General Gillmore was moving his own heavy artillery into his expanded beachhead which now included most of Morris Island. He had never admitted that his primary mission was the capture of Charleston; his purpose was the capture of Fort Sumter and the batteries and defenses on Morris and James Islands. Then the Navy could capture Charleston. He expected the Navy to do all it could to help him accomplish these secondary missions. He needed many, many more men, but the War Department could not spare additional troops from other, more vital theaters of action.

The chronic and constant personnel shortages of the monitors, due to increasing sickness and disabilities among firemen and engineers, had made constant demands on the resources of the Admiral's headquarters and other ships of the South Atlantic Squadron. The large and initially well manned *Wabash,* with a crew of 650 officers and men, had long been used as a sort of replacement training center by DuPont. She was now down to a few officers, two engineers, and a hundred men. The same was true of the large, old receiving and storeship, *Vermont,* anchored at Port Royal. Her Chief Surgeon had offered Stedman, who was ailing himself when he transferred *Nahant*'s sick to *Vermont,* an assistant surgeon's billet should he want to escape the ironclad

The turret in action.

flotilla. Stedman had turned the offer down in order to stay with the crew he knew and admired. At the same time, most of the officers of *Montauk* and *Patapsco* were being hospitalized, given a medical survey, and then invalided to home ports for treatment, rest, recuperation, and reassignment.

No monitor other than *Weehawken* had a better health record than *Nahant*. Stedman attributed the difference to the more relaxed attitude aboard *Weehawken*: minimum size night watches, more sleep for all hands, shorter working hours during daylight, more rest periods for the men, and a greater abundance of beer and grog for all hands. Commander Rodgers had recently been transferred from *Weehawken* to another billet, but his informal command attitude still prevailed when *Weehawken* also returned to Wassaw Sound to relieve *Nahant* as the watchdog at that Savannah rathole. Aboard *Nahant*, everything and everyone were still up tight.

RETURN TO BATTLE

After another series of repairs by the metal workers at Port Royal, *Nahant* was again ready for battle. General Gillmore's tactics for a victory by siege methods and attrition constantly demanded bigger and better artillery concentrations to cause even greater attrition within the hostile ranks. He already had an unprecedented number of heavy artillery pieces, army as well as naval gun batteries moved ashore. But there were still attacks to be made which required offshore bombardments. Normally, the broadsides of *New Ironsides* were sufficient, but situations constantly arose in which there was no substitute for the slow and deliberate, close-in fire of the Dahlgren 11-inch and 15-inch smoothbores. During these engagements, Admiral Dahlgren normally hoisted his flag aboard *New Ironsides* or the leading monitor. Because of the converging fire the command pennant always attracted, no monitor commander ever expressed bitterness that the Admiral did not ride with him!

After Harmony had invited him to fire a round from the 15-inch Dahlgren during the artillery duel with Wagner, Stedman had experienced a new interest in *Nahant*'s big and sluggish guns. "The turret in action," on page 165, is the way he remembered that scene. It is doubtful that this was drawn aboard ship for the grossly enlarged breech of the gun is even more grotesquely out of proportion than the guns in his previous drawings. Nevertheless, the expectant stance of the gunner and the turret commander, Harmony, peering through the peephole while motioning with his left hand to the man at the turret's turning level give the scene a more convincing quality. Stedman wisely omitted the tongs, hoisting gear, and the overhead circular track used to get the 400-pound ball and its wooden sabot to the muzzle of the gun where it would be rammed home. Including these would have added much more mechanical clutter than the scene would permit or might require. As a doctor of medicine, Stedman was consistently more interested in people than in things.

"The powder division on the berth-deck of a Monitor in action," page 169, is also a product of Gillmore's theory that heavy bombardments could produce a white flag at the target. The one man with two tongs in a tussle with the heavy cannon ball of exaggerated size conveys a feeling of driving, dynamic action—but it robs the drawing of any sense of reality. Even without Stedman's exaggeration, the ball was actually a load for at least four men for it weighed over 400 pounds. Two men, with their tongs properly adjusted, might have rolled it through the open door to the ammunition hoist at the right. Despite these inaccuracies and exaggerations, the drawing does have its merits. The viewer should keep in mind that these men are below the waterline of a ship whose armored hatches are battened down. Except for the light from the pale flames of the whale oil lamps mounted on gimbals extending from the bulkheads, the men are working in darkness. They are breathing the powder-tainted fumes from the turret above and the hot, suffocating gases from the stokehole below. The mere spectacle of that burning lamp above the carton of 15-inch powder bags is enough to fill any meditative mind, military or civilian, with dire apprehensions.

RETURN ENGAGEMENTS WITH WAGNER AND SUMTER

By August 17, General Gillmore's system of parallel and traversing trenches and their connecting saps had brought the ground troops close enough to obnoxious Battery Wagner to support another all-out

Derby Shire — Quartermaster

assault. This meant that every gun afloat and ashore that could be brought to bear would be called on to soften Wagner. The big secret: H-hour would be during twilight's first darkness. The long bombardment would prevent last minute reinforcements from across the narrow lagoon, and would also reduce the defenders to combat fatigue caused by constantly jumping from their guns into the bomb shelters. By this time, Wagner had many of these shelters. Beauregard had brought in heavy guns from elsewhere to serve as potent field batteries across the lagoon from Batteries Wagner and Gregg and to support them in any argument with the Federal forces.

Gillmore's battle plan called for the biggest concentration of fires of all calibers since the Russian surrender of Sevastapol in October 1855. The battle could last a week if need be—and it did. Monitors *Passaic, Weehawken, Nahant, Catskill,* and *Montauk* were sent from Port Royal to join the artillery battle. Guns on both sides began firing in dawn's first light on 17 August 1863. It was to be a bad day for the two Union commanders, afloat and ashore. At 5:40 AM, Dahlgren hoisted his flag on *Weehawken* and led his monitors to their firing positions off Morris Island where they could draw fire from almost all of the hostile guns from Wagner to Gregg on Cummings Point to Sumter and Moultrie. Every round drawn by the monitors was one less round that could be fired at Gillmore and his X Corps. Nothing was a greater magnet for coast artillery fire than an admiral's flag hoisted above an offshore raft with two guns on it.

At 10:20 AM, Dahlgren shifted his flag from *Weehawken* to *Passaic,* and signalled "follow me" to *Patapsco.* Both *Passaic* and *Patapsco* were armed with 150-pounder Parrott rifles instead of 15-inch Dahlgren smoothbores. They moved toward Sumter and opened fire at 1,800 yards. Dahlgren obviously wanted to see the rival heavy guns in action. Fort Sumter graciously cooperated by shifting from Gillmore's Morris Island front to the two bold visitors. At 11:40, the Admiral had seen enough, and a steam picket boat arrived to take him and his party back to *Augusta Dinsmore.* Two minutes after they went over the side, Sumter slammed two bolts against *Passaic*'s turret. As the picket boat passed *Catskill* at 12:10, Dahlgren received the voice message that Commander George W. Rodgers had been killed and that three others with him in the pilot house were dead or wounded. By 12:40, the Admiral's flag was again flying above *Augusta Dinsmore,* and her Stars and Stripes were at half-mast. All other ships followed her lead. Dahlgren was a distraught and saddened man for he had lifted Rodgers from his position as skipper of *Catskill* by promoting him and making him his fleet captain or chief of staff. When the Admiral had announced his plans the previous day, Rodgers had requested permission to return to his old command for the battle since his replacement had not arrived and because he thought he would enjoy one more go at the enemy with his old crew aboard *Catskill.* Dahlgren's anguish can be read between the lines of his official report of the action and the loss of Rodgers.

Gillmore's report of the night attack on Wagner was even worse news. Throughout the day the offshore bombardment from both the well withdrawn wooden cruisers and the closer monitors had apparently silenced Wagner's guns and driven their crews from the high and thick redoubts into the parapets and bomb shelters. The assault brigade commander was able to position his two participating regiments secretly and without any unexpected interference.

The powder division on the berth-deck of a Monitor in action.

Unfortunately, Confederate intelligence officers were performing at peak efficiency. One of their divers had gotten into the sunken *Keokuk* before the salvage teams and had lifted her signal book. The Confederates were able to decipher messages as well as to read flag signals.

Based upon their estimates derived from their analysis of signal traffic, Beauregard had reinforced Wagner's conventional coast artillery garrison during darkness with seasoned combat infantrymen from across the lagoon. They were armed with English rifles and had fixed bayonets in preparation for the expected assault. The result was slaughter in darkness. For a while, it was a gallant fight and one assault regiment had possession of one corner of the works for two hours. But, with the colonel dead and the brigade commander mortally wounded, the narrow holding had to be given up. The next day, no guns were fired at Wagner's earthworks for it was feared that more harm would come to wounded and captured Federal troops than to Confederate defenders. Wagner welcomed the respite while both sides exchanged wounded men and prisoners of war.

Gillmore and Dahlgren, however, thought that they had stockpiled enough heavy artillery ammunition to do a thorough job of demolishing Charleston's coastal and harbor defense installation regardless of whether it took a week or ten days of sustained hammering. Therefore, on with the job! Dahlgren was not aware that Colonel L. M. Keitt, commanding Battery Wagner, had reported more damage from *New Iron-sides* than from the monitors. Beauregard's Chief of Artillery Report for 21 August indicated that all but one of Wagner's guns were functional. The Confederates complained that the monitors were moving about too much making it much harder to hit the floating targets. Perhaps ammunition should be saved by ignoring them. Apparently the principles Downes had practiced with *Huron* in the Stono River were being adopted by his ironclad colleagues.

Downes, however, was nearing the end of his tour as skipper of *Nahant*. His taciturn, driving, and often unpopular personality notwithstanding, he had an enviable record. His casualties on both *Huron* and *Nahant* had been lower than those on most other ships commanded by his colleagues. Only one of the other original skippers of the monitor flotilla was still in command of his ship: Commander Ammen of *Patapsco*. All of the other monitors had been commanded by two or three different officers. Only Captain John Rodgers had been lost by promotion and transfer. One of the others had been killed, the remainder had been wounded, invalided to the hospital, and/or sent home for treatment and recuperation. Stedman, with his own increasingly repetitious chills and fever pains, darkly suspected that Commander Downes was a sicker man than Downes would admit. Downes apparently corresponded with Assistant Secretary Gustavus Fox whom he may have known when both were passed midshipmen. Fox had told him he would give him another ship if and when he officially requested relief.

By 23 August, Sumter had been whittled, cut, and hammered down to a mass of crumbled, dusty rubble. About all that held the sagging walls up were the sheltered magazines, bomb proofs, and a corner bastion or two. A week after Gillmore's failure to capture Wagner, Colonel Alfred Rhett, the fort's commander, reported to Beauregard that only one gun on the eastern face was still in service. Noting Sumter's failure to answer fire, Gillmore sent a note to Beauregard urging its surrender. The answer was, "Come take it if you can."

Dahlgren decided that a night attack by the monitors, at a time when counterfire from Moultrie, Sullivan's Island, Fort Johnson, and the Cummings Point batteries would be less effective, might enable him to administer the *coup de grace* to the old fort from 800 yards. He could then steam past it into the inner harbor. A fog aborted the entire operation although some monitors did better than others. In his last after action report from *Nahant*, Downes stated:

> *Impeded by the mistiness of the atmosphere, we did not reach our allocated position until 4 a.m. . . . we found opportunity for firing but one XI-inch shell at the fort being deterred from firing the XI-inch gun by the condition of the smoke box* [a device for keeping a muzzle flash from igniting ammunition in the turret]. . . . *During the brisk fire opened on us at intervals . . . we were struck but once on the turret heavily, starting out some eight or ten bolts. I have the*

> *satisfaction to report no one injured on this vessel during the action.*

None of the monitors achieved any part of the night's assigned mission; none was less aggressive than *Nahant*. All found themselves groping in the fog, unable to see a target, and unable to see one another. In Stedman's words:

> *After waiting till sunrise & the fog still clung to the water, we weighed & steamed out; and thus ended one of the greatest fizzles I ever was concerned with . . . whereas we were all exhausted from having been up two nights in succession with a fight intervening. A more used up, dirty faced crowd than our officers I never saw. Downes looked as peaked as an old nail, & had a dreadfully unclean mug . . . But the misery must have thawed him . . . he treated all his officers to some splendid whiskey.*

Downes actually was a very sick man and both he and his Surgeon knew it. His Executive Officer, Harmony, was also sick. Stedman bluntly told Downes that "his health was failing and he would have to go sooner or later, & he might tell the Admiral that his Surgeon thought so." About the same time he told his closer friend, Harmony, that he was sicker than their Captain and that, in effect, he was certifying him to the Medical Survey Board no matter what the Admiral's views might be concerning Downes. That is exactly the way it worked out: both of them were surveyed for relief and ordered to their home navy yards for treatment, rest, and to await orders. This meant Boston for Downes and New York for Harmony:

> *So last evening they went away. Harmony couldnt keep the tears from his eyes when he left us . . . the men crowding aft to get a shake of his hand & giving him 3 hearty cheers. Soon after a tug came for Downes—he had all the officers called on the turret, shook hands with us—the last thing he said being to tell me he would do all he could to have me relieved. The tug cast off—Carter called for 3 cheers, and we all went below feeling pretty sad. Spite of all John Downes faults, there is something so winning in his bravery and good looks that I couldnt help a pang of regret when I caught the last glimpse of him.*

In a way, that was the end of the *Nahant* saga as far as Doctor Stedman was concerned. Acting Volunteer Master William Carter, Acting Ensign Charles C. Ricker, and Stedman were almost the only remaining members of the original crew that had sailed from Boston only eight months earlier. As had already been indicated, *Nahant* had received forty-one replacements in one draft to fill to strength a crew of only seventy-five. All four of the engineer slots and the coal-heaving ratings had turned over an average of three or four times during the eight month period. The affliction that debilitated Downes and Harmony, not to mention Stedman himself, was combat fatigue, to a minor degree. The three headquarters surgeons who came to examine Downes and Harmony knew exactly what was happening although they did not use phrases found in our modern technology. They also probably looked at Stedman and wondered when they would be looking for a replacement for him.

Malaria was a new term in the medical jargon of the era. Many medical practitioners diagnosed malaria using terms such as "swamp fever," "ague," "fever and ague," "jungle fever," "marsh miasma," and "poludal poison." Different geographical areas used different names. Most doctors suspected that it was a parasitic disease; nearly all provided prescriptions which were curative, purely in the light of common practice and experience. It was not until 1880 that a French military doctor in Algeria established its parasitic character. Everyone aboard *Nahant* had fought enough mosquitoes and drunk enough unwholesome swamp water to come down with malaria, not to mention a touch of typhoid, regardless of the term applied to their chills and fever pains.

The Supply Steamer.

CHAPTER TEN Aboard USS *Circassian*

COMMANDER DOWNES had hardly departed for Boston when *Nahant*'s new skipper reported aboard. Surgeon Stedman had already met Lieutenant Commander John J. Cornwell on *Weehawken* when Cornwell was Captain John Rodger's Executive Officer. He brought *Weehawken*'s relaxed and informal attitudes with him. Within two or three weeks, Stedman was writing:

> *I play backgammon every night with our new Captain in our shirtsleeves, & the difference between the old and new regime is most startling; He says these ships are only fighting machines & when not in action the best thing we can do is to make ourselves as comfortable as circumstances will allow. I wish you could have seen him bobbing up and down in the surf the other evening when we came off the shore; and if you could have seen your husband on Ricker's shoulders coming through the surf, I think you would have laughed well. Every five or six days I see Belknap, who doesnt seem very well or strong, and who says his wife's eyes still continue to trouble her very much.*

The boat trip through the surf was made returning from a visit to the recently captured Battery Wagner. Following the costly failure to carry the redoubts in the bloody night assault on 17 August, General Gillmore, always the engineer, returned to his digging and sapping. To keep the enemy harbor forts and Confederate batteries on James Island from punishing his men while they were working, he reinforced his own artillery on Morris Island with seventeen siege and Coehorn mortars. He also added ten light siege rifles to sweep his front and to isolate Wagner with interdiction concentrations on routes of approach from Battery Gregg and James Island. Fourteen heavy Parrott rifles were brought in for counter-battery fire against Sumter, Moultrie, and the Sullivan Island batteries. The Parrotts could also help the Navy soften up Wagner during the forty-two hour bombardment to be fired prior to the next assault. The time for that artillery preparation came on 6 September when Gillmore's sappers had tunnelled themselves to positions beneath Wagner's embanked, sand redoubts.

In his description of this preparation in his post-war writings, the General for the first time voiced a warm admiration and appreciation for the naval support, for the guns the crew of *Wabash* had lugged ashore, for the offshore bombardments of the monitors, and especially for the help from *New Iron-*

All hands up anchor.

sides. But he admired his own work even more. His calcium lights, screened in the forward trenches, became footlights for the stage that was Battery Wagner; they "... brought the minute details of the fort into sharp relief." The preparation fires from all guns continued throughout the planned forty-two hour period. Gillmore admiringly described their fire "As a pyrotechnic achievement alone, the exhibition at night was brilliant and attractive, while the dazzling light thrown from our advanced trenches, the deafening roar of our guns, and the answering peals from James Island added sublimity and grandeur to the scene."

Gillmore, Admiral Dahlgren, the ironclad flotilla, and—most of all—the assault battalions all had reason to be ecstatic. In the appalling silence which followed the heavy preparatory bombardment, the infantrymen crouched in their forward positions with bayonets fixed. Then came the giant explosion of the breaching charge placed by the sappers. Blue-clad infantry ranks moved forward as one man to rush the breach and the redoubts. They encountered no resistance; the large garrison and the gunners were gone, with most of their ammunition and supplies. Only two boatloads of the enemy remained to keep the fires burning—and to surrender. It was a victory all could enjoy. The Stars and Stripes were quickly waving over both Wagner and Gregg, on Cumming's Point. All of Morris Island, the lower lip of Charleston's tight-mouthed harbor, was now in Gillmore's possession; but this merely gave him more targets to shoot

at. Charleston was still beyond his range. And, as long as General Gillmore had targets, the monitor flotilla had work to do.

This grim realization no doubt came to Stedman the moment the visiting party was through the surf and back on *Nahant*'s never hospitable armored deck. It should be noted that Cornwell, about the same age as Stedman, could happily make a game of wading through the surf to the boat while Master Ricker insisted upon carrying the Doctor high on his shoulders through the same surf to the same boat. All hands knew of his frequent bouts with headaches, ague, and remittent fevers. Ricker, the navigation officer, was obviously eager to reciprocate the care he had previously received from the Doctor.

During the weeks which followed Downes' departure, Stedman waited quietly for the change of assignment Downes had indicated he would arrange during a visit to the Navy Department in Washington. In a letter to Edith, Stedman expressed doubt that Downes had made any effort "...to have me relieved ... but I don't believe he even mentioned my name." Downes, however, during his stay in Boston, apparently told Mrs. Stedman that the Doctor would be reassigned to a naval hospital at Beaufort, South Carolina. Stedman considered this reference to be "...more or less a figment of JDs brain. I dont know that I ever heard anyone else speak of it." He dropped all hope of any further assistance from Downes.

Things went quietly back to the same old routines of shoot, accept hits, a tow to Port Royal for repairs, receive new replacements—usually engineers and coal heavers, hospitalize several patients, then back to another series of bombardments. About 20 September, autumn's first cool norther swept down the coast. It brought comfort to the men in the hot-plate ironclad flotilla; and it made Stedman feel better as well:

> *If I could only have a smart walk how I should enjoy such a fine bracing air. But the water is washing over the deck and you might as well try to walk across at Chelsea Ferry. But I'm terribly contented now—having nearly made up my mind to winter here.... What the land and sea forces do next, I can't imagine.... Mr. Read [a recently assigned, young career officer who had served on Admiral Farragut's flagship up and down the Mississippi] says Mrs. Farragut told him, her husband was coming down here to take charge as soon as Adm. Dahlgren gave out. But D. is just one of those sickly people that are always used up & never give in. The Weehawken, Patapsco, & Lehigh are at Port Royal for repairs ... when some of them return, we shall go.... I'm afraid Eversfield feels hurt that I didn't come to the Vermont & had I known I was to be here so long I would have gone at once.*

From a professional and naval career standpoint, it was a serious mistake. Doctor Charles Eversfield had a team of surgeons aboard huge, always anchored *Vermont.* One of the senior surgeons in the Navy, he took over the New York Navy Yard health services in 1864. Shortly after the war he accepted the Fleet Surgeon's billet for the European Squadron. It would seem that Stedman's best chance for career improvement would have come from picking up the towline from an older surgeon who knew the ropes.

HEALTH SURVEY AND A NEW ASSIGNMENT

Although Stedman had made up his mind to stick it out until 5 November, the date on which he would have credit for two years of continuous duty, he did not quite make it. Once again, October proved to be an unlucky month. The Army's annual health charts indicate that malaria and typhoid peaked in late September and early October 1863. Stedman became so stricken with headaches, fever, and ague that he could no longer treat the officers and men of *Nahant*, let alone himself. Captain Cornwell, exercising the normal responsibility of a line commander in such a situation, asked for a substitute surgeon. That request triggered a survey of and immediate treatment for Stedman aboard *Vermont.* When strong enough to travel and considered free of contagion, he was released and sent home for rest and recuperation, again subject to supervision and orders from Admiral Stringham's Boston Navy Yard Headquarters. As mentioned during the discussion of the earlier epidemic aboard *Nahant* and Stedman's 1862 convalescence at home, his caricature "Sent North by medical survey 'for change of climate and medical treatment'," obviously refers to recuperative leave. Though well on the way to recovery, the exhaustion that stems from such arduous service still rested heavily upon him. It is doubtful that he was home with his family by Thanksgiving, but he most certainly spent much of December and its holiday period with his family. His self portrait as a patient, with a wine bottle and a light meal among the medicines, would indicate that as a patient he was doing quite well.

As he regained his strength, Stedman undoubtedly began to wonder what his next assignment would be. This time, however, there was no need to worry about another cruise with Commander Downes for Downes had been assigned to command USS *Onward*, a comfortable armed merchantman, well suited to blockade duty. Stedman had been concerned that Downes might ask for him again, for he had written Edith in early October, prior to his relief from *Nahant* that ". . . JD will have had nothing to do with my relief & be hanged to him. If they say anything about my sailing with him, give them the contrary of encouragement. After Cornwell I dont think I could stand JD again." The younger, affable and backgammon-playing Cornwell had shown him what a skipper could be like if he desired while still running a competent ship. Although Stedman hoped to sail again with the younger breed of naval officers such as Cornwell, Harmony, and Belknap, he was soon to learn once again the futility of wishful thoughts concerning one's next commanding officer.

On 5 January 1864, USS *Circassian* arrived at the Boston Navy Yard for overhaul. She sent her crew to the receiving ship and passed to the hands of the Yard's craftsmen and mechanics. A handsome vessel, *Circassian* was a screw steamer with a 450 horsepower direct acting engine and a speed of twelve knots. She had been built in 1856 at Belfast, Ireland, for the Atlantic Royal Mail Steamship Company. Her iron hull, with clipper lines, measured 255 feet by 39 feet by 23½ feet; her weight was 1,387 tons. Her three tall masts were square-rigged with the conventional spanker on the mizzen mast. At the time of her launching, the Royal Mail steamer *Persia* had held the transatlantic record of nine days, one hour, and forty-five minutes for six years. Given reasonable luck on winds and weather, *Circassian* could easily have broken that record.

Captured while running the blockade in 1861, she was promptly converted into a cruiser, although she was too deep in the water for conventional blockade duty in Confederate waters. Although armed and manned with crews for four 9-inch smoothbores and two rifles, a 100-pounder and a 12-pounder, she was assigned to no squadron; but, instead would serve as a roving cruiser and supply ship for all squadrons. In a way, she had an open hunting license; she could board any suspicious vessel for a look at her papers. Should a Confederate commerce destroyer be reported near, *Circassian* would join in the search, and immediately

"Well done, rain water! Plug the scupper-holes, house
the awnings, pipe all hands scrub clothes."

engage the enemy in battle if the Rebel ship were encountered. In brief, the difference between *Circassian* and *Nahant* was a sailor's difference between heaven and hell. No captain could be very bad on a ship with so many virtues.

By 21 January 1864, the Navy Yard artisans had finished the overhaul; and, at 1:00 PM, the assigned officers reported aboard and the new crew arrived from the receiving ship. A happy and healthy Charles Ellery Stedman was much pleased to be aboard as Ship's Surgeon. The ship would not sail immediately for, as was commonly known, there was still much work to be done on the ship by the crew. There was also the inevitable training to be accomplished as well as eventually standing in line at various docks to receive scheduled stores ranging from beef to beans and from ice to quinine. Indeed, *Circassian* did not cast off on her first voyage of supply to the squadrons until 22 May. What a long winter of enjoyment that delay must have been for Stedman and his family! That should have been more than sufficient time for the cold winds and snows of a New England winter to cure any remnants of his long, lingering malaria from the coastal swamps of South Carolina. There was one unfortunate—for us—result of his assignment of *Circassian*: the discontinuance of his many long and interesting letters home. He knew that *Circassian* would routinely return to Boston periodically and by a foreseeable date. Most of his letters would have been in the mail bags aboard his own ship even had he written.

The ship's Captain was Acting Volunteer Lieutenant Henry B. Churchill, obviously a highly esteemed skipper from the merchant marine and in naval service only for the duration of the war. His Executive Officer was Acting Master William Williams. Deck officers were Acting Ensigns William B. Marchant, Peter Pearse, Albert Starbuck, and D. Rodney Brown. Paymaster R.C. Spalding, Chief Engineer Samuel N. Hartwell, and the Surgeon rounded out the Wardroom Mess. Within that group, Stedman fared somewhat better than he had aboard *Huron*. He clearly outranked the four deck officers, and possibly the Paymaster, for Stedman had been integrated with his rank into the Regular Navy and outranked ensigns. He also rated a larger division of hospital corpsmen and two surgeon's stewards instead of only one, as on *Nahant* and *Huron*.

THE FIRST VOYAGE

At 3:30 PM, 22 May 1864, *Circassian* cast off her mooring lines and steamed down the bay in charge of a Boston pilot. Seven days later, the ship arrived at Port Royal at noon. She spent four hours, anchor down in forty-two feet of water, transferring ammunition to the flagship, and was on her way at 5:00 PM. What was such a fast ship doing on a two day run? Her skipper was exercising his open hunting license to stop all vessels that faulted on a recognition signal in hopes that his ship might pick up a prize. During the few hours at Port Royal, Stedman recognized many familiar ships, but there was no time for renewing old friendships.

On 1 June, *Circassian* was standing into Key West, Florida. After eighteen hours, she was at sea again; and, at 7:50 PM, sighted a strange sail which she brought to with a round from one of the guns. The boarding officer, however, returned with the information that the stranger was U.S. transport *George W. Peabody* enroute to Tortugas Island to land nineteen prisoners. By early morning, 5 June, *Circassian* was at the Pensacola Navy Yard, now in the area of the squadron for which she carried the most supplies. That day, according to her log, *Potomac, Itasca,* and *Cornubia* were also at the East Gulf base. Thanks to this information, we know the time and place of the scene Stedman illustrated in "The Supply Steamer," page 173, which portrays *Circassian*'s five day sojourn in that port. The three vessels pictured are readily recognized. *Itasca,* at left was a sister of *Huron.* The low hull vessel with the high, oversize paddlewheels can only be *Cornubia,* a former blockade runner converted for blockade duty. The large, obsolete sailing vessel, at right, stripped of all standing rigging and spars above the tops, is the aging 44-gun frigate *Potomac.* Anchored for the duration, she was used as a stores ship for the Pensacola base. A stiff onshore breeze has put all vessels to heaving at the ends of taut anchor chains, complicating the transfer of stores. But, if the quarter of beef dangling over *Circassian*'s rail is lost, it will be through no fault of the alert reception committee in the boat.

"The Supply Steamer" is one of Stedman's best drawings. Stedman indicated that, "These drawings were made in 1865, some from sketches taken during the war, but mostly from memory," in his statement in 1884. That he worked entirely from memory on his caricatures of grossly exaggerated Dahlgren guns and their ammunition, one can readily accept. But other sketches, including "The Supply Steamer," have such integrity that his memory-aid sketch at the time and place must have included a considerable amount of detail. Reconstruction of the images of three ships purely from memory and with such accuracy that they are readily recognizable by class and purpose and can be so easily named from entries in a contemporary logbook not available to him, is a rather unusual accomplishment for any artist.

Circassian left Pensacola on 10 June. Enroute to New Orleans, she exchanged recognition signals with USS *Owasco,* on blockade duty; she was happy to receive some fresh meat and ice. On 18 June, *Circassian* anchored in the Mississippi off New Orleans. The bright lights of the city were too much for one bos'n's mate; he deserted. James Montgomery, rated landsman, was put in double irons on bread and water for drunkenness and fighting. The ship lingered at New Orleans until 26 June, dispensing supplies and taking on a limited amount of cargo and mail. She also received a number of seamen being invalided home or being discharged for expiration of their enlistments. There were a few others to be imprisoned pursuant to courts martial verdicts. Enroute to Boston, there was a brief pause at Pensacola to top off coal bunkers, procure fresh vegetables and fruit. The addition of more passengers—including two women, Mrs. F. J. Turner and Mrs. K.H. Clark ". . . for passage North, per order of Commodore Smith"—raised the passenger list to more than eighty.

With no additional ports of call in her sailing orders, *Circassian* was homeward bound. With great enjoyment, the bos'n's mates raced here and there piping "All Hands Up Anchor." The inevitable forecastle musician broke out his fiddle. Capstan bars were manned and spun around, gathering in the 180 feet of anchor chain Captain Churchill normally put out. The beat was called by tweets on the bos'n's mate's pipe; and the fiddler's tune was some old reliable sea chantey such as "Blow the Man Down." Stedman presents the scene, on page 175, within the homeward bound, seagoing spirit of his era. It might have been the first within Stedman's own experience. When *Huron* lifted anchor to head homeward, Stedman and most of her crew were too sick from malaria and/or typhoid to be on duty. He had been sent home from *Nahant* as a sick passenger on another ship. The homeward voyage was rather leisurely for *Circassian* apparently stopped every strange ship that failed to hoist the correct recognition signal. Moreover, as she neared her home port, rumors of a Confederate commerce destroyer along the coast involved her in a futile search. Not until the forenoon of 20 July did she anchor in Boston Harbor where she remained until 4 August. For Stedman, for Edith, and for Elly, the boy, it was a happy reunion.

THE SECOND VOYAGE

The two weeks at the Navy Yard and in Boston Harbor taking on cargo passed too quickly. *Circassian* again headed southward. There was no longer any novelty in zigzagging down the coast and outside the Gulf Stream, checking strange ships. Discharging a bit of cargo and a few passengers at a port of call such as Port Royal took but little time. Most of the important tonnage and supplies were destined for Gulf bases. By 17 August, *Circassian* was back at Pensacola, and five days later was steaming up the Mississippi toward New Orleans. Here the last of the draft of 250 men for the Gulf squadrons were checked off. *Circassian* cast off from the wharf there on the 25th and three days later anchored among the blockaders off Galveston. With all ships rolling at the end of their anchor chains, the blockaders were supplied ship to ship. According to Stedman:

> *We were detained 20 hours off Galveston when 6 would have done the business—by various complications of stupidity and red-tape; shall not make Matagorda till tomorrow & if we do not find the Aroostook a few miles below at Orangas [Aransas Pass] will have to go on to the Rio Grande after her. I wish I had nothing to do but to be at home, earning my bread & butter among people that I care about & who care for me. . . .*
>
> *The paymaster [R.C. Spalding] keeps us all alive, having come out in a very comic*

Sunday morning. Reading the Articles of War.
"..... shall be punished with death or such other
punishment as a Court Martial shall award."

light lately; the Chief Engineer Samuel L. Hartwell has a dry sort of humor which comes in with very good effect.... With the exception of D.B. Brown [Acting Ensign and Senior deck officer] the officers on the other side do not contribute much to the life of the mess.

Stedman was finding life within the supply channels less demanding but without anything approaching the camaraderie and *esprit de corps* of a combat crew geared to the weaponry of victory or defeat, or even to survival or death. That ever-present interdependence of each-upon-all and all-upon-each was lacking aboard *Circassian*. Ship routines were good; the decks were well manicured; there was an air of comfort and well-being; combat drills were scheduled and performed but with little sense of speed or precision and with no sense of urgency. It was an accepted doctrine that *Circassian* would outrun any ship she could not whip; as a supply ship, it would be her duty to do so. All was well so long as Chief Engineer Hartwell and his lads took good care of the 450-horsepower engine and the topmen were alert with the complete suit of sails for their full-rigged ship. A good breeze could add a few knots to her speed. This was a war in which *Circassian* could hardly lose anything.

Stedman obviously had a feeling of having lost some self-respect and a certain amount of respectability on the home front. He also felt far removed from the dramatic events of the war for, during his previous assignments, he had become accustomed to knowing when and where a battle was to be fought before the men and ships were deployed to fight it. Great things were now happening on all fronts, and where was Surgeon Stedman—away down on the Mexican frontier looking for a ship named *Aroostook*! As he feared, that cat had left Aransas Pass to check the other rathole she had been assigned to watch. *Circassian* followed and found *Aroostook* among many mice, doing nothing about them. All of these ships flew French colors. A French man-of-war was riding herd on seventy ships of all classes; and Her Britannic Majesty's Ship *Liverpool* was watching the French naval vessel. Napoleon III was in the midst of his effort to place Maximilian on the throne of the French-created Mexican Empire as a French puppet. A French army, reinforced by "loyal Mexican regiments" was in the process of "pacifying" northern Mexico; and a strong force, spearheaded by the infamous Foreign Legion, was landing at Matamoros. This was as close to a good military show as Stedman was to see from the deck of *Circassian*.

Stedman was becoming intrigued with the climate of the Gulf of Mexico. "The extreme beauty," he wrote, "of the sunset skies in these latitudes is a new revelation to me; the mackerel sky of small clouds of fleecy white, speckled over the pure blue in scales & winrows & mares tails, then changing to orange and lake. I never saw any like them before." He and the crew also became fond of the frequent rain squalls

Justly incensed commander, to liberty man returned on board: "Hi! come here, you sir! What's your name?"
"Name? Lor' bless yer. I aint got any name! it was shot
away at Mobile."

accompanied by no more than a cooling breeze. One squall could quickly drench the ship and clear off as suddenly as it had appeared. On such happy occasions it was, "Well done rain water! Plug the scupper holes, house the awning, pipe all hands to scrub clothes," as Stedman illustrated by the sketch on page 179.

The constant and accepted shortage of fresh water was always a problem in the ships of the Old Navy. The planning ration usually was one quart of water per man per day. In other words, twenty-five gallons of fresh water should take care of the daily needs for drinking, cooking, personal cleanliness, and washing clothes for a hundred men. Ocean water was a good rinse for clothing, but not for soaping and scrubbing. The scuttlebutt for drinking water was always near the mainmast and generously resupplied, barring an impending emergency. Rationing would be invoked without prior notice should an emergency seem remotely likely. Cautious captains often required the logbook to show how many gallons of fresh water were expended each twenty-four hours. Captain Churchill was no exception. Stedman tells us nothing about him in the few letters written on *Circassian*. Other than in line of duty, he apparently saw little of the Captain. Churchill ate alone, and left the daily routines of ship sailing to his Executive Officer, the Chief Engineer, the Paymaster, and the Surgeon, each in his own field. He appears to have been the traditional, silent, tolerant, and generous skipper in many ways; but with eyes for everything and a quick, often heavy handed, decision on matters he thought impor-

tant. Fuel and water were important in his thinking. Should the Executive Officer or the Watch Officer fail to save water by not piping the crew to the opportunity to scrub clothes during a rainy squall, a growl might be heard from Churchill.

Early marine steam engines complicated the problems of an adequate supply of fresh water at sea long before they solved it. The early condensers left much to be desired, and the low pressure equipment could develop a voracious thirst. No one was more aware of this than Chief Engineer Harwell—and Captain Churchill, for he was a master mariner with a quick eye for details. In the daily reports, for example, Churchill also required a counting of the sticks of wood consumed. One seldom finds such an entry in the log of a ship which spent as much time in port as *Circassian*. Since only the cooks used sticks of wood, the entry must have had something to do with Churchill's supervisory control of the First Cook, quite often the most mercurial character aboard. Twenty-eight sticks of wood a day appears to have been the number needed during a normal day at sea. If only ten sticks were used, it could have meant that the food was not being cooked enough or that most of the crew had eaten ashore while at a wharf.

Except for gun drills and occasional service practice, the ship was run much like a contemporary mail packet, or passenger liner. Although the ship had some space and a small dining salon for cabin passengers, emphasis was on steerage facilities used for replacements. This meant that the ship's surgeon had far more demands made upon his time than had been the case with the comparatively small crews of *Huron* and *Nahant.* His additional duty as Chaplain was called to his attention more frequently. The only divine service mentioned in the log of *Nahant* was held on Easter Sunday, just prior to the monitor attack of Fort Sumter. Captain Churchill did somewhat better; he often had a Sabbath Convocation service for all passengers, officers, and men, properly attired. However, instead of reading the Sermon on the Mount with an applicatory commentary thereon, Churchill considered a reading of the Articles of War to be a more immediate and practical sermon. In Stedman's drawing on page 183, "Sunday Morning Reading of the Articles of War . . . shall be punished with death or such other punishment as a Court Martial shall award." Captain Churchill is the bearded officer at the right with the star visible on his sleeve. Stedman, officiating as Chaplain, is reading the Articles. As a surgeon, Stedman rated a sword. On conventional, formal inspections, musters of officers, crew, and service connected travellers, he would have been required to wear it, as are the other officers in his caricature. However, in delicate appreciation of his transitory status as Chaplain, Stedman had thoughtfully omitted his personal hardware.

It was not unusual to have unwilling passengers. One convicted north-bound seaman from Farragut's flagship was in double irons when put aboard *Circassian.* The instructions that came with him were that he would always be in single irons when at sea. On one trip southbound, the ship left Boston with 250 replacements, some of whom, joining the Navy to avoid an army draft, fully intended to desert at the first opportune moment. Trouble makers could easily be found in such a group. The transport of so many at one time undoubtedly gave the wardroom officers some worry, but no actual difficulties arose.

Of course, there were the many happy, north-bound service men whose enlistments had expired months earlier but who had been necessarily held overtime awaiting a replacement or transportation. Most would re-enlist; but, in the meantime, were entitled to a bit of exuberance on the road home. Such is the situation portrayed by Stedman in " . . . 'Hi! come here, you sir! What's your name?' 'Name? Lor' bless yer, I ain't got any name! it was shot away at Mobile,' " on page 185. It is not likely that this self-proclaimed veteran of Farragut's victorious entry into Mobile Bay was put in the ship's brig on bread and water. Homeward bound, off-duty sailors will be relaxed sailors.

When Stedman was admiring the beautiful summer clouds and brilliantly colored sunsets, he perhaps did not know that August and September were the hurricane season for those waters. Such storms can be vicious anywhere south of Cape Hatteras although they occasionally make their presence felt in the northern reaches of the Atlantic. Stedman must have learned about these storms the hard way. The absence of a drenching, almost horizontal rain and the rising wave action in "Setting a Dislocated Shoulder in a

Gale," on page 189, suggests that the hurricane center has passed them by; and that they were caught in the gale-strength winds and mounting seas that follow a hurricane. This drawing was shown to a football coach who commented, "Our curative skills are not keeping up with the times. The doctors are still setting dislocated shoulders that way."

CIRCASSIAN TO THE RESCUE

Towering, tornado type clouds with white anvil-shaped tops and turbulent, blue billows blending into a black base less than a thousand feet above the surface from time to time move seaward on a wide front across the Gulf Coast. With or without a quick rain, they can kick up a hard squall which can dismast an unwary ship, crack up a flimsy craft. Such a squall caught the sternwheel steamboat *W.V. Gillum,* of New Orleans, off Sabine Pass, Texas, in early September 1864. She carried twenty-seven passengers, including two women, and had a cargo of lumber. Jerry-built, shallow-draft, riverboats such as *W.V. Gillum* often used the smaller rivers and lagoons of Louisiana for a quick, fair-weather run from Calcasieu Pass along the coast to Galveston. But *W.V. Gillum* did not make it. Though skies were clearing after the sudden squall hit her, the vessel was breaking up. The crew and passengers built an improvised life raft, thinking that they could tow it with the ship's boat; but they could make no headway. They separated to give the boat a chance to find help which could rescue those left on the raft. *Circassian,* enroute to New Or-

leans, picked up the nine oarsmen in the boat and then began to search for the raft. Captain Churchill at the same time alerted blockaders at Sabine Pass to join the search.

Because the boat and its crew had been adrift for more than three days, there was great apprehension for the people on the raft. For the next four or five days, the blockade of the coast was abandoned by *Itasca, Gertrude,* and *Penguin* to help *Circassian* find the raft and save the survivors. On the sixth or seventh day after the sinking, *Circassian* encountered the small Mexican schooner *Cora,* headed for Tampico. She had just found the raft and taken its despairing people on board. Stedman related the story as part of a long, rambling letter to Edith:

> *When Mr. Williams boarded the Schooner & ascertained that the people were there he waved his hat & all our men sprang into the rigging & gave 3 cheers. When they came over the Circassian's side they were passed over to the Dispensary & wine & water served out to them—their sunburns dressed—a big kettle of beef tea was made at once; bread and meat sent up from our pantry—old shirts and pants appeared to replace their torn & wet garments till within an hour a grin was to be seen on almost every face except the most debilitated. Some of them had been drinking salt water and were pretty low, but revived rapidly under treatment . . . it was really thrilling to hear their*

Setting a dislocated shoulder in a gale.

stories of suffering & long deferred hope. I haven't been stirred up so for a long time. Old Gragg [Will F. Gragg, First Ship's Steward] *has written a long account of it for the papers, which it is likely you will see.*

Stedman was indeed stirred by the intensity of the search for the eighteen people on the raft. Throughout his service on *Circassian*, his health was good; but, for a week or more prior to the search for survivors, he had complained of painful toothaches. But these seem to have vanished while the search was on and until the survivors were found and cared for. That night he treated the tooth, or teeth, by ". . . drinking a bottle of warm ale when they wake me up at midnight & for the first time in ages slept till 8 oclock." *Circassian* arrived in New Orleans the afternoon of 6 September and anchored off the coal wharf to wait in line for docking space at the wharf. Seventy-two hours later, she was steaming down river to Pilot Town, largely laden only with passengers, mail bags, fresh vegetables, and fruit for her own use and to distribute at ports of call. Stedman had seen a dentist; that problem was ended. His First Steward, Gragg, had provided a news reporter with details of the rescue. The final story filled a column and a half in the small newsprint of the era. Generous praise and appreciation were heaped on the ship and her gallant crew, collectively, and most particularly on Captain Churchill, Surgeon Stedman, and the other officers who had donated clothing to the suffering and destitute crew and passengers of the unfortunate steamboat,

W.V. Gillum. A faded clipping of the news report was found among Stedman's last Civil War letters.

AT LAST VICTORY SEEMS CERTAIN

The national news of the day was both good and bad. The Navy was enjoying the big headlines of the week. A few days earlier, Rear Admiral Farragut had said, "Damn the torpedoes," at Mobile Bay; and then led his fourteen wooden ships and four monitors, all new and much improved over the earlier *Nahant* class, past the guardian forts. The squadron sank or dispersed the small Confederate squadron, and captured the enemy ironclad flagship, CSS *Tennessee*. It was wonderful—but did not improve the image of General Gillmore and Admiral Dahlgren who were still locked in their campaign of attrition against Charleston. The news from other fronts was mixed. West of the Mississippi, very important news in New Orleans, the reports were generally bad. The disastrous and humiliating Red River Campaign the previous spring was under investigation by the Congressional Committee on the Conduct of the War with some of its members viewing the expedition as a cotton-grabbing venture. The inaccurate statements released by the Committee were not helping the war effort. General W. T. (War is Hell) Sherman, attacking south from Chattanooga, had pushed his opponent, Joseph E. Johnston, south of the Chattahoochee River. After the Confederate President replaced Johnston with that very rash general, John B. Hood, Sherman defeated him also and then occupied Atlanta. Sherman was destroying the industrial and transportation capabilities of the city while *Circassian* was searching for the castaways. It was very good news, indeed, especially for Abraham Lincoln whose reelection or defeat for another four year term of office was only seven or eight weeks away. Sherman was about to start his bold March to the Sea, without a supply service, but happily "living off the country." Shortly before Christmas, Sherman would be shaking hands with Admiral Dahlgren's blockade captains off Savannah, Georgia.

South of the Potomac River toward Richmond, General Grant had experienced some bad moments. While Northern newspapers screamed "Butcher Grant," he steadily kept the Confederate forces on the defensive from the Battle of the Wilderness to Spotsylvania Court House, the North Anna River, and Cold Harbor. Severely pressed, General Lee ordered General Early to duplicate Stonewall Jackson's 1862 end run up the Shenandoah Valley to threaten the capture of Washington. Early's move with his small army filled Washington's master-minding editors and maundering Congressional Committees with alarm; but Grant, unlike McClellan, refused to be drawn away from his main objectives: Richmond and Lee's army. Grant's Cavalry Corps commander, Philip Sheridan, was mopping up in the Shenandoah Valley. Grant's main force was enveloping the north, east, and south sides of Richmond with Lee's army inside its defenses. The block-point of this movement was at Petersburg, south of Richmond. Grant was forced to use the trench siege techniques employed by Gillmore against Battery Wagner, still a strong and bitter memory to Stedman. Both sides were digging and sapping under the lines of the other. Grant's engineers blew the dramatic "Petersburg Crater" under the Confederate earthworks, as Stedman had seen Gillmore do against Battery Wagner—but not with the happy results Gillmore had enjoyed with his smaller volcano. Almost everyone agreed that the war was winding down. The end seemed to be in sight, but not even the wisest of men would hazard a guess as to when that end might come.

After leaving New Orleans on 9 September with the usual ports of call at Pensacola, Key West, and Port Royal, and with the normal pauses to board suspicious vessels, it was more than two weeks before *Circassian* again steamed into Boston Harbor to anchor off the Navy Yard. This time, the visits home by officers and men were brief. Four days later, 1 October, a tugboat came alongside and put aboard seventy-nine Confederate prisoners of war; twenty-nine were officers. In a run of less than twenty-four hours, *Circassian* was in Hampton Roads and entering the James River. Well short of General Grant's headquarters at City Point, the prisoners were transferred to a river steamer which carried them on toward the front. This was part of the frequent flag of truce agreements which opposing frontline commanders made with each other to spare captured friends the dangers and discomforts of a cold Northern prison or a hot Southern stockade.

Circassian promptly cleared for the Brooklyn Navy Yard to pick up passengers and supplies. On 22 October, she cleared Brooklyn and four days later was again at Port Royal. Although nothing Stedman wrote home remains among his extant letters, during the two day stay there, he undoubtedly recognized many familiar ships and may have visited with a few friends briefly. He could not have helped noting that the siege of Charleston was still continuing as a stalemate. Dahlgren's flagship, *Philadelphia,* a comfortable, shallow draft, sidewheel steamer was at Port Royal and not at Charleston, several hours distant. Captain Balch of Stedman's favorite, *Pawnee,* came aboard *Circassian* as a passenger. By 14 November, *Circassian* was again rolling at the end of an anchor chain off Galveston, whence she worked her way again back through New Orleans and the familiar stops along the Gulf Coast and up the seaboard to Boston where she arrived on 14 December. Things were working out rather well for Assistant Surgeon Stedman. Although he had credit for almost four years of service, most of it afloat, he had been able to spend four Christmas seasons with his family and friends. But no one could envy him the fevers that had brought him home an almost broken man on two of those Christmas days.

Because her power plant and hull needed a complete overhaul, it was 5 February 1865 before *Circassian* was again ready for sea. On that date she received Rear Admiral Henry K. Thatcher and his writer aboard for transportation to Mobile where he was to

succeed Farragut. Thatcher had commanded a division of Porter's great naval and military concentration which had reduced and captured Fort Fisher and Wilmington, North Carolina, only three weeks earlier. The War was indeed winding down. But Lee's army was still in Richmond; Grant did not have enough men to close the southwestern sector of his enveloping ring. Sherman was moving north from Savannah with the ultimate objective of joining Grant. Although the Federals held Mobile Bay and its entry forts, Mobile itself was ably withstanding siege operations. Charleston, torn by bombardments, still defended its siege line and the upper stretches of the Stono River. Stedman probably first heard of the capture of Charleston by the right wing of Sherman's army about 20 February when *Circassian* was at a Florida port of call. Peace could not be too far distant.

On 16 March, Stedman was once again looking at the long, low coast of Texas at the end of the usual thirty fathoms of anchor chain always put out by Churchill. Again, and for the last time, the forecastle musician broke out his fiddle to provide the tune for getting the anchor aweigh for the homeward voyage. By the time Captain Churchill gave the command to drop anchor off the Boston Navy Yard on 12 April 1865, the papers were full of stories about the fall of Richmond and Lee's surrender to General Grant near Appomattox Court House, Virginia. General Johnson was negotiating for the surrender of his army to Sherman on the same terms. Stedman had been home only two days when the news of Lincoln's assas-

Home

sination swept across the nation.

The War was over. Nothing remained to be done except to disband the remaining minor Confederate forces, repair the damages and devastations—and put the nation back together again. Stedman had volunteered only for the War. Like most of his comrades, he was willing to leave these remaining and lesser tasks to lesser men. He promptly resigned his Regular Navy commission to return to his wife and son in their Downer Court home and resume his medical practice. The date of his resignation was 27 April 1865.

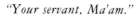

"Your servant, Ma'am."

CHAPTER ELEVEN **Through Following Years**

STEDMAN'S RESIGNATION from the Navy necessarily terminates the primary purposes and essential interests that motivated the writing and publication of this volume. Secondary interests have been restricted to an abbreviated presentation of his parentage, childhood, secondary, collegiate, and medical school years plus a small fraction of his career as a civilian doctor of medicine. He resumed this career in the spring of 1865 and continued until near the time of his death in Brookline, Massachusetts, Saturday, 24 May 1909. His span of life was seventy-eight years, two months, and three days. Accordingly, Stedman's four naval years were only a small segment of a long and useful life dedicated to the practice of medicine in Dorchester and later in Brookline.

It will be recalled that while *Circassian* was rolling in the offshore swells and he had nothing to look at but the low and hostile shoreline of Galveston Island, the often lonely Stedman wrote to Edith: "I wish I had nothing to do but be at home, earning my bread and butter among people that I care about & who care about me . . . ." There is ample evidence that throughout the long years ahead he found a full share of the domestic and professional bliss he then envisioned. But if life below the waterline on an always nearly awash ironclad was hardly one of beer and skit-tles, he found there were instances in the practice of medicine that were far short of blossoms and rosebuds. Throughout America and during the entire nineteenth century, there was little or no refuge from a general practice unless the M.D. had substantial sources of revenue from other channels. In time, a man's reputation within a certain field could enable him to set his fees somewhat higher than the average. He did it, however, at the risk of losing patients who were attracted to lower and more competitive fees from the less experienced general practitioners.

Stedman, as a returnee from the War, probably found that most of his former patients in Dorchester had become satisfied with medical attention from other doctors and showed little inclination toward an immediate return to his office, or to send word when in distress at home. It was during the remainder of 1865 that he found time for perfecting the originals of the drawings that appear in this volume. Stedman, though less productive, continued his interest in art and resumed his long standing friendship with Winslow Homer. The latter would soon be departing for France and a future fame with pigments and oils. But the Navy had failed to eradicate the teaching of Doctor Oliver Wendell Holmes that medicine was a jealous goddess who shared her devotees with no rival pursuits. Stedman's patients, when they did come to him or send word to come to them, always took priority over all else in his workaday world.

In time his reputation in medicine and curative skills within certain broad fields began to expand. This he explained in one of his few essays, probably written as a guide for a short speech to younger members of a medical society:

> But perhaps one of the best complimentaries was old Mrs. Brighams. She was 90 and had had consumption 40 years: her niece suffered from an obstinate sprain of the ankle and the old gent was kicked in the ham by a horse; but which damages I repaired. When asked by another crone how she like her surgeon, the old lady replied: "I don't know how good a family doctor he is, but he is a good doctor for legs." Then there was grandma Pope on the upper road and the last of the old fashioned Yankee farmer species, who at 84 sustained a compound fracture of the ankle. . . .One evening I had been a long time trying to relieve her heel with no great success, and she cried: "Doctor, what makes my heel ache so!" I answered in deep despair "I'm sure I don't know." "Well," said she, "go home and gitcher books, 'n read 'n find out."

In the August 1895 issue of the *Boston Medical and Surgical Journal,* Doctor Stedman expanded an earlier address to one of the medical societies into a long essay of seven or eight thousand words. Its title was "The Profession as Viewed by the Public." For the modern reader, it is a revealing picture of the problems that confronted the conscientious and ethically minded medical and surgical practitioner through the last half of the nineteenth century. As an active member of the Bay State's Obstetrical Society and the Surgical Society, Stedman was an uncompromising foe of incompetent midwives and abortionists. He was equally unsparing of well educated and properly trained physicians who dragged their feet on some religious or professional scruple in going to the aid of a person in need of treatment. That a suffering person had compounded his problems by going first to a widely recognized quack was not an acceptable excuse for ignoring or delaying a response to the patient's call. Doctor Stedman's address and resulting long essay in the *Medical Journal* stand as a sort of valedictory of a citizen and a doctor of medicine who had long served and was continuing to serve his country and fellow citizens with unstinting courage and devotion.

STEDMAN JOINS THE LOYAL LEGION

Through the four decades that followed 1865, New England could muster thousands of more or less prominent citizens who had served as commissioned officers through a part or all of the Civil War. Massachusetts alone had sent to active duty in Lincoln's armies no less than seventy-seven regiments of infantry, cavalry and heavy artillery plus seventeen bat-

A Prize at last

teries of light artillery and sixty-six separate infantry companies that were regimented with separated companies from other states. Some were for short-term calls, but more than fifty regiments were enlisted for three years or to the end of the War. The aggregate strength of all Massachusetts Volunteer Militia Regiments (National Guard in modern terms) when recomputed to a three years' enlistment standard, was 124,104 officers and men. The population of the state in 1860 was 1,231,066.

The above figures for the state's citizen soldiers do not include the sailors such as Assistant Surgeon Charles E. Stedman and his younger brother, Francis Dana Stedman. The latter served as a Naval Volunteer Third and Second Assistant Engineer, from 1862 until 1866. It has been said that the New England states provided the crews and volunteer officers for more than half of the Union's warships from the whaling fleets and merchant marine. Massachusetts certainly contributed the lion's share. It was from the commissioned officer ranks of this state's massive contributions to the Union victory that the Commandery of the State of Massachusetts of the Military Order of the Loyal Legion drew its membership and made its presence felt in the social, cultural, and even political affairs of Boston and of the state.

The Military Order of the Loyal Legion was not indigenous to the State of Massachusetts. The first state group was the Commandery of the State of Pennsylvania, formed on 4 November 1865. The fourth state group was that of Massachusetts, char-

tered on 4 March 1868. It was patterned after the patriotic tenets and fraternal purposes of the Sons of Cincinnati, an organization formed by officers of the War for American Independence. The Loyal Legion sought to continue the spirit of camaraderie; to promote an intellectual interest in military history; and to cooperate with other patriotic societies, most particularly, with the all-inclusive and more democratic Grand Army of the Republic, known to history as the G.A.R. The most frequently used vehicle toward the Loyal Legion's proclaimed objectives was the maintenance of a "unique and charming dining club" at 53 Tremont Street. There were also special commemorative dinners and picnics for survivors of sundry regiments, brigades and divisions, not to mention pilgrimages to various battlefields.

Doctor Stedman did not seek eligibility for all of these pleasant amenities until 6 November 1872. His membership number was 1,459, which most likely included prior members for the entire state rather than merely for Boston and environs. Most of them, however, lived in eastern Massachusetts.

Programs and menus for the more robust first two decades suggest a membership more interested in reliving their hardships within a comfortable atmosphere and refighting their battles with lightly penciled diagrams on table linen than in careful studies of the decisive campaigns that were being revealed by the tidal flood of published autobiographical apologies and remonstrations of erstwhile field commanders, of high and low degree, North and South. But ranks of

Thought he would trot round and tell her
and her aunt ('!) that this yarn about the
capture of Richmond is true, etc., etc.

shelved books are an essential club room decor, even today; and such military books, past, recent, and present could hardly be ignored by the management of the Loyal Legion's headquarters. The membership needed them to settle arguments. Some members died and, through lack of an interested heir, left their most treasured books and perhaps an inscrutable diary to the Massachusetts Commandery of the Loyal Legion. Few, if any, members apparently worried about this mild trend. The books were not interfering with the cuisine.

Unwittingly, the Commandery was about to go into a silent shift of synchromesh gears. Colonel Armand Augustus Rand, who had ridden away in 1861 as a second lieutenant in the 1st Massachusetts Cavalry and who returned in 1865 as the Colonel commanding the 4th Massachusetts Cavalry, failed to attend the Loyal Legion's Annual Meeting for 1882. As often happens when a responsible member of a social club is not there to defend himself, Colonel Rand was elected to the minor but onerous office of Recorder. Fortunately for posterity and for the memory of Charles E. Stedman and his caricatures, Colonel Rand worked at the minor assignment until it became a major operation.

To the Colonel, the duties of his office were explicitly within the title. He could think of nothing better to do initially than to assemble then-and-now photographs of the membership, past and present, with statements of their military or naval status, organization and commanding officers during the war years. This also involved an authentication of the sparse membership records on hand. His printed question form sent to Stedman was dated 29 March 1882. It correctly stated Stedman's rank with date of initial commission and date of resignation; i.e., 16 September 1861 and 27 April 1865. With characteristic brevity, the busy Doctor Stedman brushed the Colonel off with four lines which were considerably less than "The fullest record . . . desired" by Colonel Rand, the Recorder. They were:

> *U.S. Ship Huron, Lt. Comdg. John Downes 1862*
> *U.S. Monitor Nahant, Commander John Downes 1863*
> *U.S. Navy Yard, Boston, Adml. Stringham 1863–4*
> *U.S. Ship Circassian, Act. Lt. Comdr. Churchill 1864–5*

By its omission, it is quite obvious that the epidemic aboard *Huron* and his own illness on *Huron* and at the Boston Navy Yard was a chapter he was quite willing to forget. He also omitted Lieutenant Commander John J. Cornwell as a successor to Downes aboard *Nahant*.

Colonel Rand, with a keener sense of history and a growing interest in biography, was hardly satisfied. The Dorchester Doctor's deft pencil was known to his intimate friends within the Legion's membership. It was said of him that with a few strokes he could picture a merry friend "holding up a lamp post."

It was common knowledge in the medical profession that he had done a series of sick room and hospital caricatures for the entertainment of the Dorchester Medical Club. They were being "preserved in a volume privately printed for the club for distribution solely among its members." By 1884, in line with his own growing procurement policies for the Legion photographs and records, the Colonel had cajoled the reticent surgeon into giving the Legion an album of reproductions of his Civil War Sketches for the permanent files of the Legion. [See frontispiece.] Colonel Rand, beyond a doubt, insisted that the two photographs were within the Legion's new record and procurement policy. It is doubtful if the Colonel would have obtained the desired album of caricatures had he questioned the phoney names of ships and persons through the first three years of the sequential drawings. Indeed, Stedman provided a special cover page and title for the Legion Album. It appears as the title page of this volume as *Doctor Squillgee's Four Years in the Navy.* For the 1865 original drawings, his title page for the collection of caricatures was *Doctor Sawbones' Four Years. . . .* Certainly "Squillgee" was a far less offensive word within the medical profession than "Sawbones."

Actually, the album that Colonel Rand received contained more inaccurate names of ships and persons than the 1865 originals. It is quite obvious that as late as 1884, Doctor Stedman was willing to amuse his friends but to tell them nothing that might be held against him or the profession to which he had become more deeply devoted. Thanks to the four line key as to his ships and dates, in response to Colonel Rand's invitation to bring personal records in line with a general pattern, the phoney names and places with which Stedman embellished his drawings can usually be corrected by anyone with the time and patience to consult old logbooks in the National Archives and the *Official Records.* Somewhat more confusing was the absence of sequential numbers and the rather well shuffled and haphazard manner in which they were bound for storage in the Loyal Legion's expanding collections. Whether it was purposeful or purely accidental is immaterial. It is possible that Doctor Stedman vaguely intended to return to the album in some future day, rearrange the sketches, and beef them out into a more complicated and even romantic narrative by drawing additional and imaginary pictures. It is a tenable theory and as such it is mentioned.

There are perhaps four and certainly three stray misfits in the album. Their inclusion could be by accident. He had previously done other singles and groups of maritime drawings; the same for social scenes. The marriage picture on page 15 could symbolize his resignation from the Navy and return to marital bliss; it could be the final scene for an interwoven imaginary war romance that was never completed; or it could be a portrayal of his own wedding when he temporarily left the ranks of roistering Knights of the Punch Bowl. In this volume the last interpretation has been used. At one time or another, such an incurable draftsman must have done a sketch of his own wedding. His transitory break from the K.P.B. was emphasized by them and acknowledged by him. He was married but once and that in 1860; the picture seemed appropriate to that occasion.

Another questionable drawing is "Goodbye," on page 203. The vessel shown is a three-masted, heavy sloop-of-war, bigger and more powerful than *Huron*. She could be Commander Drayton's *Pawnee*. Stedman often saw her during the Fernandina operation and in the Stono River, while they were knocking at the back door to Charleston, S.C. His letters reveal that he admired the ship and her commander; he obviously wished he had been assigned to her rather than to *Huron*. "A Prize at Last" on page 197 cannot be other than imaginary or belonging to another series. The capturing ship is not *Huron*. The vessel being captured cannot be *Huron*'s first prize, as implied by the caption. For a time it was thought to be a portrayal of *Augusta* belatedly arriving to share the capture of the prize, *Cambria*, which was neither *Huron*'s first nor last prize. But *Augusta* had a different sail pattern and was a paddle wheel steamer.

The real puzzle is "Thought he would trot round and tell her and her aunt (!) that this yarn about the capture of Richmond is true, etc., etc.," on page 199. This plate is definitely about three other people, not to mention the horse. The week that the fall of Richmond rumors were being tossed and booted about, Assistant Surgeon Stedman was on the high seas. He could have been one of the last men in uni-form to have had definite knowledge as to Grant's occupation of Richmond.

While these imponderables are under review, we cannot discount the possibility of errors in the caption of this or that plate. They were not written in the normally miserable, quick scratching hand of the Doctor. They are in the immaculate penmanship of Colonel Rand or, most likely, an assistant. One significant error has been corrected in the light of conclusive evidence. There could have been another one or two errors in which the counter evidence was not so conclusive.

At the same time, we know Stedman to have been a man with a sly sense of humor and a mild prankster at heart. He just might have shuffled a few wild cards into the deal so as to make the game more interesting. Without prejudice to the thoughts of others, the author would like to think that this is a logical explanation.

Be that as it may, the passing years were laying heavier hands upon the busy physician and surgeon. In due time Edith presented him with two daughters, Alice and Edith. The latter married Gorham Dana, an insurance executive. The son, Ellery, born during the war and whose health gave his father so much concern, went into business. His children provided no direct descendants. Towards the end of the century, the Doctor and son Ellery enjoyed a long trip to Europe together. His wife, Edith Ellen (Parker) Stedman predeceased him by a number of years. He increasingly relied upon Gorham and Edith Dana in

Good bye!

Brookline.

Meanwhile, Doctor Stedman's sister, Lucy, had married and was getting well along with a family of her own. The closer and younger brother Frank (Francis Dana Stedman) had died of natural causes a few years after his release from the Navy. Henry Rust Stedman, eighteen years younger than Charles Ellery, had graduated from Harvard College and the University's Medical School in 1875.

In time the medical mantle of the distinguished family would pass to his shoulders. Before he died in 1926, his name was appearing in *Who's Who in America* as an outstanding neuropsychiatrist. His specialization was in the field that their father, Doctor Charles Harrison Stedman, had pioneered, "craniology and the nervous system," from the time he was appointed Superintendent of the Chelsea Naval Hospital by President Andrew Jackson.

Henry R. Stedman's daughter, Anne Bradstreet Stedman, has vivid memories of her Uncle Charles. She remembers him as always well groomed. She does not recall having ever seen him when he was not wearing the Loyal Legion's emblem, or decoration, on the lapel of his coat. Needless to say, when he died in 1909, the Flag, the Loyal Legion's squad of ceremonial lancers, buglers and drummers with muffled instruments were much in evidence at the Episcopal funeral service. He had passed away in the Brookline home of his daughter and son-in-law, Edith and Gorham Dana. He is buried in Forest Hills Cemetery.

Because Doctor Stedman's son and two daughters had passed away without a descendant, his fragmented file of letters and drawings ultimately became the divided property of Miss Anne Bradstreet Stedman and her four cousins. They knew of the album of Civil War Sketches but came to the opinion that it was irrevocably lost. Through the years, of course, the ghost of the erstwhile Assistant Surgeon was slumbering in the Loyal Legion's dusty archives under the pseudonym of "Doctor Squillgee." That is where Colonel George S. Pappas found him and the four line statement of Stedman's Civil War service. It was in sharp contrast with the scores of pages many officers had found necessary to reveal the fullness of their own services. Moreover, the caricatures fascinated Colonel Pappas from the first day he saw them.

In his light hearted, gracious, and encouraging foreword to this volume, our good friend Walter Muir Whitehill, an eminent authority on Boston and Bostonians, not to mention far wider fields in Europe and America, has told how the archives of the Loyal Legion, thanks to the zeal and interest of Colonel Pappas, became the property of the United States Government, in the custody of the U.S. Army Military History Research Collection at Carlisle Barracks, Pennsylvania.

Doctor Whitehill also comments upon Stedman's ghost having the unusual quality of appearing so often, so unexpectedly, and so many years after the *Hardy Lee* lithographs were published. As the author of this book, I have left Charles Ellery Stedman 1831–1909, properly and firmly interred in Forest

Hills Cemetery, but I cannot be so sure about his recrudescent ghost. There are other early caricatures that are not published here. Those of his post-Civil War years that I have seen were an accidental finding incident to searches for those of earlier and Civil War years. There are, beyond doubt, other post-War caricatures I have not seen. Until all have been found and published, Stedman's ghost could prove to be a rather restless spirit.

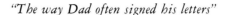

"The way Dad often signed his letters"

Glossary of Naval Terms

The Glossary of Naval Terms which follows has been taken from *A Naval Encyclopaedia: Comprising a Dictionary of Nautical Words and Phrases . . .*, published by L. R. Hamersly & Co., Philadelphia, 1881.

SQUILGEE: Formerly, a small swab. An instrument for cleaning the water from the decks . . . A lazy, mean fellow . . .

A

ABAFT, behind.

ABEAM, opposite the centre of the ship's side; on a line which forms a right angle with the keel.

AFT, abbreviation of *abaft*.

ATHWART, transversely; at right angles to the keel; across the line of the ship's course.

B

BARK, any small vessel. A three-masted vessel square-rigged on the fore and main, with fore-and-aft sails on the mizzen-mast. BARK-RIGGED, rigged as a bark, with no square-sails on the mizzen-mast.

BATTEN, slips of wood used for containing the edges of the tarpaulins over the hatches.

BATTEN DOWN THE HATCHES, to haul over the tarpaulins and secure them by nailing battens over them.

BEAT TO QUARTERS, the signal for officers and men to take battle stations.

BERTH-DECK, the deck next below the lower gun-deck.

BITTS, Vertical timbers projecting above the decks. The bitts for the cable are circular, and are coated with iron. There are generally two pairs of them, the after pair being used for the sheet-chains.

BOATSWAIN (Bos'n), . . . the title is said to be derived from *bat*, a boat, and *swan*, a swain, or servant. His symbol of office—the silver call, or whistle—was once the proud insignia of the Lord High Admiral of England, and the decorative appendage of the Admirals of the Fleet, who wore it suspended from a golden chain, and with it "were wont to cheer their men in battle." The duties of a boatswain are constant and fatiguing; his station is the forecastle, whence he can direct the men aloft. He pipes "all hands" for general work, and his mates repeat the call on their respective decks. Boatswains in the United States Navy are warrant-officers.

BOOBY-HATCH, a smaller kind of companion, but readily removable. A kind of wooden hood over a hatch, fitted with a sliding top and readily removable.

BOW, the forward part of a vessel.

BOWSPRIT, a large spar projecting over the bows to support the foremast and extend the head-sails.

BRACE, one of the ropes attached to the extremities of the yards by which they are moved about horizontally.

BULKHEAD, any partition separating apartments on the same deck. Some are very strong, and others are light and can be removed at pleasure.

BULWARK, the planking or wood-work round a vessel above the deck.

C

CAPSTAN, a machine used on shipboard when mechanical power is required for the moving or raising of heavy weights.

CAPSTAN BAR, a long lever to give an increase of power in heaving at the capstan.

CAPTAIN OF THE MAIN TOP, the name given to the leading man stationed in the main top. Captain is also the name given to certain leading men in the ship's company; as, captain of a gun, captain of the forecastle, captain of the hold, etc.

CAT-O'NINE-TAILS, an instrument formerly used for flogging in the navy. It consisted of nine pieces of cord, with three knots in each, fixed on a short piece of thick rope as a handle. With this the offender was flogged on the bare back.

COMPANIONWAY, the staircase or berthing of the ladder-way to the cabin.

D

DITTY-BOX, a small box to hold a sailor's thread, needles, brushes, combs, etc. As ditty-boxes lumber up the decks, they are not generally allowed on board a man-of-war.

DOG'S BODY, dried pease boiled in a cloth.

DOG-WATCH, the half-watches of two hours each, from 4 to 6, and from 6 to 8, in the evening. By this arrangement an uneven number of watches is made—seven instead of six in the twenty-four hours; otherwise there would be a succession of the same watches at the same hours throughout the cruise.

DOUBLE IRONS, fetters for both hands and legs.

DRAFT (or DRAUGHT), the depth of the bottom of a vessel's keel below the surface of the water.

F

FATHOM, a measure of 6 feet, roughly made by extending both arms; used in measuring cordage, depths, etc.

FLAG OFFICER, an admiral, vice-admiral, rear-admiral, or commodore.

FLOG, to punish by striking with the cat-o'nine-tails.

FORE-AND-AFT SAILS, sails which are bent to the gaffs or masts, or are hoisted upon the stays.

FOREMAST, the mast nearest the bow.

FRIGATE, a ship with a raised quarter-deck and forecastle. From these there was a descent of a few steps to the *waist*. Her forecastle extended from the stem to the *belfry*; the quarter-deck from the stern to the gangway. The open space between was the *waist*. (Armament varied based upon the period in which the ship was built.)

FROSTING, the lustreless appearance of metals, glass, etc., when not polished; this appearance somewhat resembles hoar-frost; hence the name.

G

GAFF, a small spar projecting abaft a mast, which extends the head of a fore-and-aft sail not set on a stay.

GIMBALS, pairs of brass hoops or rings which swing one within the other on diameters at right angles to each other, the pivots being on the inner surface of each successively larger hoop. Anything suspended in their centre retains a constant position relatively to the horizontal plane in whatever direction the framework is tilted; used for hanging compasses, barometers, etc.

GRAPNEL, a pronged implement used as an anchor for a boat; for the purpose of recovering an object at the bottom of a harbor; for hooking onto ropes, etc., likely to foul the screw; for securing one vessel to another when boarding is to be attempted; or to make fast a tow-line to a burning vessel, etc.

GROG, diluted spirits formerly issued to the navy. In 1740 Admiral Vernon introduced it into the British navy, and it was said to have been named from his grogram coat. Pindar, however, alludes to the Cyclops diluting their beverage with ten waters. The spirit-ration was abolished in our navy September 1, 1862.

GUN-DECK, the deck below the spar-deck, on which the guns are carried.

H

HALYARDS (HALLIARDS or HAULYARDS), the rope or purchase employed to hoist a yard or sail on its mast or stay. All yards have halliards, except the lower,—these being kept stationary ordinarily; when they are hoisted or lowered, the jeers are used.

HOWITZER, a short, light cannon, intended to throw large projectiles with comparatively small charges. . . . In the navy the howitzers are principally used in boat and in operations on shore; they would also be serviceable in repelling boarders.

I

IRISH PENNANTS, rope-yarns hanging about the rigging; loose reef-points or gaskets flying about; fag-ends of ropes.

J

JIB, a large triangular sail set on a head-stay.

JIB-BOOM, a spar rigged out through the bowsprit-cap, the heel being clamped to the bowsprit.

K

KEDGE, a small anchor used for moving a vessel from one part of a harbor to another, or for a temporary anchorage. It is usually carried out in a boat and dropped as required. *To kedge,* to move a vessel by means of a kedge.

KID, a small wooden tub.

KNOTS, the log-line is divided into *knots,* each of which bears the same proportion to a mile as 30 seconds does to an hour. Hence, in speaking of a vessel's speed, *knots* are used, meaning nautical miles. (A nautical mile measures 6080 feet compared to 5280 feet for a statute mile.)

L

LEAD, an apparatus used on board vessels to determine the depth of water. It is generally made of lead, of prismatic shape, tapering to the upper end, through which a hole is made for a strap, to which is attached a marked line.

LEADSMAN, a man stationed to heave the lead.

M

MAINMAST, the principal mast—the second from the bow.

MAN-OF-WAR, a national vessel.

MIZZEN, a term which distinguishes the mast next abaft the mainmast, and the yards, sails, and rigging belonging thereto. The name is sometimes given to the spanker.

N

NETTING, a net-work of small lines used for various purposes.

O

ORDINARY, vessels are in *ordinary* when they are out of commission and laid up.

P

PEAK, the upper after corner of a four sided fore-and-aft sail.

PENNANT, a *narrow-pennant* is worn by all government vessels in commission and commanded by an officer below the grade of commodore. This pennant is not an emblem of rank but signifies that the vessel flying it is of public character. It is worn at the main.

PETTY OFFICER, a general term, corresponding to *non-commissioned officer* in the army. He holds his position during the pleasure of the appointing authority, which is generally the commanding officer. The master-at-arms is the CHIEF PETTY OFFICER.

POWDER MONKEY, the boy who passed cartridges to the guns.

PRIZE MONEY, proceeds from the sale of captures made as prize by authority of the United States. Vessels and their cargoes captured as prize must be sent into port for an adjudication in a prize-court in the manner prescribed by law. If condemned, the property is sold by the U.S. marshal, and the proceeds, when the capture was by a vessel or vessels of the navy, disposed of according to the decree of the courts. If the prize was of equal or superior force to the vessel or vessels making the capture, the whole of the net proceeds will be decreed to the captors; and when of inferior force, one-half will be decreed to the United States and the other half to the captors.

Q

QUARTER-DECK, the upper deck abaft the mainmast. Naval etiquette requires all persons to salute on coming on a quarter-deck, and to conduct themselves in a decorous manner. The starboard side in port and the weather side at sea are reserved for the use of the commanding and executive-officers, and the officer of the deck.

QUARTERS, the stations of officers and men at the guns for battle, or for exercise, or for inspection. The stations for battle or for exercise, as though engaged in battle, are distinguished as *general quarters.*

QUARTER-WATCH, a division of one-fourth part of the ship's company. In the days when a ship carried a large number of men, a quarter-watch was sufficient to handle her in pleasant weather.

R

RECEIVING SHIP, a ship stationed permanently in a harbor for the purpose of recruiting seamen and holding them in readiness for a cruiser.

S

SABOT, a disk of wood or metal fastened to the base of a spherical projectile to keep it in the proper position while loading. All spherical shell and shrapnel in the navy have sabots, fastened to them by four straps of tinned iron, and further secured by a seizing at the base.

SALT-HORSE or SALT-JUNK, navy salt-beef; a part of the ration.

SALTWATER SOAP, soap made from cocoa-nut or palm-wood oil. It solidifies at 75 per cent of water.

SHROUD, a rope belonging to the standing rigging of a ship, generally alluded to in the plural. Each shroud is connected with another so as to form a *pair*. They are made of shroud-laid tarred hemp rope. . . .

SLIP-STOP, an arrangement for letting the anchor go. Usually, the ends of the anchor-stoppers have a tongue held in a *trip*, which is held by a trigger and controlled by a line, so that one man may detach both stoppers.

SPANKER, the aftermost sail on a ship, setting abaft the mizzen-mast, having a gaff and generally a boom.

SPAR-DECK, the upper deck of a ship extending from stern to stem.

SPLICE THE MAIN BRACE, an expression denoting the act of drinking spirits. It is the equivalent of "topping up the boom," and "sweating up the halliards."

STERN, the whole after part of the ship, as the forward part is called the bows. . . .

T

TOP, a platform of semicircular form resting upon the trestle-trees of the lower mast of a square-rigged vessel. It gives spread to the top-mast rigging, which is set up to the rim of the top. It also serves as a place for sharp-shooters during an engagement, and in a large vessel is of sufficient size for the use of a howitzer. It is of use as a landing place from which the light-yard men start in loosing or furling, as a place where topgallant and royal studding-sails are kept at sea and where men are stationed to set or take in royals, and light studding-sails when the gear is brought into the top instead of the deck.

TRUCK, . . . A circular piece of wood placed on the head of a mast of flagstaff, in which the sheave for the signal-halliards is placed.

W

WARDROOM, the apartments of the commissioned officers, including mess and state-rooms. It is on the berth-deck of frigates and sloops, but was on the gun-deck of line-of-battle ships.

WARDROOM MESS, the mess for commissioned officers.

WARP, a tow-rope or light hawser, used to move a ship about. *To warp,* to move a vessel with warps, or lines, fast to fixed points.

WINDWARD, toward the wind. The weather-side.

WING-AND-WING, before the wind with studding-sails on both sides. In a fore-and-aft rigged vessel, before the wind with the mainsail on one side and the foresail on the other.

Y

YARDS, spars suspended from a mast to which the head of a sail is bent.

Bibliographic Notes

THE ORIGINALS OF the often quoted war letters of Charles E. Stedman to his wife Edith Ellen Parker Stedman are the property of the four descendants of his sister, Lucy, and his brother, Henry. The author was provided with copies of those assembled by Miss Anne Bradstreet Stedman but is not authorized to lend these copies to others. Obituaries clipped or copied and much other vital information concerning his Harvard University years are in the alumni archives of the Widner and Countway libraries.

For Stedman's war service years the primary sources, other than his own letters and drawings, are of an official character. Among them are the logbooks of the three ships upon which he served. They can be found in the National Archives, Pennsylvania Avenue Building, Washington, D.C. Highly important are the government published *Navy Registers* for the years 1862–65 inclusive. Absolutely essential are the 30 volumes of Series I and II of the *Official Records of the Union and Confederate Navies in the War of the Rebellion*, publication beginning in 1895 pursuant to an Act of Congress, approved 31 July 1894. The last volume appeared in 1927. In connection with the siege of Charleston, South Carolina, a similar title, and with much the same publishing history, the 128 volumes of the *Official Records of the Union and Confederate Armies. . .* are helpful but not so vital as the comparable *Official Records . . . Navies.*

With reference to medical progress, its capabilities and limitations, through the earlier years of Stedman's professional experience there is nothing better than *The Medical and Surgical History of the War of the Rebellion,* Government Printing Office,

1870-88. Dr. T. F. Harrington, *The Harvard Medical School*, 1905; and Frederick Washburn, *The Massachusetts General Hospital*, 1939, are more nearly akin to Stedman's experience and growth during the great expansion of knowledge and skills that came to the profession before his death.

AUTOBIOGRAPHIES, BIOGRAPHIES, AND HISTORIES

Bostonians are prone to write readily about themselves and even more readily about one another. Few have written better about themselves than the aging, sophisticated, and overly educated Henry Brooks Adams, A.B., Harvard College, 1858. Through Headmaster Dixwell's Latin School and undergraduate years, his education was almost identical to that of Stedman and his associates. However, in his *Education of Henry Adams,* 1918, he wrote that those were fallow years productive of little or nothing toward his "education." If true, it was just as well that Stedman appears to have been doodling his way, with pencil and pad, across those frequently plowed, but never seeded fields of learning.

John Torrey Morse, *Life and Letters of Oliver Wendell Holmes,* 2 volumes, 1896; and Henry James, *Charles W. Eliot; President of Harvard University, 1869–1909,* 2 volumes, 1930; and others tell an entirely different story about Harvard. Morse graduated with the Class of 1860 and James with the Class of 1899, and an LL.B., 1904. Charles W. Eliot was only a year or two behind Stedman through the Latin School and Harvard College. In the light of their testimony and that of many others, we can only assume Henry Adams waited too long and too near the end of the road before his decision to plumb and to record the depths of his truly vast learning. That is why his opinions are rejected in favor of the majority in reviewing the education of Stedman in this volume. In the two books mentioned above, James offers the better bibliography for further reading or study.

For linking Stedman's Boston with modern Boston three titles are suggested: Justin Winsor (Editor), *The Memorial History of Boston, 1630–1880,* 5 volumes, 1880. Its maps should be correlated with up-to-date city and road maps. The other two books are Walter Muir Whitehill, *Boston in the Age of John Fitzgerald Kennedy,* 1965; and Cleveland Amory, *The Proper Bostonians,* 1947. Both supply the reader with ample bibliographies. One caution concerning Amory's book: at times he is so charmed by the froth that billows over the rim of his mug that he ignores the substantial ale under the foam.

The Atlantic Coast during the Civil War and the prolonged siege of Charleston, S.C., have a literature of their own. Rear Admiral Daniel Ammen, erstwhile commander of monitor *Patapsco,* wrote one of the best autobiographies that came from the war; *The Old Navy and the New,* 1891. His earlier book, *The Atlantic Coast,* 1883, is adequate but hardly in a class with the autobiography. In the same series Stedman must have enjoyed reading and largely agreeing with A.T. Mahan, *The Gulf and Inland Waters,* 1883; and J. R. Soley, *The Blockade and the Cruisers,* 1883. James P. Baxter III, *The Introduction of the Ironclad Warship,* 1933; and H.W. Wilson, *Ironclads in Action,* 1895, are important books.

The well known and well illustrated *Battles and Leaders of the Civil War,* 4 volumes, 1884–88, were written by former officers of the armies and navies of both belligerents, under the editorship of *Century Magazine.* Generals Beauregard for the South and Gillmore for the North, and others, wrote their divergent narratives concerning Charleston. Among them Rear Admiral C.R.P. Rodgers, at the time Fleet Captain aboard *New Ironsides,* was allowed to chime in with a brief review of the Union ironclads in their attacks upon the defending forts. Otherwise, DuPont's other broader and more significant operations elsewhere are generally ignored.

Rear Admiral John A.B. Dahlgren's second wife was the widow of an Ohio congressman with a literary reputation of her own. This, combined with the heavy ordnance that bears his name, have given him a better press and more fame than came to his rival, Admiral S.F. DuPont. Madeleine Vinton Dahlgren, *A Memoir of John·A. Dahlgren,* 1882, is informative. Written by a distinguished kinsman, Henry A. DuPont, *Rear Admiral Samuel Francis DuPont,* 1926, is a better book about the better of the two naval commanders who failed to capture Charleston, though the army commanders necessarily share the blame with both admirals. For the army problems see Major General Quincy A. Gillmore, *Engineering and Artillery Operations against Charleston,* 1868. For the problem as seen from the deck of *New Ironsides,* see George E. Belknap, "Reminiscent of the Siege of Charleston," *Papers of the Military Society of Massachusetts,* volume 12, 1902, pp. 155–207. Robert M. Thompson and Richard Wainwright (editors), *The Confidential Correspondence of Gustavus Vasa Fox, Assistant Secretary of Navy, 1861–65,* 2 volumes, 1919, is significant. The attitude of the Navy Department toward the monitors and their use is further revealed in Gideon Welles, *The Diary of Gideon Welles,* 3 volumes, 1903. There are more recent and expanded editions of this title.

At least a few titles should be mentioned in recognition of the men who so often slipped through the always watching cordons of Union blockaders. Among the best were: John Wilkinson, *The Narrative of a Blockade Runner,* 1877; and August C. Hobart-Hampton ("Captain Roberts") *Sketches of My Life,* 1887.

Wilkinson was a Confederate naval officer from Virginia who had resigned from the U.S. Navy "to go South." Hobart-Hampton was a British naval officer and an incurable adventurer. Jim Dan Hill, *Seadogs of the Sixties; Farragut and Seven Contemporaries,* 1935; and Perpetua Books edition, 1961, contains biographical studies of four Northern and four Southern naval officers, each selected for the type of naval mission to which he was ordered.

In the writing of Stedman's war story, the two reference titles most frequently consulted were produced by the Naval History Division of the Navy Department. *The Civil War Naval Chronology,* Government Printing Office, Washington, 1971. It was initiated in paperback sections for the Civil War Centennial Years by Rear Admiral John B. Heffernan (Ret.); continued by Rear Admiral Ernest M. Eller (Ret.). The Naval History Division's other indispensable title is the multi-volume *Dictionary of American Naval Fighting Ships.* It was initiated by Ernest M. Eller and is being carried forward vigorously by Edwin B. Hooper. The present six volumes carry the individual ship histories from A through Q. The handsome volumes are on the Government Printing Office "Best Seller List." Complete sets of these volumes will become rare book items on collectors' lists within a few years after the publication of the last volume.

Index

216